Computer Professional's
Quick Reference

Other McGraw-Hill Titles of Interest

Computer Professional's Quick Reference

M. S. Vassiliou
Thousand Oaks, California

J. A. Orenstein
Boston, Massachusetts

McGraw-Hill, Inc.
New York   St. Louis   San Francisco   Auckland   Bogotá
Caracas   Lisbon   London   Madrid   Mexico   Milan
Montreal   New Delhi   Paris   San Juan   São Paulo
Singapore   Sydney   Tokyo   Toronto

Library of Congress Cataloging-in-Publication Data

Vassiliou, M. S.
    Computer professional's quick reference / M. S. Vassiliou,
J. A. Orenstein
       p.   cm.
    Includes bibliographical references and index.
    ISBN 0-07-067211-3 (hc) — ISBN 0-07-067212-1 (pbk.)
    1. Operating systems (Computers) 2. Computer interfaces
3. Computer networks. I. Orenstein, J. A. II. Title.
QA76.76.063V37 1992
005.4'3—dc20   91-34128
                                         CIP

1 2 3 4 5 6 7 8 9 0 DOC/DOC 9 7 6 5 4 3 2 1

ISBN   0-07-067211-3 {HC}
ISBN   0-07-067212-1 {PBK}

*The sponsoring editor for this book was Jeanne Glasser, the editing
supervisor was Frank Kotowski, Jr., and the production supervisor
was Suzanne W. Babeuf.*

Printed and bound by R. R. Donnelley & Sons Company.

To our families near and far.

Contents

List of Tables   xiii
List of Figures   xvii
Preface   xix

Section 1   Common Operating System Commands   1

Chapter 1. UNIX   3

    1.1   Files and Filenames   4
        1.1.1 Valid Filenames   4
        1.1.2 Directory Structure and Pathnames   5
        1.1.3 Wild Cards   5
    1.2   List Out Directory Contents   6
    1.3   Copy a File   6
    1.4   Rename a File   7
    1.5   Delete a File   7
    1.6   List Contents of File on the Screen   7
    1.7   Print a File   8
    1.8   Create a New Directory   8
    1.9   Remove a Directory   8
    1.10 Move to Another Directory   8
    1.11 Edit a File (Line Mode)   8
    1.12 Compile and Run a Program   10
    1.13 Command Procedures   11
        1.13.1 Invoke a Command Procedure Interactively   12
        1.13.2 Invoke a Command Procedure in Batch   12
        1.13.3 Check on the Progress of a Job   12
        1.13.4 Stop a Batch Job   12
    1.14 Abort Operation   13
    1.15 Redirection of Input and Output   13
    1.16 Bibliography   14

Chapter 2. VAX-VMS   15

    2.1   Files and Filenames   15
        2.1.1 Valid Filenames   15

	2.1.2 Directories and Full File Specification	16
	2.1.3 Wild Cards	17
2.2	List Out Directory Contents	17
2.3	Copy a File	18
2.4	Rename a File	18
2.5	Delete a File	18
2.6	List Contents of File on the Screen	19
2.7	Print a File	19
2.8	Create a New Directory	20
2.9	Remove a Directory	20
2.10	Move to Another Directory	20
2.11	Edit a File (Line Mode)	20
2.12	Compile and Run a Program	22
2.13	Command Procedures	22
	2.13.1 Invoke a Command Procedure Interactively	22
	2.13.2 Invoke a Command Procedure in Batch	23
	2.13.3 Check on the Progress of a Job	23
	2.13.4 Stop a Batch Job	23
2.14	Abort Operation	23
2.15	Bibliography	23

Chapter 3. MVS-TSO		**25**
3.1	Files and Filenames	26
	3.1.1 Valid Filenames ("Data Set Names")	26
	3.1.2 Partitioned Data Sets	27
	3.1.3 Wild Cards	27
3.2	List Out Directory Contents	28
3.3	Copy a File	29
3.4	Rename a File	29
3.5	Delete a File	29
3.6	List Contents of File on the Screen	30
3.7	Print a File	30
3.8	Create a New Directory	30
3.9	Remove a Directory	31
3.10	Move to Another Directory	31
3.11	Edit a File (Line Mode)	31
3.12	Compile and Run a Program	32
3.13	Command Procedures	34
	3.13.1 Invoke a Command Procedure Interactively	34
	3.13.2 Invoke a Command Procedure in Batch	35
	3.13.3 Check on the Progress of a Job	35
	3.13.4 Stop a Batch Job	35
3.14	Abort Operation	35
3.15	Bibliography	35

Chapter 4. VM-CMS   37

4.1	Files and Filenames	37
	4.1.1 Valid Filenames ("File Identifiers")	37
	4.1.2 Directory Structure and Pathnames	38
	4.1.3 Wild Cards	39
4.2	List Out Directory Contents	39
4.3	Copy a File	40
4.4	Rename a File	41
4.5	Delete a File	41
4.6	List Contents of File on the Screen	41
4.7	Print a File	42
4.8	Create a New Directory	42
4.9	Remove a Directory	42
4.10	Move to Another Directory	42
4.11	Edit a File (Line Mode)	42
4.12	Compile and Run a Program	42
4.13	Command Procedures	43
4.14	Bibliography	43

Chapter 5. MS-DOS   45

5.1	Files and Filenames	46
	5.1.1 Valid Filenames	46
	5.1.2 Directory Structure and Pathnames	47
	5.1.3 Wild Cards	48
5.2	List Out Directory Contents	49
5.3	Copy a File	50
5.4	Rename a File	51
5.5	Delete a File	52
5.6	List Contents of File on the Screen	52
5.7	Print a File	53
5.8	Create a New Directory	53
5.9	Remove a Directory	53
5.10	Move to Another Directory	53
5.11	Edit a File (Line Mode)	54
5.12	Compile and Run a Program	55
5.13	Command Procedures	57
5.14	Abort Operation	57
5.15	Move to Another Drive	57
5.16	Format a Disk	57
5.17	Duplicate a Disk	58
5.18	Verify a Disk	59
5.19	Redirection of Input and Output	59
5.20	Bibliography	59

Chapter 6. Macintosh   61

6.1   Versions of the System and the Finder   61
6.2   Abort Operation   62
6.3   Fundamental Shortcuts   62
6.4   Move a Window without Selecting It   63
6.5   A Neater CLEAN UP   64
6.6   Close All Windows   64
6.7   TRASHing Files   64
6.8   Attractive Accents and Punctuation Marks   64
6.9   The Command Symbol   65
6.10 The Dominant Disk   65
6.11 Multifinder Miscellanea   65
6.12 Remarks on Fonts   66
      6.12.1 Traditional Screen Fonts   66
      6.12.2 Printer Fonts   66
      6.12.3 Adobe Type Manager and Truetype   67
      6.12.4 Font Identifications   67
6.13 Graphics Formats   68
      6.13.1 Paint Format   68
      6.13.2 PICT   68
      6.13.3 PICT2   69
      6.13.4 TIFF   69
      6.13.5 EPS   69
      6.13.6 Converting from One Format to Another   70
6.14 Bibliography   75

Chapter 7. System Characteristics   77

7.1   UNIX   77
7.2   VAX-VMS   77
7.3   MVS-TSO   78
7.4   VM-CMS   78
7.5   MS-DOS   78
7.6   Macintosh   78
7.7   DEC PDP-11/RT-11   78
7.8   DECSYSTEM-10 and DECSYSTEM-20   78
7.9   PRIME 50 series—PRIMOS   79
7.10 UCSD pSystem   79
7.11 CDC Cyber Systems—NOS   79
7.12 CP/M-80   79

Section 2   Data Communications and File Transfer   81

Chapter 8. Interfaces, Connections, and Modems   83

8.1   RS-232 Serial Interface   83
      8.1.1 Generalities   83

8.1.2 Useful Subsets of RS-232   84
8.1.3 Remarks on Connecting Computers to Modems   85
8.1.4 Typical Connection for Two Computers   86
8.1.5 RS-232 Implemented with a 9-Pin Connector   87
8.2   RS-422 Serial Interface   89
8.3   Interconnecting Macintoshes, IBM-PC's, and Other Computers   92
8.4   Centronics Parallel Printer Interface   96
8.5   IEEE 488   97
8.6   SCSI Interface on Apple Macintosh Computers   98
8.7   Modem Topics   102
8.7.1 Modem Standards   103
8.7.2 Smart Modems   106
8.7.3 Transmission Speed   107
8.7.4 Communication Characteristics of Some Systems   109
8.8   Bibliography   110

Chapter 9. Worldwide Networks   113

9.1   Descriptions of Important Networks   113
9.1.1 The Internet   113
9.1.2 BITNET   115
9.1.3 DECnet Internet   115
9.1.4 UUCP   116
9.1.5 USENET   116
9.1.6 JANET   116
9.1.7 JUNET   116
9.1.8 EUnet   116
9.2   Important Computers   116
9.3   Electronic Mail Addresses   117
9.4   Obtaining Internet Information   118
9.5   Bibliography   119

Chapter 10. Kermit   121

10.1   A Sample Kermit Session   121
10.2   Remarks on Kermit Commands   124
10.3   The connect Command   124
10.4   The set Command   125
10.4.1 set baud   125
10.4.2 set delay   125
10.4.3 set duplex   125
10.4.4 set escape   125
10.4.5 set file   125
10.4.6 set flow   126
10.4.7 set handshake   126
10.4.8 set IBM   126
10.4.9 set parity   127
10.5   The send Command   127
10.6   The receive Command   127

10.7   The get Command   128
10.8   Kermit Operation and Packet Format   128
10.9   Bibliography   130

Chapter 11. FTP   131

11.1   A Sample FTP Session   131
11.2   A Subset of Essential FTP Commands   133

Section 3   Standards   135

Chapter 12. Standards Organizations and Procedures   137

12.1   Standards Organizations   138
        12.1.1 International Organizations   138
        12.1.2 European Organizations   140
        12.1.3 National Organizations   141
        12.1.4 Professional and Industry Organizations   143
12.2   Addresses of Standards Organizations   144
        12.2.1 International Organizations   144
        12.2.2 European Organizations   145
        12.2.3 National Organizations   145
        12.2.4 Professional and Industry Organizations   146
12.3   Bibliography   146

Chapter 13. Character Codes and Typography   149

13.1   ASCII   149
13.2   EBCDIC   150
13.3   ISO 646 and International Versions of ASCII   150
13.4   The Eight-Bit Code ISO 6937   151
13.5   The Eight-Bit ISO Alphabets 8859/1 to 8859/9   152
13.6   Manufacturers' "Extended ASCII's"   153
13.7   Accented Letters in ISO Alphabets and Manufacturers'
        "Extended ASCII's"   153
13.8   Character Code Tables   156
13.9   Letter Frequency   188
13.10   Digital Typography   190
        13.10.1 Units   190
        13.10.2 Other Typographic Terminology   191
        13.10.3 Resolution   192
        13.10.4 Representation of Fonts   193
13.11   List of Standards Relating to Character Codes   193
13.12   Bibliography   195

Chapter 14. Floating-Point Format   197

14.1   Precision and Range   197
14.2   Bias   198

14.3	ANSI/IEEE Single-Precision Formats	198
14.4	ANSI/IEEE Double-Precision Formats	199
14.5	List of Floating-Point Standards	200
14.6	Bibliography	200

Chapter 15. Network Standards   203

15.1	Open Systems Interconnection (OSI) Model	203
15.2	TCP/IP and the OSI Model	205
15.3	IEEE Local Area Network Standards	206
15.4	List of Network Standards	207
	15.4.1 General OSI Reference Model	208
	15.4.2 Application Layer	208
	15.4.3 Session Layer	209
	15.4.4 Transport Layer	210
	15.4.5 Network Layer	210
	15.4.6 Data-Link Layer	211
	15.4.7 Data-Link Layer: IEEE LAN Standards	211
	15.4.8 Physical Layer	213
15.5	Bibliography	214

Chapter 16. Programming Language Standards   215

16.1	Ada	215
16.2	BASIC	216
16.3	C Language	218
16.4	COBOL	218
16.5	FORTRAN	219
16.6	Pascal	220
16.7	List of Programming Language Standards (ANSI, ISO)	222
16.8	Programming Language Standards under Development	224
16.9	Bibliography	225

Chapter 17. Other Hardware and Software Standards   227

17.1	Operating Systems	227
17.2	Microprocessors	228
17.3	Software Engineering	228
17.4	Computer Graphics	229
17.5	Text and Document Processing	230
17.6	Data Communications	231
	17.6.1 EIA Standards	231
	17.6.2 ISO and National Bodies	232
	17.6.3 CCITT Recommendations	233
	17.6.4 European Communications Standards (NETs)	243
17.7	Standard Paper Sizes	244

Glossary of Acronyms   247

Index   251

List of Tables

Cross-Reference of Common Operating System Commands   2

TABLE 8.1
RS-232 (EIA 232)/CCITT V24 Pin Assignment   85

TABLE 8.2
Possible RS-232 Connection of Two Computers Both Configured as DTE   87

TABLE 8.3
Making an Adapter Cable from PC/AT DB-9 to PC DB-25   88

TABLE 8.4
Making an RS-232 Null Modem when One Port is a DB-9 and the Other
is a DB-25   89

TABLE 8.5
Making an RS-232 Null Modem when Both Ports are DB-9   89

TABLE 8.6
Making an Adapter Cable from Macintosh DB-9 to Mini-DIN   91

TABLE 8.7
Pin Assignments for Macintosh SE and II Serial Interfaces
(Mini-DIN Connector)   91

TABLE 8.8
Pin Assignments for Macintosh Plus Serial Interface (Mini-DIN Connector)   92

TABLE 8.9
Pin Assignments for Macintosh 512K Serial Interface (DB-9 Connector)   92

TABLE 8.10
Connecting a Macintosh 512K to an IBM-PC   93

TABLE 8.11
Connecting a Macintosh Plus, SE, or II to an IBM-PC   93

TABLE 8.12
Connecting a Macintosh 512K to an IBM-PC/AT, PS/2, or Similar
Model Using a DB-9 Connector   93

TABLE 8.13
Connecting a Macintosh Plus, SE, or II to an IBM-PC/AT, PS/2, or
Similar Model Using a DB-9 Connector   94

TABLE 8.14
Connecting a Macintosh 512K to a Tandy Model 100 Laptop, or
to an Apple Imagewriter   94

TABLE 8.15
Connecting a Macintosh Plus, SE, or II to a Tandy Model 100 Laptop,
or to an Apple Imagewriter   94

TABLE 8.16
Connecting a Macintosh 512K to a Hayes Modem   95

TABLE 8.17
Connecting a Macintosh Plus, SE, or II to a Hayes Modem   95

TABLE 8.18
Connecting a Macintosh 512K to a Macintosh Plus, SE, or II   95

TABLE 8.19
Connecting Together Two Macintosh 512K's   96

TABLE 8.20
Connecting Together Two Macintosh Plus, SE, or II's   96

TABLE 8.21
Pin Assignment of Centronics Interface   97

TABLE 8.22
Pin Assignment of IEEE 488 Bus Connector   98

TABLE 8.23
Pin Assignment of the Internal SCSI Interface on Macintosh Computers 100

TABLE 8.24
Pin Assignment of External SCSI Connector on Macintosh Computers   102

TABLE 8.25
AT&T Bell Series Modems   103

TABLE 8.26
CCITT V-Series Modems   104

TABLE 8.27
Modem Signal Frequencies   105

TABLE 8.28
Frequencies for Telephone Touch-Tone Dialing   105

TABLE 8.29
Hayes Smartmodem 1200™ Commands   106

TABLE 8.30
Hayes Smartmodem 1200™ Result Codes   107

TABLE 8.31
Illustration of Data Transfer Rates   109

TABLE 8.32
Communication Characteristics of Various Systems   110

TABLE 9.1
Some Common E-Mail Address Formats   118

TABLE 13.1
ASCII and EBCDIC Table   156

TABLE 13.2
Hexadecimal-to-Decimal Conversion   160

TABLE 13.3
ASCII and EBCDIC Nonprintable Control Characters   162

TABLE 13.4
EBCDIC Control Characters Without Direct ASCII Equivalents   163

TABLE 13.5
Graphical Representations of Normally Nonprintable ASCII Control
  Characters   164

TABLE 13.6
Replacement Characters for British Version of ASCII   167

TABLE 13.7
Replacement Characters for German Version of ASCII   167

TABLE 13.8
Replacement Characters for French Version of ASCII   167

TABLE 13.9
Replacement Characters for Italian Version of ASCII   168

TABLE 13.10
Replacement Characters for Spanish Version of ASCII   168

TABLE 13.11
Replacement Characters for Swedish Version of ASCII   168

TABLE 13.12
Replacement Characters for Danish Version of ASCII   169

TABLE 13.13
Replacement Characters for Norwegian Version of ASCII   169

TABLE 13.14
ISO 6937/2 Character Set   170

TABLE 13.15
ISO Standard Alphabets 8859/1, 8859/2 and 8859/3   170

TABLE 13.16
ISO Standard Alphabets 8859/4 and 8859/9   174

TABLE 13.17
ISO 8859/5, Latin/Cyrillic Alphabet   177

TABLE 13.18
ISO 8859/6, Latin/Arabic Alphabet   178

TABLE 13.19
ISO 8859/7, Latin/Greek Alphabet   179

TABLE 13.20
ISO 8859/8, Latin/Hebrew Alphabet   180

TABLE 13.21
Manufacturers' Extended Character Sets   181

TABLE 13.22
IBM PC and PS/2 Extended Character Sets   184

TABLE 13.23
Baudot Code   187

TABLE 13.24
Binary Codes for Decimal Digits   188

TABLE 13.25
Letter Frequency Distributions in English   189

TABLE 13.26
Highest-Frequency Letters in Various Languages   189

TABLE 13.27
Conversion Between Typographical Units   191

TABLE 16.1
Programming Language Standards   223

TABLE 17.1
International Paper Sizes: "A" Series   244

TABLE 17.2
International Paper Sizes: "B" Series   245

TABLE 17.3
International Paper Sizes: "C" Series   245

List of Figures

FIG. 6.1
Macintosh Graphics Format Conversions Currently Possible Using
Commercially Available Software   71

FIG. 6.2
Macintosh Graphics Format Conversions Currently Possible Using
Adobe Photoshop 1.1   72

FIG. 6.3
Macintosh Graphics Format Conversions Currently Possible Using
Deneba Canvas 2.1   73

FIG. 6.4
Macintosh Graphics Format Conversions Currently Possible Using
Supermac Pixelpaint 2.0   74

FIG. 6.5
Macintosh Graphics Format Conversions Currently Possible Using
Supermac Pixelpaint Professional 1.0   75

FIG. 8.1
Pin Numbering for a DB-25 Connector   84

FIG. 8.2
Pin Numbering for a DB-9 Connector   88

FIG. 8.3
Pin Assignments on the Macintosh Mini-DIN Connector   90

FIG. 8.4
Pin Assignments for the Centronics Parallel Interface Connector   96

FIG. 8.5
Pin Assignments for the IEEE 488 Interface Connector   98

FIG. 8.6
Pin Assignments for the Internal SCSI Interface Connector
on Macintosh Computers   99

FIG. 13.1
Illustration of Accented Letters in ISO Alphabets   165

FIG. 13.2
Illustration of Typographical Terminology   192

FIG. 15.1
ISO OSI and ARPA/Internet Reference Models   206

FIG. 15.12
Relationship Between IEEE 802 Standards and ISO OSI Model   207

Preface

Computer users and programmers often suffer from a shortage of processing power, a shortage of disk space, or a shortage of main memory. Perhaps the only thing in the world of computers which is never in short supply is incompatibility. Despite the proliferation of a large number of desirable standards in hardware, software, and data communications, the scientists, engineers, or hobbyists who find themselves working on more than one computer or system can also find themselves hopelessly confused.

Consider the case of operating systems. Until recently, there was no standard at all to govern development in this area. It was only in 1988 that the IEEE released its standard operating system interface, POSIX (based on UNIX), and it remains to be seen what impact this standard will have. Operating systems have developed separately from each other over the last thirty years, occasionally borrowing ideas from each other and occasionally working in a similar manner to solve common problems—but separately nonetheless. As a result, operating systems are often similar enough to make moving between them feasible for the user, and different enough to make doing so annoying, confusing, and sometimes dangerous. Moving from one computer system to another is a bit like changing from one car to another. But it is far worse than switching, say, from a Honda Accord to a Chevrolet Caprice; it is more like changing from an Accord or a Caprice to a car where the steering wheel is on the floor, the accelerator is hand-operated and hangs from the roof, and the brakes are in the door handle.

One aim of this book, addressed in Sec. 1, is to make the task of working on an unfamiliar or semifamiliar system a bit easier. VMS users who find themselves on a UNIX system, for example, and want only to perform a few simple operations without becoming experts, should find this section useful. So will UNIX people who have to do a quick job on an IBM mainframe; or MVS users who must use an IBM-PC from time to time. We present working subsets of five major operating systems: UNIX, VAX-VMS, VM-CMS, MVS-TSO, and MS-DOS. In addition, there is a chapter on Macintosh shortcuts and tips. Finally, Chap. 7 summarizes the fundamental characteristics of several computer systems, including some systems not covered in detail in this book.

We do not cover all commands, by any stretch of the imagination; and we do not illustrate every possible usage for the commands we do cover. We eschew general syntactic forms, preferring to present the material through various concrete examples. We concentrate on the often-used basics: listing directories; copying files, renaming them, deleting them, and editing them; compiling and running programs; and other such operations.

Section 2 of the book concentrates on data communications. The aim of Sec. 2 is related to that of Sec. 1: to provide information useful to the multi-system programmer or user. Such individuals must not only cope with different operating systems, but also with different hardware interfaces, file transfer protocols, networks, etc. Chapter 8 treats interfaces and connections (e.g., PC to Mac), and also provides information on modems. Chapter 9 covers worldwide networks such as BITNET and the Internet. Chapters 10 and 11 cover file transfer with Kermit and FTP.

Another important aim of this book is to acquaint the reader with the world of information technology standards—those forces working against incompatibility (often without success). Section 3 of the book, and some of Sec. 2, is devoted to this purpose. Section 3 covers standards organizations and standardization procedures, and lists many important standards in information technology. The reader will find many useful tables in Sec. 3, including standard and nonstandard character codes (Chap. 13), and floating-point formats (Chap. 14). There are also some discussions not explicitly related to the subject of standards, but related to the topics of the individual chapters—for instance, the discussion of digital typography in the character codes chapter. Chapter 15 discusses network standards, and Chap. 16 describes the history and development of programming language standards.

In general, this book is not tutorial in nature, and is not for the inexperienced beginner, although much information contained herein will be useful to beginners and advanced professionals alike. The book is intended to be a somewhat heterogenous but useful compendium of information for experienced users. It is unlikely that you will find all the information in this book anywhere else in one place.

M. S. Vassiliou
J. A. Orenstein

1

Common Operating System Commands

This section provides working subsets of five major operating systems: UNIX, VAX-VMS, VM-CMS, MVS-TSO, and MS-DOS. In addition, there is a chapter on Apple Macintosh shortcuts and useful information. The treatment is not comprehensive, and is example-driven rather than general in nature. The intent is to give the user the ability to do simple things simply. The generality and comprehensiveness of fuller treatments can often be distracting for the user who only needs to navigate briefly through a system and perform a few simple tasks.

In addition to a summary of common commands, each chapter also provides a short survey of the history and development of the operating system in question, and an outline of the different versions or dialects of that system (e.g., Berkeley UNIX vs. AT&T UNIX, DOS 2.0 vs. 4.0, etc.). Important differences between dialects are noted in the text.

The table below provides a quick cross-reference to some of the commands covered. To locate these and other commands, the reader is referred to the index, and the chapter table of contents. In the index at the back of the book, commands are listed by function, and under the entries for the individual operating systems.

Cross-Reference of Common Operating System Commands

Function	UNIX (Chap. 1)	VAX-VMS (Chap. 2)	MVS-TSO (Chap. 3)	VM-CMS (Chap. 4)	MS-DOS (Chap. 5)
List directory	ls	DIR	LISTCAT	LISTFILE	DIR
Copy a file	cp	COPY	COPY	COPYFILE	COPY
Rename a file	mv	RENAME	RENAME	RENAME	RENAME
Delete a file	rm	DELETE	DELETE	ERASE	ERASE
List file contents	cat	TYPE	LIST	TYPE	TYPE
Print file	lp,lpr	PRINT	DSPRINT	PRINT	PRINT
Create a directory	mkdir	CREATE/ DIRECTORY			MKDIR
Remove directory	rmdir	DELETE[1]			RMDIR
Change directory	cd	SET DEFAULT			CD
Line editor	ed	EDT, EDIT	EDIT	EDIT	EDLIN

Note: 1. Appropriate protection parameters must first be set.

The final chapter in this section summarizes some fundamental characteristics of several operating systems, including, but not limited to, the six systems covered in detail in this book.

1

UNIX

UNIX is a popular operating system, written mostly in the C programming language. It was developed at AT&T Bell Laboratories by two talented individuals, Dennis Ritchie and Ken Thompson, and first introduced in 1969. It incorporated ideas from Multics, MIT's CTSS, and other innovative operating systems of the time, and introduced significant innovations of its own. It has enjoyed a huge success, and now runs on literally every type of computer: micros, workstations, minis, mainframes, and supercomputers. More than a million UNIX systems have been shipped. UNIX has heavily influenced other operating systems, and has formed an important basis for POSIX, the new ISO/IEC Operating System Interface standard [ISO/IEC 9945-1 (1990), adapted from IEEE 1003.1 (1988)—see Chap. 17].

UNIX has always been an open system, and many individuals and teams have contributed to its development over the years. Although countless organizations have been involved in UNIX research and development, there have been three major development streams, two at AT&T and one at the University of California at Berkeley. These streams have both diverged from each other and influenced each other.

Within AT&T, UNIX has continued to develop under the *aegis* of its original developers in the Research Group, and this "Research UNIX" is now in its Ninth Edition (1987). Meanwhile, a UNIX Support Group at AT&T has also worked continuously on developing its own versions, using the Research 6th Edition as a starting point around 1977. These versions from the UNIX Support Group have led to the commercial products licensed by AT&T, starting with System III in 1982 and System V in 1983. By 1989, AT&T System V UNIX was in its fourth release.

In addition to the AT&T efforts, a major research program was under way at the University of California at Berkeley, and the first Berkeley VAX version, 3 BSD UNIX, was ready in 1978 (BSD stands for Berkeley Software Distribution). DARPA (Defense Advanced Research Projects Agency) funded the development of 4 BSD, starting at the end of the 1970s. The latest Berkeley version is 4.3 BSD (1987).

Thus, the UNIX world is full of variations, extensions, and versions. However, there are really only two broad "flavors" of UNIX in common use: AT&T UNIX (System V), and Berkeley UNIX (4 series BSD). These have much in common, although there are important differences. For instance, command-language programming ("shell programming") is different in the two systems. For the basic subset of commands we cover below, the differences are, as a rule, not terribly important.

UNIX provides online help for the commands described below. The command is man (for manual). For example, to find out about the ls command, type

```
man ls
```

→ **Warning**

Before we proceed, we must note that UNIX is *case sensitive*. Jones is different from jones. The user should exercise extreme care in typing.

1.1 Files and Filenames

1.1.1 Valid Filenames

Filenames may be up to 14 characters long on System V, and up to 255 characters long on Berkeley systems.

Splitting a file up into a basename and an extension, separated by a period, is optional, but it is a common practice, and may be required by certain applications, e.g., compilers. For example, the filename myprog.c may refer to the C program myprog. myprog is the basename, c is the extension.

1.1.2 Directory Structure and Pathnames

UNIX has a hierarchical file system, and the complete specification of a file showing its position in the system is a pathname. The pathname

/usr/fred/text/chapter

is an absolute pathname specifying the file named chapter. This file is inside the directory called text, which is inside the directory fred (which happens to be the individual user directory for fred); this in turn is in the directory usr, which is the directory containing the identifications and file systems of all users on the system. usr itself is but a subdirectory in the root directory. Since the above is an absolute pathname, it can be used to specify the file chapter, no matter where you are in the system. Suppose, however, you happen to be in the directory /usr/fred: then a relative pathname

text/chapter

would be sufficient to specify the file. If you happen to be in /usr/fred/text, then chapter alone is sufficient.

The directory above the current directory can be referred to using a double-period, "..". For example, if the current directory is /usr/fred/text, then .. refers to /usr/fred. The current directory can be referred to using one period, although this is less useful.

1.1.3 Wild Cards

- * Matches any sequence of characters
- ? Matches any single character
- [ ] Matches characters enclosed within [ ].

The following examples will clarify the above.

a*	Any filename beginning with a.
a*b*c*	Any filename beginning with a, ending with c, and having a b somewhere in the middle.
a?	Any two-character filename beginning with a.
abc[def]	The filenames abcd, abce, or abcf.
a[a-z]	A filename beginning with a and ending in any lowercase letter.

1.2 List Out Directory Contents

The basic command is

```
ls
```

which will produce a listing of the files in a directory (note that on some older Berkeley systems, the ls command was denoted lc). There are many options to augment the basic commands. The most useful is

```
ls -l
```

which will list all the files in long format, i.e., with additional information as shown in the following example. This is a single entry in the directory listing; it shows the information for the file myprog.c:

```
-rwxrwxrwx 1 fred      15432  Jan 2 00:36 myprog.c
```

The - at the beginning means the file is an ordinary one; a d would have indicated a directory. rwxrwxrwx means that read (r), write (w), and execute (x) access are allowed to the file, for the file's owner, the owner's user group, and the rest of the world. As another example, consider rwxr-xr--. This would indicate that the owner had read, write, and execute access; the group had read and execute access but no write access (could not modify the file, only read it and run it); and the rest of the world had only read access. The 1 following the access codes in the example above indicates the number of links to the file. The 15432 is the size of the file in bytes. The date and time indicate when the file was last modified. Sometimes, in between the owner and the size, you might see the owner's group affiliation. System V will insert this field automatically, while Berkeley systems must be requested to do so, via option -g (e.g., ls -lg).

1.3 Copy a File

To copy the contents of the file old into the file new, while leaving old intact, use the command

```
cp old new
```

This overwrites new if it already exists. If new is a directory, then the result is to place a copy of old into the directory new.

You may use the cp command with wild cards. For example,

```
cp *.c mydir
```

will copy all files located in the current directory and having extension .c into the directory mydir.

1.4   Rename a File

To rename the file oldfile so that its filename is newfile, type

    mv oldfile newfile

If newfile already exists, it will be deleted and replaced with oldfile. To move oldfile from the current directory into the immediate subdirectory mydir, use

    mv oldfile mydir

As with cp, you may use wild cards in file specifications.

1.5   Delete a File

Follow these examples:

rm myfile	Delete the file myfile.
rm -f myfile	Delete myfile even if I have write protection on it.
rm *	Delete all files. (DANGEROUS!)
rm -i *	Delete all files, but ask me if I really want to do so before each one. (Be careful! Some older versions do not recognize this.)
rm -r mydir	Delete directory mydir, along with all its files and subdirectories.

CAUTION: Be careful when using wild cards. Suppose you want to remove all files ending in .c. The correct way to accomplish this is to type

    rm *.c

If you make a mistake and type instead

    rm * .c

with a space between the wild card and the .c (not a difficult mistake to make), you will lose all your files. The system will see rm * first , and do it.

1.6   List Contents of File on the Screen

To list the file myfile, type

    cat myfile

Using cat will display the whole file, nonstop. If you want to view the file one screenful at a time, do the following:

more myfile	Operates on Berkeley systems. Typing a space will display the next screenful. Typing a carriage return will scroll one line. CTRL-C will abort.
pg myfile	Operates on AT&T systems. Typing either a carriage return or a space will display the next screenful.

1.7 Print a File

`lp myfile`   (System V) Print the file `myfile` on the system printer.

`lpr myfile`   (Berkeley Systems) Print the file `myfile` on the system printer.

1.8 Create a New Directory

Create a new subdirectory named `mydir`, to be located in the current directory:

```
mkdir mydir
```

Create a new subdirectory `mydir`, to be located in `/usr/fred/text`:

```
mkdir /usr/fred/text/mydir
```

1.9 Remove a Directory

Remove the subdirectory `mydir`, located in the current directory:

```
rmdir mydir
```

Remove the subdirectory `mydir` as specified by an absolute pathname:

```
rmdir /usr/fred/text/mydir
```

Note: `mydir` must be empty (i.e., it must contain only the entries . and ..). `rm -r` (see Sec. 1.5) does not have this requirement.

1.10 Move to Another Directory

Move from the current working directory to subdirectory `mydir` (located in the current directory):

```
cd mydir
```

Move from the current working directory to the subdirectory `hisdir`, located in the subdirectory `dox`, which in turn is located in `steve`'s user directory:

```
cd /usr/steve/dox/hisdir
```

If you are not sure which directory you are currently in, type the command `pwd`; this will print the name of your current working directory. To move back to your home directory (your user directory—the place you start in when you log in), just type `cd` alone, without a directory name.

1.11 Edit a File (Line Mode)

Berkeley UNIX has a full screen editor called `vi` (visual). It was quite good when it was first introduced in the late seventies, but it pales compared to modern full-screen editors on microcomputers. If you use Berkeley UNIX constantly, it would be a good idea to learn vi. If not, the line editor ed, and its more modern extended version ex, should suffice. ed is the basic editor which should be available on any UNIX system; ex is an extended line editor generally available on Berkeley systems, and used in conjunction with vi.

If you know other line editors, you will have no problem with ed or ex. In the discussion below, we use ed as the model, but much applies equally to ex. For the really basic editing functions with which we are concerned, ed and ex are similar. (Note that we are not implying that experienced users should use ex just as they would ed—that would not be taking full advantage of ex's greater power).

If the file myfile.dat does not exist and you type

```
ed myfile.dat
```

then you will create a new file by that name. If the file you want to edit does exist, ed will let you make changes to it. Suppose you are editing an existing file myprog.f. You would get into the line editor by typing :

```
ed myprog.f
```

The prompt in line mode is an asterisk * for ed, and a colon : for ex. Here are examples of editing commands in line mode:

!ls	Execute a normal UNIX ls command from within the editor. You can pass commands from the editor to the UNIX shell by preceding them with an exclamation point.
1p (1n)	Go to the top of the file, and display the first line. Using p causes line to be displayed without line number; using n causes line number to be displayed along with the line.
23p (23n)	Go to line 23 and display line 23.
-11	Move up 11 lines, and display new line.
+12	Move down 12 lines, and display new lines.
4,10p (4,10n)	Display lines 4 through 10.
6,$p (6,$n)	Display entire file starting at line 6.
15d	Delete line 15.
15,50d	Delete lines 15 through 50.
15,31t10	Copy lines 15 through 31 and put them after the present line 10 (in ex, t can be coded as co instead).
12,14m20	Move lines 12 through 14 to the position after the present line 20.
i	Get into insert mode. You will not receive the normal * prompt. You may type in your desired text, which will be placed immediately before your current position in the file.

a	Get into insert mode. You will not receive the normal * prompt. You may type in your desired text, which will be placed immediately after your current position in the file.
.	Get out of insert mode and back into line-edit mode.
/Jones/p	Find the next occurrence of the string Jones.
//p	Find the next Jones (after you have already issued the command /Jones/ above).
3,/Jones/p	Display file from line 3 through the first line containing Jones.
//	Find the next Jones (after you have already issued the command /Jones/ above).
g/Jones/p	Find and display all lines in the file containing the string Jones.
s/me/you/p	Change first occurrence of me on the current line to you.
s/me/you/gp	Change all occurrences of me on the current line to you.
3,7s/me/you/g	Change me to you in lines 3 through 7.
1,$s/me/you/g	Change me to you throughout the file. Adding a p to the end of the command would cause the last line changed to be displayed.
6r /usr/fred/junk.dat	
	Copy the external disk file /usr/fred/junk.dat and put it after line 6 in the file you are editing. To put the disk file above the first line in your edited file, use line number 0 (0r).
10,40w my.dat	Copy lines 10 through 40 into an external disk file called my.dat.
w	Save changes permanently. Does not cause exit from editor.
q	Exit editor without saving changes since the last w. When you are ready to stop, and you want to save all changes you have made, use w followed by q.

1.12   Compile and Run a Program

Suppose you have written a C program with three modules, say main.c, sub1.c, and sub2.c (files ending in .c are assumed to be C source programs). You can compile and link all of them as follows:

```
cc main.c sub1.c sub2.c
```

Notice that there are no commas separating the filenames. The compiler will create object files main.o, sub1.o, and sub2.o, and produce an executable file with the standard name a.out (which you may want to change to something else). To run the program, simply type the name of the executable file:

```
a.out
```

Note that if you want the executable file to be called something other than a.out to begin with, you can specify your desired name using the -o option:

```
cc  main.c subl.c sub2.c -o xxxexe
```

The above command creates an executable file xxxexe, which you can run simply by typing

```
xxxexe
```

FORTRAN 77 source programs should be created with extension .f, e.g., main.f, subl.f, and sub2.f. The UNIX FORTRAN 77 compiler command is f77 (many other names are possible), and its syntax is similar to that of the cc command, e.g.:

```
f77  main.f subl.f sub2.f
```

Again, the default name of the executable file is a.out, and you can run the program just by typing a.out.

To aid modular program development, UNIX provides an extremely powerful program called make, which automatically keeps track of files that have changed, and recompiles them when necessary. It is a fairly safe bet that, in a directory containing a file named makefile or Makefile, make can be used to construct executables in that same directory. For example, to remake an executable called xxxexe, simply type

```
make xxxexe
```

or sometimes just

```
make
```

For more information on make, consult online help (man make), your system manuals, or tutorial books on UNIX (e.g., Kochan and Wood, 1989; McGilton and Morgan, 1983).

1.13   Command Procedures

UNIX command files are known as "shell scripts" or "shell programs." There are currently three major different UNIX shells, (i.e., three different languages for creating command files):

1. The Bourne shell, sh   Currently distributed with AT&T System V.

2. The Korn shell, ksh   A newer shell compatible with sh, and which may be distributed as a standard shell by AT&T in the future.

3. The C shell, csh   Incompatible with sh or ksh; distributed with Berkeley UNIX.

1.13.1   Invoke a Command Procedure Interactively

Suppose you are working in the Berkeley system (C shell) and there is a command file called `mycom`. You can run it by typing

```
csh mycom
```

Similarly, if the file is written in the Bourne shell:

```
sh mycom
```

or in the Korn shell:

```
ksh mycom
```

1.13.2   Invoke a Command Procedure in Batch

To run some command file called `mycom` in batch ("in the background"), do the following (assume now we are running Berkeley UNIX and `mycom` is a C shell script):

```
csh mycom&
```

The ampersand `&` tells UNIX to run in background, i.e., to start `mycom` running and accept new commands from the terminal immediately (note that the ampersand is not limited to running command files in background—it can be used to run any command in background). When you type `csh mycom&`, the system will print out a process identification number on your terminal.

1.13.3   Check on the Progress of a Job

To check on the progress of the background process, try

```
ps
```

which will list information on the processes you have running, including the process id numbers. The command

```
ps -al
```

will give you more complete information (1 option) , about all processes (a option), not just your personal ones. The `ps` commands given above should work in both Berkeley and System V, but other `ps` command options are different in the two systems.

1.13.4   Stop a Batch Job

First, find out the PID (process identification number) of your job by issuing a `ps` command as described above. Suppose your PID is 1128. The command

```
kill 1128
```

should kill the job. If the job is very stubborn and seems to be doing its best to stay alive (it happens sometimes), try

```
kill -9 1128
```

which is the surest way to kill the job.

1.14   Abort Operation

CTRL-C can often function as an interrupt key.   Pressing it can abort an undesired operation.

1.15   Redirection of Input and Output

It is often useful to capture output from some command or program in a file, or to use the output of one command as input to another. UNIX offers general-purpose facilities to accomplish these tasks.
   The command

    ls > files

lists the files in the current directory, but instead of printing the listing on the monitor, captures the result in the file `files` located in the current directory.   Any existing contents of `files` will be lost. To append to an existing file, the command is

    ls >> files

Input can also be redirected.   A command or program that reads input from the console can be used to accept input from a file.   For example

    prog < f

feeds file `f` as input to program `prog`, which normally reads input from the console.
   Output from one program can be used as input to another program using a pipe.   For example, `more` is a UNIX program that takes input and displays it one screenful at a time.   The user must type a space to obtain the next screenful of the input.   This command

    ls | more

produces a directory listing a screen at a time.
   Some UNIX programs are designed to accept either files or redirected input. `grep` is a program that searches files for lines containing a given string.   This command

    grep "Fred" phone-book

searches the file `phone-book` for lines containing `Fred`, and prints out all such lines.   The command can also be given as follows:

    cat phone-book | grep "Fred"

`cat phone-book` lists the contents of `phone-book`.   Each line is passed, via the pipe, to the `grep` command which prints out lines containing `Fred`.
   Any number of programs can be chained together with pipes and redirection.   For example, this sequence

    cat phone-book | grep "Fred" | sort > freds

produces, in the file `freds`, a sorted listing of the those lines in `phone-book` containing `Fred`.   The reader may consult Kochan and

Wood (1989), or McGilton and Morgan (1983) for more information on redirection and pipes.

1.16   Bibliography

Anderson, G., and P. Anderson (1986), *The UNIX C Shell Field Guide*, Prentice-Hall, Englewood Cliffs, New Jersey.

Christian, K. (1988), *UNIX Command Reference Guide*, John Wiley, New York, New York.

Hewlett-Packard Co. (1990), *The Ultimate Guide to the vi and ex Text Editors*, Benjamin Cummings, Redwood City, California.

Kochan, S. G., and P. H. Wood (1989), *Exploring the UNIX System*, Second Edition, Hayden Books, Indianapolis, Indiana.

Leffler, S. T., M. K. McKusick, M. J. Karel, and J. S. Quarterman (1989), *The Design and Implementation of the 4.3 BSD UNIX Operating System*, Addison-Wesley, Menlo Park, California.

McGilton, H., and R. Morgan (1983), *Introducing the UNIX System*, McGraw-Hill, San Francisco, California.

Morgan, C. R. (1990), *Inside Xenix* (reprint of 1986 work), The Waite Group, Carmel, Indiana.

2

VAX-VMS

VAX-VMS, or simply "VMS," has historically been the primary operating system on DEC's VAX line of computers, although UNIX has been penetrating the market. VMS is somewhat similar to PDP-11 RSX. The VAX is a virtual-memory machine, and VMS features virtual storage management.

VMS is a reasonably friendly system. It also has some unique features, such as automatic generation of new versions of files. VMS provides online help for the commands described below. For example, to find out about the COPY command, type

```
HELP COPY
```

2.1 Files and Filenames

2.1.1 Valid Filenames

Filenames are composed of a name, followed by an extension, followed by a version number, for example:

```
MYPROG.FOR;23
```

where MYPROG is the name and FOR is the type. In this example, version 23 of MYPROG.FOR is designated. If you omit the version number, VMS will assume that you are referring to the latest version of the file. Note the period separating the name from the extension, and the semicolon separating the extension from the version number. The version number may be up to five decimal digits with a value between 1 and 32767. The name may be up to 39 alphanumeric characters. The extension may also be up to 39 characters long, but it is typically only three characters long, as per the following suggested defaults (partial list only):

BAS	BASIC source code
C	C source code
COM	Command file
DAT	Data file, e.g., containing input data for a FORTRAN program.
DIR	Subdirectory
EXE	Executable file
FOR	FORTRAN source code
LIS	Listing created by compiler or assembler
LOG	Information file created by (e.g.) a batch job
MAI	File storing mail message
MAR	MACRO assembler source code
OBJ	Object code

2.1.2   Directories and Full File Specification

VMS has a hierarchical file system, and the complete specification of a file will indicate the directories and subdirectories in which it is contained. For example, the specification of MYPROG.FOR, contained in the subdirectory called SOURCE, in turn contained in the subdirectory called PERSONAL, all in the user directory of user FRED, would read as follows:

[FRED.PERSONAL.SOURCE]MYPROG.FOR;23

Again, the version number is optional. The square brackets, however, are essential. If you happen to be in the subdirectory SOURCE, then MYPROG.FOR is sufficient to specify the file.

In fact, the long specification given above is not actually the most complete specification. The specification may also include a node name, identifying the computer in question from among many in a network, and a device name (generally a fixed disk) where your user directory is located. Suppose FRED is on disk drive DDA1 (device names contain up to four alphanumeric characters), on node TACOS. Then the full specification of file MYPROG.FOR is as follows:

TACOS::DDA1:[FRED.PERSONAL.SOURCE]MYPROG.FOR;23

In general, if you are working only in your own user directory, you will not need to specify the node or the device name to access your files.

2.1.3 Wild Cards

- * Matches any sequence of characters
- % Matches any single character

Examples:

*.BAS	Any file of type BAS
MYPROG.FOR;*	All versions of MYPROG.FOR. Useful in DELETE commands.
A%.FOR	Any file of type FOR, beginning with A, followed by any one character

The above wild cards are the two that VMS supports for general file-matching, although more are supported for the purposes of directory searching (see below).

2.2 List Out Directory Contents

The basic command is
```
DIRECTORY
```
which will produce a listing of the files in a directory. DIRECTORY may be abbreviated DIR. There are many options to augment the basic command. Some of the useful ones are:

DIR/SIZE	Give the size of each file
DIR/DATE	Show when each file was created
DIR/FULL	Show complete information on each file

DIR/FULL will give the following information on each file: Size, protection status, creation date, and the date the file was last modified, as well as other information.

For the purpose of directory searching, VMS supports some wild cards in addition to the ones discussed in Sec. 2.1.3. It supports the ellipsis ..., which searches down a directory hierarchy, and the hyphen -, which searches up a directory hierarchy. Some examples will clarify this:
```
DIR [FRED.SOURCES...]*.DAT
```
This will list information on all files of type DAT contained in FRED's directory SOURCES or any of its subdirectories.

```
DIR [...]
```
will list information on all files in your current directory and all subdirectories.
```
DIR [-]
```
will list information on all files in the directory above the one in which you are currently located. Suppose you are user FRED, and you have three subdirectories, D1, D2, and D3. Suppose further that you are currently located in D1. Then the command
```
DIR [-.D2...]
```
will list information on all the files in subdirectory D2, and all its subdirectories.

2.3 Copy a File

To copy the contents of the file OLDFILE.DAT into the file NEWFILE.DAT while leaving OLDFILE.DAT intact, use the command
```
COPY OLDFILE.DAT NEWFILE.DAT
```
If NEWFILE.DAT already exists, VMS will create a new version of it. Suppose you are user FRED. To copy the contents of the file OLDFILE.DAT into another file named OLDFILE.DAT, located in the directory MYDIR, in your user directory, you may use
```
COPY OLDFILE.DAT [FRED.MYDIR]OLDFILE.DAT
```
You may use the COPY command with wild cards. For example,
```
COPY *.DAT [FRED.MYDIR]
```
will copy all files of type DAT into FRED's directory MYDIR. You may also use the . . . and - wild cards discussed above.

2.4 Rename a File

To rename the file OLDFILE.FOR so that its filename is, say, NEWFILE.FOR, type
```
RENAME OLDFILE.FOR NEWFILE.FOR
```
To move OLDFILE.DAT from the current directory into the directory MYDIR contained in your user directory FRED, use
```
RENAME OLDFILE.DAT [FRED.MYDIR]OLDFILE.DAT
```
As with COPY, you may use wild cards in file specifications.

2.5 Delete a File

Suppose you want to delete your file MYPROG.FOR. If you simply use the DELETE command, and type
```
DELETE MYPROG.FOR
```
it will not work! The reason is that you have not specified a version number. In this case, VMS does not make its customary assumption

that you are referring to the current (highest-numbered) version.
You must specify a version number explicitly, e.g.,

```
DELETE MYPROG.FOR;3
```

This will, however, delete only version 3 of MYPROG.FOR. To delete
all versions of the file, type

```
DELETE MYPROG.FOR;*
```

Should you want to delete all versions of the file MYPROG.FOR except
the current (highest-numbered) one, use the PURGE command:

```
PURGE MYPROG.FOR
```

The command

```
PURGE/KEEP=3 MYPROG.FOR
```

will purge all but the latest three versions of MYPROG.FOR. Issuing a
PURGE command without a file specification will cause VMS to
delete all old versions of all files in the current directory. VMS, by
keeping old versions of files, makes your life as a programmer
somewhat easier, but does tend to consume large amounts of disk
space. You are likely to be issuing PURGE commands often to free up
space. Returning to the DELETE command, be careful when using
wild cards. The command

```
DELETE *.*;*
```

will delete all the files in your current directory. To protect yourself
from yourself, you may want to use the /CONFIRM option, for
example:

```
DELETE/CONFIRM *.BAS;*
```

This will delete all files of type BAS, but will cause VMS to ask you
for confirmation before deleting each one.

2.6   List Contents of File on the Screen

To list the file MYPROG.FOR, type

```
TYPE MYPROG.FOR
```

Using TYPE will display the whole file, nonstop. CTRL-S will pause
the listing, and CTRL-Q will continue it. If you want to view the file
one screenful at a time, do the following:

```
TYPE/PAGE MYPROG.FOR
```

2.7   Print a File

To print a hard copy of the file MYPROG.FOR, simply type

```
PRINT MYPROG.FOR
```

2.8   Create a New Directory

Create a new subdirectory named MYDIR, to be located in the current directory:

```
CREATE/DIRECTORY [.MYDIR]
```

Create a new subdirectory MYDIR, to be located in [FRED.TEXT]:

```
CREATE/DIRECTORY [FRED.TEXT.MYDIR]
```

2.9   Remove a Directory

Removing directories is a bit less straightforward than other operations in VMS. As an example, suppose you want to remove the subdirectory MYDIR, located in the current directory (which we assume here is your user directory FRED). You must go through several steps. First, if the subdirectory is not empty, you must delete all the files inside it. Then, you must reset the protection code on MYDIR, giving its owner (you) the right to delete it. This is necessary because VMS protects subdirectories from inadvertent deletion. To reset the protection, type:

```
SET PROTECTION = (O:D) MYDIR.DIR
```

Now, delete the directory:

```
DELETE MYDIR.DIR;1
```

Note that the version number is needed. Notice also that in both commands above, we needed to use the extension DIR to specify a subdirectory—something we do not do routinely.

2.10   Move to Another Directory

Move from the current working directory to subdirectory MYDIR (located in the current directory):

```
SET DEFAULT [.MYDIR]
```

Move from the current working directory to the subdirectory HISDIR, located in the subdirectory DOX, which in turn is located in STEVE's user directory:

```
SET DEFAULT [STEVE.DOX.HISDIR]
```

2.11   Edit a File (Line Mode)

The VMS editor is called EDT, sometimes called EDIT. It has both a line mode and a full-screen mode. Here, we cover the line mode. If the file MYFILE.DAT does not exist and you type

```
EDT MYFILE.DAT
```

then you will create a new file by that name. If the file you want to edit does exist, EDT will let you make changes to it. Suppose you are editing a preexisting file MYPROG.FOR. You would get into the line editor by typing :

EDT MYPROG.FOR

The prompt in line mode is an asterisk *. If you type a c, you will go into full-screen mode; to get back to line mode, issue a CTRL-Z. Here are examples of editing commands in line mode:

1	Go to the top of the file, and display the first line.
23	Go to line 23 and display line 23.
-11	Move up 11 lines.
+12	Move down 12 lines.
Carriage-return	Move down 1 line and display new line. Equivalent to +1.
D 15	Delete line 15.
D 15:50	Delete lines 15 through 50.
CO 15 TO 76	Copy line 15 and put it above the present line 76.
CO 15:31 TO 10	Copy lines 15 through 31 and put them above the present line 10.
M 44 TO 107	Move line 44 to the position above the present line 107.
M 12:14 TO 20	Move lines 12 through 14 to the position above the present line 20.
I	Get into insert mode. You will not receive the normal * prompt. You may type in your desired text, which will be placed immediately above your current position in the file.
CTRL-Z	Exit insert mode and return to line-edit mode. Also exit screen mode and return to line-edit mode.
RES	Renumber lines in file in increments of 1 (insertions and deletions complicate the numbering system, and you can use this to resimplify the situation).
'xxxyy'	Find first occurrence of string xxxyy.
S/X1/X2/	Change the string X1 to the string X2.
S/X2/X30/1:10	Change X2 to X30 in lines 1 through 10.
S/ME/YOU/W	Change ME to YOU throughout the file.
S/ME/YOU/W/Q	Change ME to YOU throughout the file, but ask for permission before making each change. Answer Y or N.
INCLUDE J2.DAT	Copy the external disk file J2.DAT and put it above your current position in your edit file.
WR MY.DAT 10:40	Copy lines 10 through 40 into an external disk file called MY.DAT.
QUIT	Exit editor without saving changes (BE CAREFUL!).

EX   Exit editor, with all changes saved. VMS will create a
                      new version of your file.

2.12   Compile and Run a Program

FOR is the VAX FORTRAN 77 compiler command. Suppose you
have a FORTRAN program consisting of three modules,
MYPROG.FOR, SUB1.FOR, and SUB2.FOR. The following sequence
will compile and link the program and create an executable module
MYPROG.EXE:

```
FOR MYPROG
FOR SUB1
FOR SUB2
LINK MYPROG,SUB1,SUB2
```

Note that the FOR command assumes the extension .FOR. The FOR
commands above create the object modules MYPROG.OBJ, SUB1.OBJ,
and SUB2.OBJ. The LINK command assumes the default extension
.OBJ in the filenames, and links the three together. Note that the
LINK command automatically searches several libraries, so that
you need not worry about specifying (say) the library containing
FORTRAN intrinsic functions such as SIN or COS. This does not
mean you cannot link libraries of your own. Suppose you often use
LINPACK, which resides (say) in SYS$UTIL, and you know that the
linker does not automatically search it; you can specify it in the
LINK:

```
LINK MYPROG,SUB1,SUB2,SYS$UTIL:LINPACK.LIB
```

After the link command completes without errors, you will have an
executable file MYPROG.EXE. To execute it, simply type

```
RUN MYPROG
```

The procedure for other languages is similar. Suppose MYPROG.C,
SUB1.C, and SUB2.C are C programs. You could use the sequence

```
CC MYPROG
CC SUB1
CC SUB2
LINK MYPROG,SUB1,SUB2
RUN MYPROG
```

2.13   Command Procedures

2.13.1   Invoke a Command Procedure Interactively

Consider a command procedure called MYCOM.COM [coded in Digital
command language (DCL)]. To invoke it interactively, type:

```
@MYCOM
```

2.13.2 Invoke a Command Procedure in Batch

To submit MYCOM.COM for batch (background) execution, type

    SUBMIT MYCOM

To submit it for batch (background) execution starting at (say) 9:00, type

    SUBMIT/AFTER=9:00 MYCOM

2.13.3 Check on the Progress of a Job

To check on a job's progress,

    SHOW QUEUE SYS$BATCH

This assumes the job is running on the system queue SYS$BATCH. On your system, the default system queue might be called something else. You also have the option to submit your job to a specific queue using the /QUEUE= option to the submit command; more information can be found in the system manuals, or in Bynon and Shannon (1987).

2.13.4 Stop a Batch Job

First, find out the ENTRY number of the job by issuing a SHOW QUEUE as described above. Suppose the entry number is 218. The command

    STOP/ENTRY=218

should kill the job.

2.14 Abort Operation

The interrupt key is CTRL-Y. This will stop an executing process. CTRL-C can also be used to abort a process, which can then be restarted by typing CONTINUE. CTRL-Z often works as an exit key for some applications programs or operation modes.

2.15 Bibliography

Bynon and Shannon (1987) is a good introduction to basic VMS commands. Kenah and Bate (1984) is an in-depth discussion of the VMS operating system (*not* a user's guide). Those who need to write their own command procedures can consult Anagnostopoulos (1989).

Anagnostopoulos, P. C. (1989), *Writing Real Programs in DCL*, VAX Users Series, Digital Press, Bedford, Massachusetts.

Bynon, D. W., and T. C. Shannon (1987), *Introduction to VAX/VMS,* Professional Press, Spring House, Pennsylvania.

Kenah, L . J., and Bate, S. F. (1984) *VAX/VMS Internals and Data Structures*, Digital Press, Bedford, Massachusetts.

MVS-TSO

MVS is one of IBM's two principal operating systems for its mainframe computers. The other is VM-CMS (Chap. 4). MVS, which first appeared in 1974 on the System/370, stands for multiple virtual storages; each user has a separate 16-Mbyte virtual address space. The older versions of the System/370 architecture had 32-bit words but only 24-bit addresses, rather small by today's standards. In 1982, IBM introduced the System/370 "Extended Architecture," with 31-bit addresses. MVS/370 was modified to MVS/XA to take advantage of the larger address space.

MVS is an efficient large-scale batch-processing system, but it is not terribly good for interactive work. MVS's interactive command-line interface, TSO, can be quite slow. Those who work extensively with MVS must usually learn job-control language (JCL), a complicated affair. We do not cover any JCL below. Neither do we cover IBM's ISPF, a menu-driven system interface for MVS-TSO. ISPF is more user-friendly, and has a respectable full-screen editor, but can be excruciatingly slow to use. The beginner is probably better off using a few simple commands in TSO. MVS-TSO provides some online help. To find out about the LISTCAT command, for example, type

```
HELP LISTCAT
```

3.1   Files and Filenames

3.1.1   Valid Filenames ("Data Set Names")

Files in TSO are referred to as "data sets." The name of a data set can be up to 44 characters long. There are some restrictions on the form of a data set name: it must be composed of one or more sections, known as "qualifiers," each of which is no more than eight characters long; the qualifiers are separated by periods. The following are valid names for data sets:

```
MYFILE
MYFILE.DATA
MYFILE.NEW.DATA
MYFILE.NEW.OCT.DATA
```

The data sets above (in order from top to bottom) are said to have one, two, three, and four "levels of qualification," with the leftmost levels being "higher." In the name

```
MYFILE.NEW.DATA
```

for example, `MYFILE` is the "highest level of qualification," and `DATA` is the "lowest level of qualification."

UNIX and VMS users, please note: The "levels of qualification" are *not* indicators of a directory structure—they are only components of a filename. `MYFILE.NEW.DATA` is only a filename. `.NEW` is not a directory, or anything remotely resembling one. The last qualifier in the data set name generally denotes the type of the data set (e.g., `DATA` in the example above). The following are a few commonly used data set types:

ASM	Assembly-language source code
CLIST	Command file
CNTL	Batch file containing JCL (job-control language) commands
COBOL	COBOL source code
DATA	Uppercase text, usually for use as input to application programs
FORT	FORTRAN source code
OBJ	Executable object module
TEXT	Upper and lowercase text

The above conventions for naming files are MVS conventions. TSO, which as we have said is the command-line interface to MVS, adds a few of its own. In TSO, the data set name also includes the user identification. Suppose your user identification is `TSOFRD1`; then the full names of the files in the example above are

```
TSOFRD1.MYFILE
TSOFRD1.MYFILE.DATA
TSOFRD1.MYFILE.NEW.DATA
TSOFRD1.MYFILE.NEW.OCT.DATA
```

Note that TSO attaches the user identification automatically, so that you should not include it. If you were to refer to the first data set as `TSOFRD1.MYFILE`, for example, TSO would think you were referring to `TSOFRD1.TSOFRD1.MYFILE`! You can suppress TSO's automatic appending of the user identification by putting the filename in single quotes. The proper way to refer to the first data set above, if you want to include the user identification, is `'TSOFRD1.MYFILE'`.

3.1.2   Partitioned Data Sets

MVS does not support a full hierarchical file system of the type to which UNIX or VMS users are accustomed.   There are no directories, subdirectories, etc.   MVS does provide a single-level directory-like structure in the form of what is called a "partitioned data set" (PDS). A PDS is a data set that contains other data sets known as "members." Members may not themselves be PDSs, but only ordinary files.   As an example, suppose you have a FORTRAN program called `MYPROG.FORT`, which is composed of a main program `MAIN` and two subroutines, `SUB1` and `SUB2`. You may make `MAIN`, `SUB1`, and `SUB2` the members of the PDS called `MYPROG.FORT`. You would refer to them as follows:

```
MYPROG.FORT(MAIN)
MYPROG.FORT(SUB1)
MYPROG.FORT(SUB2)
```

In each case, the member name is enclosed in parentheses. Member names may be one to eight characters long. The name of the PDS itself (i.e., `MYPROG.FORT` in this example) follows the naming conventions described above. Note that we have omitted the user identification from the beginning, as TSO appends it automatically (see above).

3.1.3   Wild Cards

In MVS-TSO, the asterisk * functions as a wild card. However, it can only replace one section of a filename (one level of qualification).

`*.DATA`   Any file of type `DATA` having a total of two qualifiers, excluding the user identification: e.g., `MYFILE.DATA`, `YOURFILE.DATA`, etc.

..DATA   Any file of type DATA having a total of three qualifiers,
                    excluding the user identification: e.g., MYFILE.NEW.DATA,
                    YOURFILE.OLD.DATA, etc.

3.2   List Out Directory Contents

The basic command is

    LISTCAT

which will produce a listing of the files in your user identification.
LISTCAT may be abbreviated LISTC. There are many options to
augment the basic command. Some of the most useful are
illustrated by examples. The command

    LISTC ALL

will list complete information concerning each file in the user
identification, including the name, the creation date, the volume
serial, the device type, and other things. The command

    LISTC ENTRIES (MYPROG.FORT MYFILE.DATA)

will cause TSO to list information on the files specified inside the
parentheses, in this case MYFILE.FORT and MYFILE.DATA. The
ENTRIES option can also be used with wild cards:

    LISTC ENTRIES (*.FORT)

will list information on all files of type FORT with one other level of
qualification in the filename (excluding the user identification).

    LISTC LEVEL (MYFILE.NEW)

will list information on all files whose names begin with
MYFILE.NEW. Note that the option ALL can be combined with the
options LEVEL or ENTRIES. Thus, the following commands are also
valid:

    LISTC LEVEL (MYFILE.NEW) ALL
    LISTC ENTRIES (*.FORT) ALL

You can obtain more information about individual data sets by
using the LISTDS command. For example,

    LISTDS MYFILE.DATA

will show the record format, logical record size, block size, data set
organization, and volume serial number for MYFILE.DATA.
LISTDS can also be used to list the names of all members of a
partitioned data set, by specifying the option MEMBERS. For example:

    LISTDS MYPROG.FORT MEMBERS

will produce, in addition to the usual information, a list of names of
all the members of the PDS MYPROG.FORT.

3.3 Copy a File

Suppose you want to copy the file OLDFILE.DATA, a sequential (non-partitioned) data set, into the new file NEWFILE.DATA while leaving OLDFILE.DATA intact. You may accomplish this as follows:

```
COPY OLDFILE.DATA NEWFILE.DATA
```

NEWFILE.DATA should not already exist before you issue the command.

If OLDFILE.DATA were a PDS, then NEWFILE.DATA *could* be an already existing partitioned data set. The members of OLDFILE.DATA would all be copied into NEWFILE.DATA. NEWFILE.DATA would not have to be empty before the command was issued, but if any of its members had the same names as members of OLDFILE.DATA, they would be replaced.

You are also allowed to specify members of a PDS directly in the COPY command. The command

```
COPY MYPROG.FORT(MAIN) NEWPROG.FORT(F1)
```

will create a new member F1 in NEWPROG.FORT, which will be identical to member MAIN of MYPROG.FORT. If member F1 already exists, it is replaced.

Believe it or not, the COPY command may not be available at all TSO installations. Although it is unlikely that you will find an installation without this command, there is a chance that its format will be different from what we have described here.

3.4 Rename a File

Consider the following examples:

```
RENAME OLDFILE.FORT NEWFILE.DATA
RENAME MYPROG.FORT(MAIN) MYPROG.FORT(INANE)
```

The first command gives the file OLDFILE.FORT the new name NEWFILE.DATA. The second renames member MAIN of the PDS MYPROG.FORT, so that its new name is INANE. The second command could also be written

```
RENAME MYPROG.FORT(MAIN) (INANE)
```

3.5 Delete a File

To delete the file OLDFILE.DATA, type simply

```
DELETE OLDFILE.DATA
```

This will usually produce the desired result, unless the expiration date of the file has not passed. If that is the case and you still need to delete the file, use

```
DELETE OLDFILE.DATA PURGE
```

You may specify a list of files to be deleted. The command:

```
DELETE (OLDFILE.DATA NEWFILE1.DATA MYDATA.DATA) PURGE
```

will delete all three files in the parentheses. The DELETE command also accepts limited wild card specifications. For example,

```
DELETE OLDFILE.* PURGE
```

will delete all files whose names begin with OLDFILE and that have one additional level of qualification. In other words, the command immediately above will delete OLDFILE.DATA, OLDFILE.FORT, OLDFILE.COBOL, etc. Note that an asterisk can only replace one level of qualification (see Sec. 3.1.1), and that level cannot be the highest one.

3.6 List Contents of File on the Screen

To list the file MYPROG.FORT, type

```
LIST MYPROG.FORT
```

Or, for the individual member MAIN of the PDS PROG.FORT,

```
LIST PROG.FORT(MAIN)
```

Some TSO installations may not have the LIST command.

3.7 Print a File

The command is DSPRINT, another essential command that some installations may not have! DSPRINT has many options and directives, but if all you want is a simple hard copy of your file, you need only know the name of your file and the name of the printer (defined by the installation at which you are working). Unfortunately, you will have to find out the name of the printer yourself. Suppose the name of the printer at your installation is IBMXXXX1, and the file you want to print is MYFILE.DATA

```
DSPRINT MYFILE.DATA IBMXXXX1
```

If you want to print out the member MAIN of the PDS PROG.FORT,

```
DSPRINT PROG.FORT(MAIN) IBMXXXX1
```

To print out only part of the file, you can specify the range of line numbers you want. For example, to print lines 10 through 200 of MYPROG.COBOL,

```
DSPRINT MYPROG.COBOL IBMXXXX1 NUM(1,6) LINES(10:200)
```

NUM(1,6) tells DSPRINT that line numbers start at position 1 and are 6 bytes long (appropriate for a COBOL file).

3.8 Create a New Directory

This is not applicable, because MVS-TSO does not have a UNIX-like hierarchical file system.

The closest thing MVS-TSO has to a directory structure is the partitioned data set. The easiest way to create one of those is to find an existing one and copy it.

3.9   Remove a Directory
This is also not applicable.

3.10   Move to Another Directory
This is also not applicable.

3.11   Edit a File (Line Mode)
ISPF has a full-screen editor, but it may be faster and easier to use the TSO line editor, especially for short jobs.

To create and edit a new file called MYPROG.FORT(MAIN), type
```
EDIT MYPROG(MAIN) FORT NEW
```
Notice that you do not enter MYPROG.FORT(MAIN) as the file specification. To edit an existing file MYPROG.FORT(SUB1), type
```
EDIT MYPROG(SUB1) FORT OLD
```
You actually do not need to specify OLD or NEW; the editor will assume OLD for existing members and NEW for nonexistent ones. For a new file, the editor will put you in input mode, and you can type in data one line at a time, entering a carriage-return (enter key) after each line. For an old file, the editor will put you in edit mode.

A very few important commands which you can issue in edit mode are illustrated by the examples below:

LIST	Display entire file.
LIST 26	Display line 26.
LIST 4 10	Display lines 4 through 10.
RENUM 10 2	Renumber lines in your file, starting at line number 10 with an increment of 2. RENUM by itself means RENUM 10 10.
DELETE 15	Delete line 15.
DELETE 15 50	Delete lines 15 through 50.

INPUT 112   Enter input mode and place new text after line 112. Note that new line numbers are created as you enter text. It is your responsibility, unfortunately, to make sure there are enough unused line numbers to accommodate the new lines you are adding. Try renumbering your file using RENUM with a large increment. Also, you can specify an increment for the INPUT command, e.g., INPUT 112 1, which tells the editor to accept input, place it after line 112, and number new lines with an increment of 1. Leave input mode by entering only a carriage return on your final line.

CHANGE 12 /ME/YOU/
                  Change first occurrence of string ME to YOU on line 12. Note: the delimiter does not have to be a slash, /. It can be any character that does not occur in either of the strings. Note also that if the first character of either string is an asterisk *, the delimiter *must not* be a slash, because TSO will think /* marks the beginning of a comment.

CHANGE 12 20 /ME/YOU/
                  Change first occurrence of string ME in lines 12 through 20 to YOU.

CHANGE 30 /ME/YOU/ ALL
                  Change all occurrences of ME on line 30 to YOU.

CHANGE 12 20 /ME/YOU/ ALL
                  Change all occurrences of string ME in lines 12 through 20 to YOU.

END SAVE   Exit editor and save changes to file permanently.

END NOSAVE   Exit editor without saving changes.

3.12 Compile and Run a Program

Compiling, linking, and running a program in MVS-TSO is difficult. Unlike the case of (say) UNIX, where the procedure involves typing two lines, the user must worry about fairly low-level system details such as allocating space, allocating files, freeing files, and so on. Of course, there are probably "canned" JCL procedures available at most installations to do the job in background, or "canned" command files (CLISTs) written in TSO CLIST language (in fact, the commands we show below provide a reasonable idea of what might go into such a CLIST).

However, to illustrate what is involved, we present the commands as if you actually had to type them in at the terminal. We give an example for FORTRAN, although the situation for other languages is similar. Unfortunately, we must issue a *caveat*: these procedures are so complicated that there is much room for parts of them being superseded. They are not *guaranteed* to work—they must unfortunately be nothing more than a starting point.

Suppose you have a program with three modules (a PDS with three members), MYPROG.FORT(MAIN), MYPROG.FORT(SUB1), MYPROG.FORT(SUB2). Naturally, you must compile all three modules. The first thing you must do is perform some system allocation functions:

```
ALLOC F(SYSUT1) NEW SPACE 100 BLOCK(1050)
ALLOC F(SYSUT2) NEW SPACE 100 BLOCK(4096)
ALLOC F(SYSTERM) DA(*)
```

SPACE 100 tells MVS to allocate 100 blocks. This should be adequate for a reasonable-size program, but you may need to use a different number. As for the numbers in the BLOCK parameter (1050 and 4096), it is best for you to type them as is and not tamper with them.

Next, you must perform some additional allocations, and issue the command to compile the main program MYPROG.FORT(MAIN)

```
ALLOC F(SYSIN) DA(MYPROG.FORT(MAIN))
ALLOC F(SYSLIN) DA(MYPROG.OBJ(MAIN))
CALL 'SYS1.FORTVS.LOADLIB(IFEAAB)'
```

The last line above calls the FORTRAN 77 compiler. By replacing FORTVS with FORTH, you could call the old FORTRAN 66 compiler, if you were so inclined. You must repeat the above procedure for the other two modules. Let us begin with MYPROG.FORT(SUB1):

```
ALLOC F(SYSIN) DA(MYPROG.FORT(SUB1))
ALLOC F(SYSLIN) DA(MYPROG.OBJ(SUB1))
CALL 'SYS1.FORTVS.LOADLIB(IFEAAB)'
```

and then MYPROG.FORT(SUB2)

```
ALLOC F(SYSIN) DA(MYPROG.FORT(SUB2))
ALLOC F(SYSLIN) DA(MYPROG.OBJ(SUB2))
CALL 'SYS1.FORTVS.LOADLIB(IFEAAB)'
```

Finally, issue the command

```
FREE F(SYSLIN SYSIN)
```

You have now compiled the three modules of your program, and generated object code in the PDS MYPROG.OBJ, with members MAIN, SUB1, and SUB2. You must now link them ("link-edit," in MVS parlance). Once again, you must perform certain system tasks first:

```
FREE SYSUT1
FREE SYSUT2
FREE SYSTERM
FREE SYSLIN
ALLOC DDN(SYSTERM) DSN*
ALLOC DDN(SYSPRINT) DSN*
```

```
ALLOC DDN(SYSUT1) DSN(SYSUT1) UNIT(SYSDA) SPACE(2,1) CYLINDERS
                                                        DELETE
```
The last command is meant to be on a single line, with a space between CYLINDERS and DELETE. SPACE(2,1) CYLINDERS requests an allocation of two cylinders, with an extra one in reserve. You may want to change the parameters. DELETE denotes that the space allocation is temporary. Continuing, we must specify libraries to be searched:
```
ALLOC DDN(SYSLIB) DSN('SYS1.FORTLIB')
```
The above line requests that the usual system FORTRAN library be searched. If you have other libraries, say, e.g., one called SYS1.SUBLIB, you can include them as well:
```
ALLOC DDN(SYSLIB) DSN('SYS1.FORTLIB' 'SYS1.SUBLIB')
```
Continuing:
```
ALLOC DDN(SYSLIN) DSN(MYPROG.OBJ(MAIN)
          MYPROG.OBJ(SUB1) MYPROG.OBG(SUB2))
ALLOC DDN(SYSLMOD) DSN(MYPROG.LOAD(MAIN))
CALL 'SYS1.LINKLIB(IEWL)'
```
(The first ALLOC is intended to lie on one line.) You have now, if all has gone well, compiled and linked your program. The executable file is MYPROG.LOAD(MAIN). Before you run your program you must perform further allocations. For example, you may want to assign the terminal for reading and writing. The following two lines assign the terminal to FORTRAN unit number 5 for reading, and unit number 6 for writing:
```
ALLOC F(FT05F001) DA(*) SHR
ALLOC F(FT06F001) DA(*) SHR
```
Suppose you also need to read from an existing data file MYDAT.DATA. The following line assigns unit 10 to MYDAT.DATA (TSOFRD1 is the user identification in this example):
```
ALLOC F(FT10F001) DA('TSOFRD1.MYDAT.DATA') SHR
```
When you have done all the above, you are ready to run your code:
```
CALL MYPROG.LOAD(MAIN)
```

3.13   Command Procedures

3.13.1   Invoke a Command Procedure Interactively

Suppose the command procedure is called MYCOM.CLIST. To invoke it, type
```
EXEC MYCOM
```
To invoke it with a listing on the screen, type
```
EXEC MYCOM L
```

3.13.2   Invoke a Command Procedure in Batch

This involves job-control language (JCL) and is not covered here.

3.13.3   Check on the Progress of a Job

This also involves job-control language (JCL) and is not covered here.

3.13.4   Stop a Batch Job

This also involves job-control language (JCL) and is not covered here.

3.14   Abort Operation

The PA1 key on the IBM 3270 terminal can act as an interrupt key for many TSO operations.

3.15   Bibliography

Lowe (1984) provides a good introduction to basic concepts and commands. Those who need a reference for job-control language can consult Lowe (1987). Nirmal (1990) covers CLISTs (command procedures). Katzan and Tharayil's book (1984) covers MVS in greater depth, discussing the basic architecture of the system; however, it is not an appropriate reference for basic commands.

Katzan, H., and D. Tharayil (1984), *Invitation to MVS: Logic and Debugging*, Petrocelli Books, New York, New York.

Lowe, D. (1984), *MVS TSO*, Mike Murach & Associates, Fresno, California.

Lowe, D. (1987), *MVS JCL*, Mike Murach & Associates, Fresno, California.

Nirmal, B. K. (1990), *MVS-TSO, Mastering CLISTs*, QED Information Sciences, Wellesley, Massachusetts.

4

VM-CMS

VM is one of IBM's two major operating systems for its mainframe computers, the other being MVS (Chap. 3). VM stands for "virtual machine"—each user has the illusion of having his own complete computer system. The real machine *appears* to be several machines. VM manages IBM 370 family hardware. Each user can choose a different operating system, each on its own virtual machine. Under VM, a user can actually run MVS, or TSO (MVS's command-line interface), although we do not show how to do this. We assume the user is running CMS (conversational monitor system), and what we cover below is a working subset of CMS commands. Note that CMS has an online help facility that can be accessed by issuing a HELP command.

4.1 Files and Filenames

4.1.1 Valid Filenames ("File Identifiers")

A "file identifier" in CMS consists of three parts: The filename, the file type, and the file mode. The three parts are separated by spaces. For example, in the identifier

```
MYPROG FORTRAN A1
```

MYPROG is the filename, FORTRAN is the file type, and A1 is the file mode.

The filename component of the file identifier (MYPROG in the example above) may be from one to eight characters long. Valid characters for filenames are upper and lower case letters (which are treated as equivalent), the digits 0 to 9, and the characters _, -, :, @,#, +, and $.

The file type component of the file identifier may also be from one to eight characters long, with the same set of allowable characters as the filename. The user may assign his own file type, but more commonly he will employ one of the following reserved types (partial list):

ASSEMBLE	Assembly-language source code
BASIC	BASIC source code
COBOL	COBOL source code
EXEC	Command file
FREEFORT	FREEFORM FORTRAN source code
FORTRAN	FORTRAN source code
LISTING	Print output
MACRO	Macro definition
MEMO	Text
MODULE	Executable file
TEXT	Object code

The third field of the file identifier is the file mode (A1 in the example above). The file mode is a two-character code. The first character is a letter identifying the *minidisk* on which the file resides. A minidisk is essentially a virtual hard disk—a portion of the system's disk storage set aside to emulate a separate direct-access storage device (DASD). The second character is a file mode number. You, the user, do not typically have to worry about this number, and need not specify it. For example,

    MYPROG FORTRAN A

is an acceptable specification. The possible values of the file mode number are from 0 to 6. The default value is 1, denoting that the file is eligible for read and write access. A value of 0 indicates a private file: only users with read and write access to the minidisk may view such a file.

4.1.2   Directory Structure and Pathnames

VM-CMS does not support a full hierarchical file system in the manner of UNIX, but each user can have several minidisks (virtual disks), each with its own files. Thus the system emulates a two-level directory structure.

4.1.3 Wild Cards

The asterisk * functions as a wild card character in CMS. It is used to replace either the filename, file type, or file mode of the file identifier. Consider the following examples:

* FORTRAN A	All FORTRAN files on disk A
MYPROG * A	All files on disk A whose name is MYPROG, regardless of the file type
MYPROG * *	All files, on any disk, whose name is MYPROG, regardless of the file type
* * A	All files on disk A
* * *	All files

4.2 List Out Directory Contents

To obtain a listing of the files on your current minidisk (say it is disk A), use

```
LISTFILE * * A
```

or simply

```
L * * A
```

The output will include the full file identifier for each file. To obtain more information, use

```
L * * A (LABEL
```

(Yes, use only one parenthesis!). This will cause the following additional data to be displayed for each file: the record format (F = fixed length, V = variable length), the logical record length, the length of the file in records, the number of physical blocks occupied by the file, the date and time the file was created, and the CMS volume serial number for the minidisk containing the file.

You may have noticed that the commands above have wild cards in them. This is because the LISTFILE command, unlike similar commands in other operating systems, is designed to be used with a file identifier. It is not used in the same way as an unqualified UNIX ls, for example. To obtain information for one particular file—say, FORTRAN code MYPROG on disk A, you can use

```
L MYPROG FORTRAN A
```

or

```
L MYPROG FORTRAN A (LABEL
```

You may use wild cards to obtain partial directory listings:
Consider the following:

```
L * FORTRAN A
```

will give you a listing for all FORTRAN files on your minidisk.

```
L * * *
```

or

```
L * * * (LABEL
```

will list information on all files, in all minidisks.

4.3 Copy a File

The command is COPYFILE, often abbreviated COPY. Note that it
will generally not copy over an existing file, unless you specify the
(REPLACE option. The COPYFILE command has many options and
can be used in many ways. Consider the following examples:

```
COPYFILE MYPROG FORTRAN A MYPROG FORTRAN B
```
> Makes a copy, on your B disk, of the program MYPROG
> FORTRAN on your A disk.

```
COPYFILE MYPROG FORTRAN A = = B
```
> Same as the previous command. The first equals sign tells
> CMS that the filename (MYPROG) is the same, and the second
> equals sign tells CMS that the file type (FORTRAN) is the same.

```
COPYFILE MYPROG FORTRAN A MYPROG FORTRAN B (REPLACE
```
> Makes a copy, on your B disk, of the program MYPROG
> FORTRAN on your A disk, even if a file MYPROG FORTRAN B
> already exists.

```
COPYFILE MYPROG FORTRAN A NEWPROG FORTRAN B
```
> Makes a copy, on your B disk, of the program MYPROG
> FORTRAN on your A disk, and calls the new file NEWPROG
> FORTRAN.

```
COPYFILE * FORTRAN A = = B
```
> Copies all FORTRAN files currently on your A disk onto your B
> disk.

```
COPYFILE * FORTRAN A = CPY B
```
> Copies all FORTRAN files currently on your A disk onto your B
> disk, and makes their file type CPY rather than FORTRAN.

```
COPYFILE * FORTRAN A BIGFILE FORTRAN B
```
> Copies all FORTRAN files currently on your A disk onto your B
> disk, putting them all into one file called BIGFILE FORTRAN.
> The COPYFILE command can thus be used to concatenate
> files.

4.4 Rename a File

The command
```
RENAME MYPROG FORTRAN A URPROG FORTRAN A
```
will give the file MYPROG   FORTRAN   A the new name URPROG
FORTRAN A. The command
```
RENAME MYPROG FORTRAN A URPROG = =
```
will have precisely the same effect in this case. The = symbol in
each field means there is no change in that field from the old name
to the new name. The command
```
RENAME * FORTRAN A = BADSTUFF =
```
causes all files of type FORTRAN on minidisk A to be renamed so that
they are now of type BADSTUFF, which is not a standard file type, but
one defined by the user for his own purposes. The command
```
RENAME * FORTRAN A = BADSTUFF = (TYPE
```
Will do the same thing we have just discussed, but it will display the
new names on the screen as the command executes, so that you may
monitor the progress of the command.

Note that despite its similarity to, say, the UNIX mv, the RENAME
command *cannot* be used to move a file from one minidisk to
another. In other words, a command such as
```
RENAME MYPROG FORTRAN A MYPROG FORTRAN B
```
is *illegal.*

4.5 Delete a File

To delete the file MYPROG FORTRAN B, type simply
```
ERASE MYPROG FORTRAN B
```
You may use wild cards. For example, the command
```
ERASE * FORTRAN B
```
will delete all FORTRAN files on minidisk B. As another example,
```
ERASE * FORTRAN *
```
will delete all FORTRAN files in all minidisks.

4.6 List Contents of File on the Screen

To list the contents of the file MYPROG FORTRAN B, type
```
TYPE MYPROG FORTRAN B
```
If you issue the command
```
TYPE MYPROG FORTRAN *
```
then CMS will search through all your minidisks alphabetically
until it finds the file; then it will display the file on the screen.

To stop a listing (e.g., if you have already seen what you want and
do not want more), type
```
HT
```

CMS will respond with a MORE message. When you see this, press the function key PA2.

4.7   Print a File

To print a hard copy of the file MYPROG FORTRAN A, type
```
PRINT MYPROG FORTRAN A
```

4.8   Create a New Directory

This is not applicable.

4.9   Remove a Directory

This also is not applicable.

4.10   Move to Another Directory

This also is not applicable.

4.11   Edit a File (Line Mode)

Most editing in CMS is done with XEDIT, a screen editor. The CMS line editor, EDIT, is seldom used, and rather difficult to find documentation for. Since we do not cover screen editors here, we refer the user to appropriate works covering XEDIT, such as Eckols (1988b).

4.12   Compile and Run a Program

Suppose you wish to compile your program MYPROG FORTRAN A. First, you need to make sure you have enough virtual storage for the compiler. To do this, issue the command
```
QUERY STORAGE
```
VS FORTRAN requires about 3 Mbyte. If the system tells you you do not have that much, then issue the command
```
DEFINE STORAGE 3M
IPL CMS
```
(Press ENTER key twice)
The command to compile MYPROG FORTRAN is
```
FORTVS2 MYPROG
```
The compiler will create a list file MYPROG LISTING, and an object file called (oddly enough) MYPROG TEXT. You are now almost ready to run your program, but you must first warn CMS about which

libraries the system will need to run the program properly. This is accomplished using the GLOBAL command. The appropriate GLOBAL command depends both on the programming language and on the particular VM-CMS installation, so some research is required on the part of the user. For VS FORTRAN the GLOBAL commands will probably resemble the following:

```
GLOBAL TXTLIB VSF2FORT CMSLIB
GLOBAL LOADLIB VSF2LOAD
```

(Typically you will put the appropriate GLOBAL commands in a command file of some kind.)   To run your program, type the command

```
LOAD MYPROG (START
```

4.13   Command Procedures

Command procedures are of type EXEC. Suppose there is a command procedure called MYCOM EXEC A. In order to invoke it interactively, type

```
EXEC MYCOM EXEC A
```

If the CMS system on which you are working has the "implied execution option" in effect, you may execute the procedure simply by typing its name:

```
MYCOM
```

4.14   Bibliography

A good coverage of basic commands is available in Eckols (1988a) and IBM (1986). Fosdick (1987) is somewhat more exhaustive in coverage. Eckols (1988b) is devoted solely to the CMS editor XEDIT.

Eckols, S. (1988a), *VM-CMS, Commands and Concepts*, Mike Murach & Associates, Fresno, California.

Eckols, S. (1988b), *VM-CMS XEDIT Commands and Features*, Mike Murach & Associates, Fresno, California.

Fosdick, H. (1987), *VM-CMS Handbook*, Hayden Books, Indianapolis, Indiana.

IBM, Inc. (1986), *VM/System Product CMS Primer, Release 5*, Item SC24-5236-3, International Business Machines Corp.

5

MS-DOS

MS-DOS is the dominant operating system for IBM-style microcomputers using the Intel 80x86 family of microprocessors, (which includes the 8088). The use of MS-DOS, which is not a terribly sophisticated system, is enormously widespread. Chances are you can probably find an MS-DOS machine anywhere in the world. This is because of the huge success of the IBM-PC, the PC's open architecture, the proliferation of low-cost IBM-PC clones, and the enthusiastic development of a very large base of third-party application software.

MS-DOS is continuously and rapidly evolving. There are several "versions" in circulation, and people often become confused. The versions *are* different. Usually, the variations do not affect routine commands, but this is not always the case. Some of the differences are even apparent in the small subset of commands we cover below; These important ones are indicated.

Briefly, the history of MS-DOS is as follows. First of all, let us distinguish between MS-DOS, a Microsoft product, and PC-DOS, packaged under the IBM name. Although PC-DOS has essentially been equivalent to MS-DOS, subtle differences in the versions have cropped up from time to time. MS-DOS (and PC-DOS) Version 1.0 ran on the original IBM PC in 1981, and supported only single-sided, single-density floppies. Version 1.25 (PC-DOS v. 1.1) added some bug fixes and support for double-sided floppy disks. MS-DOS (PC-DOS) v. 2.0, released in 1983, added many new features, including a hierarchical file system and support for hard disks. MS-DOS v. 2.01 and v. 2.11 added support for international characters, and PC-DOS v. 2.1 was released with the ill-fated IBM PCjr. In 1984, MS-DOS (PC-DOS) v. 3.0 was introduced with the IBM PC/AT, and provided support for larger hard disks and for 1.2-Mbyte floppies. Interestingly, MS-DOS v. 2.25 was introduced in 1985, after v. 3.0. It did not have v. 3.0's extra features, but it had increased support for Japanese and Korean character sets. MS-DOS (PC-DOS) v. 3.1, introduced in 1984, had support for Microsoft networks. In 1986, MS-DOS (PC-DOS) v. 3.2 added support for 3.5-in floppy disks. Since then, Version 3.3 has made changes to at least ten commands, and Version 4.0 has introduced the DOS shell and hard-disk partitions greater than 32 Mbyte in size. Version 5.0, released in mid-1991, offers a number of improvements including a screen-editor (in addition to the archaic line editor EDLIN), and improved memory management, allowing the use of memory above 640K. DOS 5 also includes command-line editing, allowing the user to modify or reexecute previous commands quickly. Users of DOS 5 can also recover erased files, and recover inadvertently formatted disks.

MS-DOS is still alive and well. Although OS/2 was released in 1988, wholesale conversion from DOS to OS/2 has not occurred in the last three years—at least not to the extent some people expected. An alternative to OS/2, Windows 3.0 is available from Microsoft. It is a fairly complete operating system in its own right, but it relies on MS-DOS for file manipulation.

5.1   Files and Filenames

5.1.1   Valid Filenames

Names of files in MS-DOS may be one to eight characters long. They may include, in addition, a three-character extension separated from the filename by a period. A filename may not include any of the following characters:

```
= + < > ? * , . : ; | / \
```

or the space character. A filename may also not be identical to the following reserved device names:

```
AUX  COM1,  COM2, etc.,   CON  LPT1,  LPT2, etc.
NUL  PRN  PRT  USER
```

Typical filename extensions (which must be separated from the filename by a period) include:

ASM	Assembly-language source code
BAK	Backup file (often created by word processors)
BAS	BASIC source code
C	C source code
DAT	Data file, e.g., for input to application programs written by the user
EXE	Executable file
FOR	FORTRAN source code
H	C language header file
LST	Listing file, e.g., created by a compiler
MAP	Load map created by a linker
OBJ	Object code, e.g., created by a compiler
PAS	Pascal source code
SYS	Device drivers
TMP or $$$	Temporary file
TXT	Text file

Note that a file specification may need to include the name of the disk drive. The drivename is a letter followed by a colon, as these examples show:

    A: B: C:

If you are working on drive A: and drive A: contains the file MYFILE.DAT, then

    MYFILE.DAT

is an adequate specification. If you move to drive B: however, and you want to access this same file, then you must include the drivename in your specification:

    A:MYFILE.DAT

5.1.2 Directory Structure and Pathnames

Note: Only later versions of DOS (MS-DOS 2.1 to 4.0; PC-DOS 2.0 to 3.3; and IBM DOS 4.0) have a hierarchical file system.

Each drive has a root directory that can contain subdirectories, which can in turn contain other subdirectories, and so on. A full file specification is thus given by a pathname, which includes information about where the file is located in the directory structure. Suppose you have a file CHAP1.TXT, located in the subdirectory BOOK, which is in turn located in the directory WRITING, on drive C:. The proper way to specify the full, absolute pathname (assume you are on drive C:) is

    \WRITING\BOOK\CHAP1.TXT

If you are not on drive C:, the specification must include the drivename:

```
C:\WRITING\BOOK\CHAP1.TXT
```

The initial \ is needed to specify that the directory WRITING is in the root directory of drive C:. MS-DOS records the current directory for each drive, so C:WRITING\BOOK\CHAP1.TXT (no \ preceding WRITING) refers to the WRITING directory in the current directory of drive C:. If the current directory of drive C: is \, then the two forms are equivalent. But if the current directory is, say, WORK, then C:WRITING\BOOK\CHAP1.TXT also refers to C:\WORK\WRITING\BOOK\CHAP1.TXT. The current directory is a convenience, but its use can lead to files being misplaced. When in doubt, specify an absolute path. (Note that pathnames can become very long as the level of nesting increases—and bear in mind that DOS commands are limited to 128 characters in length!)

If a pathname does not begin with a drive specification or a \, then the pathname is said to be relative to the current drive and directory. For example, if your current drive is C:, and your current directory is \WRITING\BOOK, then CHAP1.TXT can be referred to directly. It is customary for the MS-DOS prompt to display both the current drive and directory, so you can judge which form of pathname is appropriate. Note that the MS-DOS prompt can be customized, so there is no guarantee that the prompt will display the current drive and directory.

There are two other symbols that can be used to navigate through the file system. The period refers to the current directory. More useful is a double-period, "..," which refers to the parent directory. The following examples summarize these forms of addressing, (assume that the current drive is C: and the current directory is \WRITING\BOOK). The left column is a pathname, and the right column shows the corresponding absolute pathname.

```
\                 C:\
CHAP1.TXT         C:\WRITING\BOOK\CHAP1.TXT
.                 C:\WRITING\BOOK
..                C:\WRITING
C:CHAP1.TXT       C:\WRITING\BOOK\CHAP1.TXT
C:..              C:\WRITING
```

5.1.3 Wild Cards

Note: Wild cards are supported by the following versions of DOS: PC-DOS 2.0 to 3.3, MS-DOS 2.1 to 4.0, and IBM DOS 4.0.

The asterisk wild card character * replaces arbitrary strings, but with certain limitations. Basically, an asterisk can substitute for any string of characters needed to complete a filename or an extension. This is best illustrated by examples. The following uses of * are correct:

*.DAT	Any file of type DAT
E*.DAT	Any file of type DAT, whose name begins with E
EAR*.FOR	Any file of type FOR, whose name begins with EAR
MYPROG.*	Any file whose name is MYPROG, regardless of its type (this might include, e.g., MYPROG.FOR, MYPROG.OBJ, MYPROG.EXE, etc.)
B*.*	Any file, of any type, whose name begins with B
.	Any file of any type

The following uses of * will not generally produce the desired effects:

A*	This will not specify every file beginning with A, but only those files beginning with A and having no extension. The correct way to specify any file beginning with A is A*.*
A*B*C	In UNIX, this will specify any file beginning with A, ending with C, and having a B in the middle. In DOS, it will not work.

Note that in the special case of the DIR command, the user has more flexibility in the use of wild cards. The * wild card will replace anything that follows it, including the extension.

Another important wild card is the ?, which can replace a single character, for example,

A???.FOR

which will specify all files of type FOR, whose names begin with A, and include any three other characters.

5.2 List Out Directory Contents

The basic command is

DIR

which will produce a listing of the files in the current directory of the current drive. If you need a directory listing for another directory and drive, you can move to that directory (see Sec. 5.10) and issue a DIR. Alternatively, you can stay in your current drive and provide a pathname. For example, if you are on drive A: and you need a listing for the root directory of drive B:, you may type

```
DIR B:\
```
Note that the contents of the current directory of drive B: will be listed if the \ is omitted.

The `DIR` command causes the following information to be listed about each file: the filename, the filename extension (e.g., BAS, DAT, etc.), the size of the file in bytes, and the date and time when the file was last modified. DOS Versions 2.0 and higher have an option / P, e.g.,
```
DIR /P
```
which causes the directory contents to be listed one screenful at a time (see Sec. 5.19 for a more general technique). You may obtain a listing of a particular subdirectory, for instance the WRITING subdirectory on drive C:, by issuing a command such as
```
DIR C:\WRITING
```
You may use wild cards to obtain information on particular subsets of files. For example,
```
DIR *.DAT
```
will list information on all files, in your current drive and directory, of type DAT. Note that the DIR command can use wild cards with greater flexibility than can other commands. The * wild card can replace any string at all, with no limitations imposed by file extension. For instance,
```
DIR B:\WRITING\C*
```
Will cause information to be displayed about all files beginning with C, in the WRITING directory on drive B:.

5.3 Copy a File

Consider the following examples (assume MYFILE.DAT resides on drive A:, which is the current drive):

COPY MYFILE.DAT B:	Copies MYFILE.DAT from the current directory of the current drive to a new file of the same name, in the current directory of drive B:.
COPY MYFILE.DAT B:NEWFILE.DAT	Copies MYFILE.DAT from the current directory of the current drive to a new file called NEWFILE.DAT in the current directory of drive B:.
COPY MYFILE.DAT NEWFILE.DAT	Copies MYFILE.DAT into a new file called NEWFILE.DAT on the same drive (A:).
COPY *.DAT B:	Copies all files of type DAT in the current directory of the current drive into files of the same names, in the current directory of drive B:.

COPY *.* B: Copies all files in the current directory
                                  of the current drive to files of the same
                                  name in the current directory of drive
                                  B:.

COPY MYFILE.DAT B: /V   Copies MYFILE.DAT from the current
                                  directory of the current drive to a new
                                  file of the same name, in the current
                                  directory of drive B:. The /V option
                                  tells DOS to verify the integrity of the
                                  copy.

COPY MYFILE.DAT \DIR1\X.DAT   Copies MYFILE.DAT from the current
                                  directory of the current drive to a new
                                  file called X.DAT in directory DIR1 of the
                                  current drive.

It is also possible to use the COPY command to concatenate files. For
example, the command

    COPY FILE1.DAT + FILE2.DAT + FILE3.DAT NEWFILE.DAT

will create the file NEWFILE.DAT and fill it with a concatenation of
FILE1.DAT, FILE2.DAT, and FILE3.DAT.

Note that if the source file and target file are in the same directory,
you must give the target (i.e., the proposed copy) a new name. Note
also that if you are copying to another directory, and you specify a
target filename that exists in that directory, the existing file will be
replaced.

5.4 Rename a File

The command is RENAME or REN. Consider the following examples
(assume MYFILE.DAT resides on drive A:, which is the current
drive):

RENAME MYFILE.DAT YERFILE.DAT   Renames MYFILE.DAT to YERFILE.DAT

RENAME B:\DIR1\HISFILE.DAT YERFILE.DAT
                                 Renames HISFILE.DAT in directory
                                 DIR1 on drive B: to YERFILE.DAT (in the
                                 same directory)

RENAME *.DAT *.FOR   Renames all files of type DAT to files of
                                 the same names, with extension FOR

Although RENAME accepts wild cards, as shown above, you cannot use
wild cards to add characters. For example, suppose you have the
files MY1FILE.DAT and MY2FILE.DAT in your current directory, and
you issue the command

    REN MY?.DAT MYX?.DAT

hoping to rename the files to MYX1FILE.DAT and MYX2FILE.DAT; it will not work.

Unfortunately, RENAME cannot be applied to directories. You must create a new directory with the desired name, copy the files, delete the files from the original directory, and then delete the old directory.

5.5 Delete a File

The command is issued either as DEL, DELETE, or ERASE. Some versions do not recognize DELETE. Examples:

ERASE MYFILE.DAT	Deletes MYFILE.DAT
ERASE B:\DIR1\YERFILE.DAT	Deletes YERFILE.DAT which is in directory DIR1 on drive B:
ERASE *.DAT	Deletes all files of type DAT in the current directory
ERASE *.*	Deletes all files in the current directory

Note: MS-DOS v. 2.1 and later, and PC DOS v. 2.0 and later, allow you to delete all files in the directory just by specifying the path to the directory, without needing to code *.*. For example, the command

ERASE B:\DIR1\DIR2

will delete all files in the subdirectory DIR2. If the directory is the current one, you can represent it simply with a period.

Note: MS-DOS v. 4.0 and IBM DOS v. 4.0 allow a /P option to the DEL command. This option will cause the system to ask you for permission before deleting files. For example,

ERASE *.DAT/P

will not just delete all the files of type DAT; the system will ask you for permission to delete each individual file.

Directories cannot be removed using the ERASE command. Instead, use the RMDIR (or RD) command. The directory must be empty before it can be removed.

5.6 List Contents of File on the Screen

To list the contents of the file MYFILE.DAT, type

TYPE MYFILE.DAT

CTRL-S will pause the listing, and CTRL-Q will continue it.

Note: MS-DOS v. 2.11 and later, PC-DOS v. 2.0 to 3.3, and IBM DOS v. 4.0 all allow the listing of a file one screenful at a time. When the screen fills up, the system waits for any key to be pressed before it resumes. CTRL-C aborts the listing. To list MYFILE.DAT one screenful at a time, type

```
MORE<MYFILE.DAT
```

(MORE is an external command, also discussed in Sec. 5.19.) Another way is to use the TYPE command with a pipe, as follows:

```
TYPE MYFILE.DAT|MORE
```

Pipes, and related topics are discussed in Sec. 5.19.

5.7 Print a File

To print a hard copy of the file MYFILE.DAT, type

```
PRINT MYFILE.DAT
```

(The PRINT command can also be used in many other ways.)

5.8 Create a New Directory

The command is MD or MKDIR:

`MD DIR1`	Creates subdirectory DIR1, in the current directory
`MD C:\DIR1\DIR2`	Creates subdirectory DIR2 in DIR1 on drive C:

5.9 Remove a Directory

The command is RD or RMDIR:

`RD DIR1`	Removes subdirectory DIR1, in the current directory
`RD C:\DIR1\DIR2`	Removes subdirectory DIR2 in DIR1 on drive C:

In order for a subdirectory to be removable, it must contain no files, must have no children, and must not itself be the current directory.

5.10 Move to Another Directory

The command is CD. Examples:

`CD DIR1`	Go to subdirectory DIR1 contained in the current directory.
`CD B:\NEWDIR\DIR1\DIR2`	Go to subdirectory DIR2 in DIR1 in NEWDIR on drive B:.
`CD ..`	Go up one level.

CD ..\SUB1	Go up one level, then down into directory SUB1 (presumably, you know that SUB1 exists in the directory above you). Easy way to move "sideways."
CD	Find out which directory is current.
CD B:	Find out which directory is current on drive B: (suppose you are in drive A:).

5.11   Edit a File (Line Mode)

There are so many different excellent screen editors and word processors for MS-DOS machines that the line editor EDLIN may seem like a dinosaur. It is. But, as with all the other operating systems we have been considering, it is essential knowledge. It is always available, conceptually simple, and easily summarized. If you have any familiarity with line editors, just looking at the material below will enable you to navigate through EDLIN and do fast editing jobs when you have no idea how to use the latest word processor.

If the file MYFILE.DAT does not exist and you type

    EDLIN MYFILE.DAT

then you will create a new file by that name. If the file you want to edit does exist, EDLIN will let you make changes to it. Suppose you are editing a preexisting file MYPROG.FOR. You would get into the line editor by typing:

    EDLIN MYPROG.FOR

The prompt in line mode is an asterisk *. Here are examples of EDLIN commands. *Note*: EDLIN is case-sensitive in searching.

4,10L	Display lines 4 through 10.
L	Display a screenful.
-5,+6L	Display lines ranging from five lines above current line to six lines below current line.
15D	Delete line 15.
15,50D	Delete lines 15 through 50 .
-5,+6D	Delete lines ranging from five lines above current line to six lines below current line.
15,31,10C	Copy lines 15 through 31 and put them before the present line 10 .
12,14,20M	Move lines 12 through 14 to the position before the present line 20.

I	Get into insert mode. You will receive a line number and the * prompt. You may type in your desired text, which will be placed immediately before your current position in the file.
CTRL-Z	Get out of insert mode and back into line-edit mode. The CTRL-Z must be followed by a carriage return.
5,25SJones	Find the string Jones, searching from line 5 through line 25.
5,25?SJones	Find the string Jones, searching from line 5 through line 25, and asking each time whether to stop the search. User types Y to stop, N to continue.
3,40RJonesCTRL-ZSmith	From line 3 through line 40, change the string Jones to the string Smith.
3,40?RJonesCTRL-ZSmith	From line 3 through line 40, change the string Jones to the string Smith, while asking for permission to stop search. User types Y to stop, N to continue.
6TB:JUNK.DAT	Copy the external disk file JUNK.DAT, which resides on drive B: and put it before line 6 in the file you are editing.
E	End editing session and save changed file to disk.
Q	Get out of editor without saving changes .

EDLIN also provides an easy way for the user to replace a given line. To position yourself at a particular line, simply type the line number followed by a carriage return. This will cause EDLIN to prompt you to retype the line in question.

5.12   Compile and Run a Program

There are a number of programming environments available for MS-DOS; many of these (e.g. Turbo Pascal) have their own conventions for program compilation and linking. Still, several environments follow the "traditional" compile–link sequence familiar to users of other operating systems such as UNIX or VMS. MS-DOS has its own linker, and it is good to know the basics of how to use it. Before linking, of course, one must compile the modules to be linked, and here even the "traditional" compilers will differ among themselves. Consider, for the sake of illustration, Microsoft Pascal. Suppose you have a program consisting of a main program MYPROG.PAS and two subroutines SUB1.PAS and SUB2.PAS. The compile command for MYPROG.PAS might look something like

    PAS1 MYPROG,MYPROG,MYPROG,MYPROG

The four MYPROGs in the command specify the following, in order: (1) take MYPROG.PAS as the input; (2) produce object code with the name MYPROG.OBJ; (3) produce a source listing with the name

MYPROG.LST; and (4) produce an object listing with the name MYPROG.COD. If the command were

```
PAS1 MYPROG, O1, L1, C1
```

Then the compiler would take MYPROG.PAS and compile it to an object module named O1.OBJ, with a source listing L1.LST and an object code listing C1.COD. A NUL in place of any parameter suppresses that parameter. For example,

```
PAS1 MYPROG,MYPROG,NUL,NUL
```

would tell the compiler to compile MYPROG.PAS into MYPROG.OBJ, and produce no source listing or object listing. It is conceivable that in some compilers the default extensions .PAS (or .FOR, .BAS, or whatever), .OBJ, etc. may not be assumed, and you may have to type the entire name for each parameter, e.g.,

```
COM MYPROG.FOR, O1.OBJ, NUL.LST, NUL.COD
```

where COM is the compile command for some particular compiler. It is also possible that the compiler has more than one pass (that is the case with Microsoft Pascal and Microsoft FORTRAN), and you may need to type something like

```
PAS1 MYPROG,MYPROG,NUL,NUL
PAS2
PAS3
```

This assumes, of course, that the PAS1, PAS2, and PAS3 programs are on your hard disk—if there is no hard disk on your machine, you will probably have to shuffle floppy disks in and out and specify the drive where PAS1, PAS2, etc., are residing (e.g., issue command B:PAS2).

The above discussion gives some flavor of how Microsoft-style compilers work under MS-DOS, but note that there are useful shortcuts that we have not covered. Also, do exercise caution and use whatever manual may be available, because, as we have said, compilers do differ. Microsoft QuickBasic, for example, has a compiler command BC, which only takes three parameters (no object code list file), for example:

```
BC MYPROG, O1.OBJ, MYPROG
```

which would compile MYPROG.BAS to object code in a file named O1.OBJ, and produce a source listing MYPROG.LST.

One reason for concentrating somewhat on Microsoft-style compilers is that the Microsoft MS-DOS linker has a similar syntax and spirit. Suppose you have compiled your programs and you now have three object files MYPROG.OBJ, SUB1.OBJ, and SUB2.OBJ. You must use the linker to link them together and resolve external references. Your link command might look like this:

```
LINK MYPROG+SUB1+SUB2,MYPROG,NUL.MAP,PASCAL.LIB+MATH.LIB
```

The first and last arguments can each be used to specify multiple files, separated by + signs. The first argument MYPROG+SUB1+SUB2 specifies the modules to be linked. If there were only one module called MYPROG.OBJ, the argument would simply be MYPROG. The second argument specifies that the executable file should be named MYPROG.EXE. The third argument tells the linker not to produce a load map. If this argument were MYPROG instead of NUL.MAP, then a load map MYPROG.MAP would be produced. The fourth argument PASCAL.LIB+MATH.LIB specifies libraries to be searched to resolve external references—in this case the Pascal library and the Math library. Note that in some cases you might not need to specify any libraries at all, since the appropriate ones might be searched automatically.

The LINK command noted above should, if it completes without error, create the executable module MYPROG.EXE. To run your program, you would simply type

    MYPROG

If the executable module were not on your current drive, you would have to specify a drive, e.g.,

    B:MYPROG

5.13 Command Procedures

Suppose there is a command procedure ("batch file") called MYCOM.BAT. In order to invoke it interactively, simply type its name:

    MYCOM

5.14 Abort Operation

CTRL-C or CTRL-BREAK will interrupt a batch file while it is executing, and may also act as an exit key for a number of application programs. CTRL-ALT-DEL is a drastic way to interrupt what you are doing: it will cause the system to reboot.

5.15 Move to Another Drive

If you are on drive A: and you wish to move to drive B:, simply type

    B:

5.16 Format a Disk

Before you can write to a new floppy or hard disk, you must format it. The command is FORMAT:

FORMAT A: Format the disk in drive A: to the full capacity of the drive

FORMAT A:/S   Format the disk in drive A: to the full capacity of the drive,
                   and transfer the operating system to the disk (make it a
                   system disk)

As DOS evolved, so did floppy disks and disk drives. Newer
models of IBM and compatible personal computers had disk drives
with ever-increasing capacity. It is possible to use the FORMAT
command to format a disk to less than its full capacity, for use in
older machines. Useful examples for 5.25" drives:

FORMAT A:/1/8   Format the disk in drive A: to be one-sided with eight
                   sectors per track (DOS 1.0)

FORMAT A:/1   Format the disk in drive A: to be one-sided with nine
                   sectors per track (DOS 1.1)

FORMAT A:/8   Format the disk in drive A: to be two-sided with eight
                   sectors per track (320-kbyte—DOS 2.0–2.1)

Note: In DOS v. 3.3 the number of tracks and the number of
sectors per track can be explicitly specified. Example:

FORMAT A:/T:80/N:9   Format the disk in drive A: to have 80 tracks and 9
                     sectors per track (e.g., for a 3.5" 720-kbyte disk in a
                     1.44-Mbyte drive).

Note: In DOS v. 4.0 you can simply tell the system the capacity (in
kbyte) to which you want the disk formatted, using the /F option:

FORMAT A:/F:360 Format the disk in drive A: to have 360-kbyte capacity

5.17 Duplicate a Disk

The command
    DISKCOPY A: B:
copies the contents of the disk in drive A: onto the disk in drive B:.
The disk in drive B: need not be formatted. Note that DISKCOPY is
an external command (like MORE and CHKDSK, for example) that
invokes the DOS program DISKCOPY.COM. You must ensure that
the program is on your hard disk, or system floppy.

5.18   Verify a Disk

The command

```
CHKDSK  B:
```

checks the condition of the file allocation table and directories on the disk in drive B:. Like DISKCOPY, CHKDSK is an external command, and you must make sure you have it on your system disk.

5.19   Redirection of Input and Output

It is often useful to capture output from some command or program in a file, or to use the output of one command as input to another. MS-DOS offers general-purpose facilities to accomplish these tasks.

The command

```
DIR > FILES.TXT
```

lists the files in the current directory, but instead of printing the listing on the monitor, captures the result in the file FILES.TXT located in the current directory. Any existing contents of FILES.TXT will be lost. To append to an existing file, the command is

```
DIR >> FILES.TXT
```

Input can also be redirected. A command or program that reads input from the console can be used to accept input from a file. The command

```
SORT < PHONES.TXT
```

sorts and then prints the contents of PHONES.TXT (SORT is an MS-DOS external command).

Output from one program can be used as input to another program using a pipe. For example, MORE is an MS-DOS external command that takes input and displays it one screenful at a time. The user must type a space to obtain the next screenful of the input. This command

```
DIR | MORE
```

produces a directory listing a screen at a time. The effect is similar to DIR /P. Any number of programs can be chained together with pipes. For example, this sequence

```
DIR | SORT | MORE
```

produces a sorted listing of the files in the current directory, one screen at a time.

5.20   Bibliography

There are very many books on MS-DOS on the market. Kamin (1989) is one of the best references available. Duncan (1988a) is a definitive work, but also very thick and rather expensive. Duncan (1988b) provides good coverage of advanced techniques. Those who need to write their own command procedures (batch files) can consult Richardson (1988). The arrival of DOS 5 has spawned a profusion of books describing the new features; Kamin (1991) and Nelson (1991) are examples.

Duncan, R. (1988a) (ed.), *The MS-DOS Encyclopedia*, Microsoft Press, Redmond, Washington.

Duncan, R. (1988b), *Advanced MS-DOS Programming*, Second Edition, Microsoft Press, Redmond, Washington.

Kamin, J. (1989), *DOS up to and Including DOS 4.0*, Expert Advisor Series, Addison-Wesley, Menlo Park, California.

Kamin, J. (1991), *DOS 5, Everything You Need to Know*, Prima Publishers, Rocklin, California.

Nelson, K. Y. (1991), *The Little DOS 5 Book*, Peachpit Press, Berkeley, California.

Richardson, R. (1988), *MS-DOS Batch File Programming, Including OS/2*, Windcrest Books, Blue Ridge Summit, Pennsylvania.

6

Macintosh

The Apple Macintosh operating system is hardly one that needs extensive documentation. It is so easy to use that many consider it a model of what a small-computer operating system should be. It would be a sheer waste of space to cover basic operations such as file copying, deleting, etc., the way we have done for other systems.

However, with the user-friendliness of the Macintosh comes an undeniably high overhead, and relatively slow performance given the power of the hardware. Many experienced users might seek occasionally to bypass some of the easy—but slow and cumbersome—ways of doing things, and perform operations faster.

In this section, which is something of a hodgepodge, we concentrate not on basic operations, but on handy shortcuts for experienced users, as well as useful miscellaneous information. Note that we do not cover the new System 7 in detail, although the information below should still be relevant. (Section 6.1 lists some of the new features of System 7.)

6.1 Versions of the System and the Finder

The System file contains the basic Macintosh operating system and interacts directly with the ROM. The Finder is a higher-level component of the operating system: it manages the Macintosh desktop, and accepts and interprets user commands. Both the Finder and the System have evolved continuously since the

Macintosh was introduced. Unfortunately, some Finder/System combinations are incompatible, and newer versions may not work on older machines. The following list provides some guidelines:

Mac II	Acceptable combinations include Finder 6.1/System 6.0; Finder 6.0/System 4.2; Finder 5.5/System 4.1. Combinations of earlier versions of System and Finder not recommended.
Mac SE	Acceptable combinations include Finder 6.1/System 6.0; Finder 6.0/System 4.2; Finder 5.5/System 4.1; Finder 5.4/System 4.0. Combinations of earlier versions of System and Finder not recommended.
Mac Plus	Acceptable combinations include Finder 6.0/System 4.2; Finder 5.5/System 4.1; Finder 5.4/System 4.0; Finder 5.3/System 3.2. Other combinations not recommended.
Mac 512K	Finder 5.3/System 3.2 recommended.
Mac XL	Finder 5.3/System 3.2 recommended.
Mac 128K	Finder 4.1/System 2.0 recommended.

As this book was in the final stages of preparation, Apple released System 7, a truly major revision of the Macintosh system software. Although we do not cover System 7 in detail here, it is worth noting some of its new features. System 7 eliminates the control panel, allowing more direct manipulation of the system configuration. It also eliminates the FONT/DA Mover. Fonts can now be installed directly into a folder in the system folder. System 7 implements Apple's new Truetype font technology, allowing sharper rendering of fonts on the screen (see Sec. 6.12). System 7 allows much more extensive multitasking, and background printing. It also allows "live" copy-and-paste between applications, and supports virtual memory.

6.2   Abort Operation

You can often interrupt what you are currently doing by holding down the COMMAND key (the ⌘ key) and pressing the period key: ⌘-..

6.3   Fundamental Shortcuts

These shortcuts speed up basic finder operations by avoiding the necessity to select a command from the pull-down menus using the mouse. Some of these work from within popular application programs as well. In the list below, ⌘-N (for example), means hold down the ⌘ key (known also as the COMMAND or CMD key), and press the N key. ⌘-SHIFT-1 means hold down the ⌘ and SHIFT keys, and press the 1 key.

⌘-A	Select all items in the current window.
⌘-C	Copy into clipboard.
⌘-D	Duplicate selected item in current window. NOTE: To duplicate items into a different window (rather than simply moving them there), depress the OPTION key while dragging.
⌘-E	Eject selected floppy.
⌘-SHIFT-1	Eject floppy in drive 1 (internal).
⌘-SHIFT-2	Eject floppy in drive 2 (external).
⌘-I	Get information on selected item.
⌘-N	Create new (empty) folder in current window.
⌘-O	Open selected item.
⌘-P	Print selected item.
⌘-Q	Quit application.
⌘-V	Paste contents of clipboard.
⌘-X	Move (cut) selection into clipboard.
⌘-Z	Undo
⌘-SHIFT-3	Place image of the screen into a MacPaint file. You can do this up to 10 times. Successive screen dumps will be named Screen 0, Screen 1, etc. This may not always work.
⌘-SHIFT-4	Print the current window on an Imagewriter printer.
⌘-SHIFT-4	(With CAPSLOCK pressed) Print the entire screen on an Imagewriter printer.

6.4   Move a Window without Selecting It

A Macintosh desktop is typically cluttered. It is often desirable to change the position of various windows, but the user can become very frustrated when he finds that dragging on a window causes it to become active. To move a background window around on the screen without causing it to become active (which would make it cover up your current window), simply hold down the ⌘ key while you are dragging.

6.5 A Neater CLEAN UP

Depressing the OPTION key while selecting CLEAN UP from the SPECIAL menu will lead to a more thorough cleaning up.

Another tip to keep your desktop neat and organized is to hold down the ⌘ key while dragging items. This causes the items to move only to discrete points on an invisible grid—hence items stay aligned.

6.6 Close All Windows

You can close all windows by depressing the OPTION key while you close your current window.

6.7 TRASHing Files

TRASHing files often results in time-consuming warning messages. Also, one cannot delete a locked file by simply dragging it to the TRASH. To bypass warning messages and delete locked files, simply depress the OPTION key while you drag your items to the TRASH.

It sometimes happens that the Macintosh refuses to TRASH a given item and persists in issuing "file in use" messages. It may be necessary in such cases to restart the computer.

6.8 Attractive Accents and Punctuation Marks

Many users find it difficult to get attractive accents and quotation marks on a Macintosh (unless they use TEX). There are some relatively little-known tricks that can create good accents and quotation marks. For example,

To get:	à	use OPTION-`, then depress a
To get:	á	use OPTION-E, then depress a
To get:	â	use OPTION-I, then depress a
To get:	ä	use OPTION-U, then depress a
To get:	ã	use OPTION-N, then depress a
To get:	"	use OPTION-[
To get:	"	use OPTION-SHIFT-[
To get:	'	use OPTION-]
To get:	'	use OPTION-SHIFT-]
To get:	...	use OPTION-;

To get: –   use OPTION-DASH (this produces a longer dash)

To get: —   use OPTION-SHIFT-DASH (this produces an even longer dash)

6.9 The ⌘ Symbol

To produce the ⌘ symbol, hold down the CONTROL key (*not* the OPTION key, and *not* the ⌘ key), and type a lowercase q, in the Chicago font (note that the original Mac keyboards associated with the original Mac and Mac Plus do not have a CONTROL key). This may not work on all word processors.

6.10 The Dominant Disk

The "dominant disk" is generally the startup disk, containing the System and the Finder. Its icon appears in the upper-rightmost corner of the screen. When you perform certain operations from another disk, the Macintosh may return to the dominant disk for additional instructions. If the dominant disk is not a hard disk, and has been ejected, you may have to swap the dominant disk in and out. It is possible to force the Macintosh to designate another disk as dominant. If the startup disk is a hard disk, the newly-designated dominant floppy may only stay dominant temporarily.

To change the designation of dominant disk, do the following:

1. Open the system folder on the disk which is to be designated dominant.

2. Holding down ⌘-OPTION, double-click on the finder in the system folder.

6.11 Multifinder Miscellanea

Multifinder requires considerable memory to be effective. It is best used with 2 Mbytes of RAM, or greater.

* If you run out of memory, quitting all applications and reopening them *may* help, by defragmenting existing memory.

* Use GET INFO to examine and change memory allocation settings if necessary.

* If you want to keep Multifinder off even when it is switched on in SET STARTUP, hold down the ⌘ key while the Macintosh is powering on.

* If you want to turn Multifinder on for your session, even if it is switched off in SET STARTUP, hold down OPTION and ⌘, and double-click on Multifinder in the System folder.

- You can launch several programs simultaneously under Multifinder without creating a permanent startup set. You may do this by selecting all the icons in question (via SHIFT-CLICK: hold down the SHIFT key and click the mouse), and choosing OPEN from the FILE menu.

6.12   Remarks on Fonts

One of the Apple Macintosh's best features is the ease of document preparation, with a variety of type styles and sizes. A few facts about fonts are often misunderstood. First of all, there is an important distinction between *screen* fonts and *printer* fonts, although this distinction has recently become blurred with the advent of Adobe Type Manager and Truetype. Let us first consider the traditional distinction between bitmapped screen fonts and outline-coded printer fonts.

6.12.1   Traditional Screen Fonts

A screen font is one that is designed for display on the Macintosh screen, to give the user a close approximation of what will be printed on the actual page. Screen fonts are displayed naturally at screen resolution, which is about 72 dots-per-inch (dpi)—much lower than the 300 or more dpi typical for laser printers. Screen fonts on the Mac have traditionally been stored as bitmaps. For the best screen effect, a given typeface should be installed directly (via the Font/DA Mover, except in the case of System 7) at each point size for which it is likely to be used. If the system only has, Times Roman at 12 points, and the user wants to display it at 9 point, then the Mac's graphics software will try to scale the 12-point font down to 9 points, and it is not likely to look very good—it may be barely legible.

6.12.2   Printer Fonts

Unless you want a direct printed version of your screen font at 72 dpi, your laser printer must be equipped with the appropriate corresponding printer font. The Apple Laserwriter and other printers use PostScript fonts, which are outline-coded, fully scaleable, and stored permanently in ROM. It can also use downloadable fonts, which are stored in the Mac system and shipped to the printer as needed. The important point to note is that having a screen version of a font is not enough—a printer version is also required.

6.12.3 Adobe Type Manager and Truetype

The traditional situation for screen fonts described in Sec. 6.12.1 has been changed by the advent first of Adobe Type Manager (ATM) and then of Apple's Truetype font technology. Both utilities produce good displays at screen resolution using the information in outline-coded font files. The user thus need no longer store separate bitmaps for each font at each point size. Truetype and ATM are competing technologies that produce a roughly comparable quality of screen output (Tinkel, 1991). The two competing font formats, Adobe Type 1 and Truetype, differ in that the former implements the outlines as cubic Bezier splines, and the latter uses quadratic B-splines. It is also worth noting that ATM is implemented as an INIT, whereas Truetype is an integral part of System 7 (Truetype too was an INIT in Systems 6.05 and 6.07).

6.12.4 Font Identifications

In the Macintosh system, each font is assigned an identification number. Unfortunately, when the Mac was first designed, it only had 128 kbyte of RAM and 64 kbyte of ROM, and no one really predicted the future explosive proliferation of fonts, so that provision was made for only 256 font identification numbers. Of these, 0 through 127 were reserved for system use, so that new fonts could only be assigned identification numbers between 128 and 255. The reason this is important is that on older systems one could easily run out of identification numbers. On such systems the Font/DA Mover, if it detects an identification number collision when it is installing a new font, will typically reassign the identification number of the new font to something else. This can conceivably cause problems for a user printing output on someone else's system, which does not know about the reassigned identification number for the user's new font.

On newer systems, the user need not worry about the above considerations. In 1986 Apple introduced the FOND/NFNT resource combination, replacing the old FONT resource (a "resource" on the Macintosh system is simply a form of structured data, with a four-letter resource name and an identification number). The FOND resource contains information on kerning, spacing, and other such details for an entire family of fonts represented as NFNTs. For example, Helvetica could be represented as a FOND, with the specific constituent fonts such as ten-point Helvetica or twelve-point Helvetica being represented as NFNTs. The older FONTs can also be constituents of a FOND. If a

FONT is a constituent of a FOND, its identification number is the same as that of the parent FOND. This is not the case with the NFNT representation. NFNT identification numbers typically change as fonts are moved, but each FOND maintains a list of its current associated NFNTs. A FOND with NFNTs attached has an identification number ranging from 1024 to 16383, with numbers from 3072 to 16383 reserved by Apple for commercial type foundries. The importance of all this to the user is that the Apple Macintosh can accommodate a large number of typefaces, and care need only be exercised to avoid identification-number conflicts when working on old machines and systems.

6.13   Graphics Formats

The plethora of painting, drawing, and illustrating programs available for the Macintosh (e.g. MacDraw, MacPaint, Adobe Illustrator, Aldus Freehand, and so on) has led to a profusion of graphics file formats. These formats are generally incompatible with each other, and the situation can become very confusing for the user. Parascandolo and Abernathy (1990) have written a very useful article on the topic in a recent issue of *MacUser* magazine, to which we refer the interested reader.

There are five major categories of file formats for Macintosh graphics: paint, PICT, PICT2, tagged image file format (TIFF), and encapsulated PostScript (EPS). Each of these can also have subcategories.

6.13.1   Paint Format

A MacPaint file, referred to also simply as a paint file, is a compressed bit map. Each pixel can be either black or white. The images stored are thus black and white, with a resolution of 72 dots per inch, and are 8 × 10 inches large (vertically oriented). The data compression and expansion is effected by Macintosh system utilities PackBits and UnPackBits. The paint format is the most basic of all the formats.

6.13.2   PICT

PICT files can comprise both bit maps and object-oriented, resolution-independent graphics. The object-oriented graphics are encoded in QuickDraw, the Macintosh system's graphics language. PICT sets no limits on the resolution of bit maps, although application programs may set ones of their own. PICT files can be black and white, or any one of eight colors.

6.13.3   PICT2

PICT2 is a full-color extension of PICT. PICT2 has basic subtypes: 8-bit PICT2 (256 colors) and 24-bit PICT2 (16.8 million colors). In Figs. 6.1 to 6.5 we further divide PICT2 according to whether the file contains object-oriented drawings or bit maps.

6.13.4   TIFF

TIFF (tagged image file format) is a versatile representation used also on IBM personal computers. TIFF files are bit maps, and do not store object-oriented graphics. There are three subtypes:

Monochrome TIFF	Each pixel black or white only
Gray-scale TIFF	Each pixel chosen from 256 grays
Color TIFF	Each pixel chosen from 16.8 million colors (24-bit color)

6.13.5   EPS

An EPS (encapsulated PostScript) ASCII file is one which essentially contains a PostScript program to produce an image. Usually, an EPS ASCII file also contains a PICT version of the image so that it can be previewed on the Macintosh screen. As an example, consider the illustrations in this book. Typically, each illustration was produced in Adobe Illustrator. It was then copied to the clipboard as encapsulated PostScript (by holding down the OPTION key while selecting the COPY command—a handy trick), and pasted into the word processor used to produce the book. The PostScript program in the EPS file allows the illustration to be reproduced at the full resolution of the laser printer when the page is printed. The PICT representation allows the illustration to be previewed on the screen at screen resolution when editing the file.

EPS files can also be binary. Binary EPS files typically contain a PICT preview of the image for screen viewing, as do ASCII EPS files. However, instead of containing a PostScript program to draw the image, binary EPS contains a stream of hexadecimal numbers describing the bit map (binary EPS files can be very large).

6.13.6   Converting from One Format to Another

Typically, most Macintosh graphics programs work with a handful of the file formats. MacPaint works only with paint files, and MacDraw works with its own MacDraw representation and with PICT files. In their *MacUser* article, Parascandolo and Abernathy (1990) present a detailed table showing which conversions can be performed by which programs. We do not reproduce this entire table here. Instead we notice that four programs, namely Adobe Photoshop, Pixelpaint, Pixelpaint Professional, and Canvas 2.1, are the most versatile. Figures 6.2 through 6.5 show the format-conversion capabilities of these four programs.

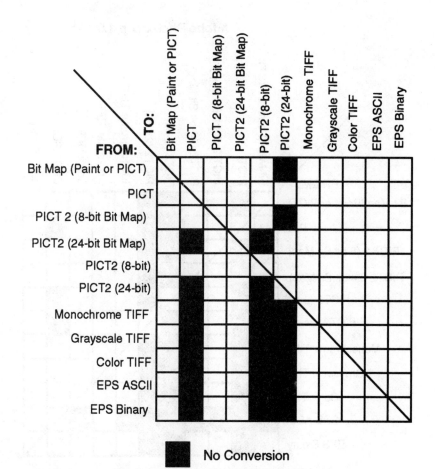

Fig. 6.1 **Macintosh graphics format conversions currently possible using commercially available software.**

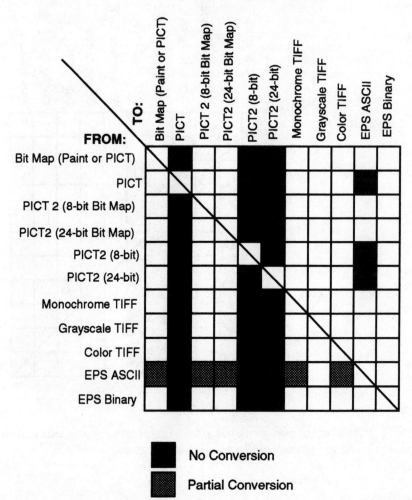

Fig. 6.2 Macintosh graphics format conversions currently possible using Adobe Photoshop 1.0.

Deneba Canvas 2.1

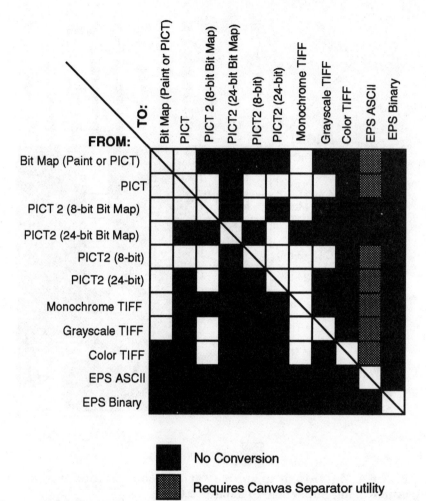

No Conversion

Requires Canvas Separator utility

Fig. 6.3 Macintosh graphics format conversions currently possible using Deneba Canvas 2.1.

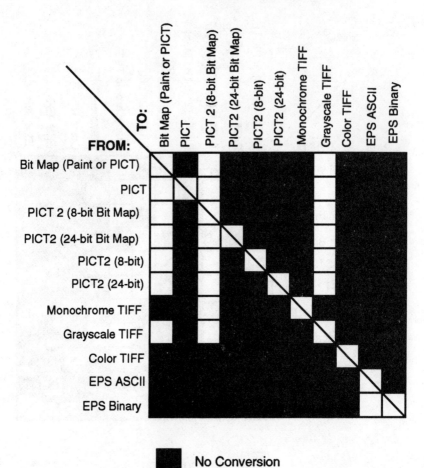

No Conversion

Fig. 6.4 Macintosh graphics format conversions currently possible using Supermac Pixelpaint 2.0.

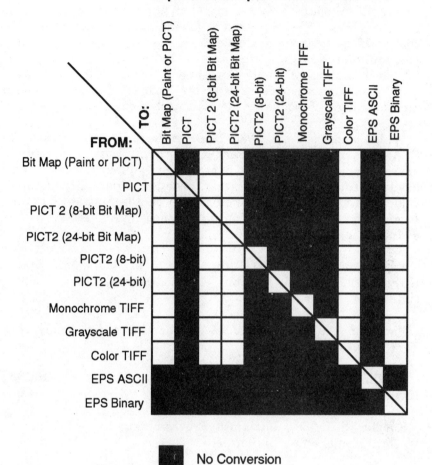

Fig. 6.5 Macintosh graphics format conversions currently possible using Supermac Pixelpaint Professional 1.0.

6.14 Bibliography

Lu (1988) provides an excellent overview of Macintosh hardware and software. Apple Computer (1990) is a definitive guide to hardware. Harriman and Calica's (1989) book is a good source of advanced tips and useful information difficult to find elsewhere. Harriman (1988) is useful for those who are interested in data sharing and networking between Macintoshes and MS-DOS computers.

Often, the easier a computer is to use, the more difficult it is to program. Macintosh systems and application programming is quite involved, with Pascal and C generally being the languages of choice. Many tools are available to aid the programmer. For those who are interested in delving into the Macintosh system in depth, the five volumes of Apple Computer's *Inside Macintosh* are a fundamental reference. Knaster (1988) discusses useful programming techniques for the Macintosh toolbox.

Apple Computer Corp. (1985–1990), *Inside Macintosh, Volumes 1–5*, Addison Wesley, Menlo Park, California. (Note: All volumes are available separately in paper cover; volumes 1–3 are also available bound together as a hardcover. A separate index to all volumes and to other Apple literature on the Macintosh, called *Inside Macintosh X-Ref* and also published by Addison-Wesley, is available in addition).

Apple Computer Corp. (1990), *Guide to the Macintosh Family Hardware*, Second Edition, Addison-Wesley, Menlo Park, California.

Harriman, C. (1988), *The MS-DOS-Mac Connection*, Brady, New York, New York.

Harriman, C., and B. Calica (1989), *The Macintosh Advisor*, Hayden Books, Indianapolis, Indiana.

Knaster, S. (1988), *Macintosh Programming Secrets*, Addison-Wesley, Menlo Park, California.

Lu, C. (1988), *The Apple Macintosh Book*, Third Edition, Microsoft Press, Redmond, Washington.

Parascandolo, S., and A. Abernathy (1990), "MacUser Guide to Graphics Formats," *MacUser*, Sept. 1990, 266–276.

Tinkel, K. (1991), "Dueling Font Standards," *MacUser*, Oct. 1991, 165–177.

7

System Characteristics

Below are some notes on the systems covered in this book, as well as some others. The information concentrates on word size, the method of coding text, marking end-of-line, etc. It is far from complete, and it is certainly subject to change, but it might be useful to the unfamiliar user who is taking his first steps in a system, or who is perhaps attempting a file transfer. The information below can be found in da Cruz (1987) (see Chap. 10 bibliography).

7.1 UNIX

UNIX runs on so many different machines that it would be futile to try and specify a word size. Text byte size is 8 bits. Text is coded as 7-bit ASCII, with the 8th (high-order) bit generally set to 0. End-of-line is marked with a line-feed. An accurate byte count of file size is maintained in the directory

7.2 VAX-VMS

Word size is 32 bits, and text byte size is 8 bits. Text is coded as 7-bit ASCII, with the 8th (high-order) bit generally set to 0. VMS offers a variety of file organizations. Usually, records are variable and padded to an even length; end-of-line is implied via attributes of the directory. An accurate byte count of file size is maintained in the directory.

7.3   MVS-TSO

Word size is 32 bits, and text byte size is 8 bits. Text is coded in EBCDIC. End-of-line in variable records is marked by a special record-control word, as is end-of-file.

7.4   VM-CMS

Word size is 32 bits, and text byte size is 8 bits. Text is coded in EBCDIC. End-of-line in variable records is marked by a special record-control word, as is end-of-file.

7.5   MS-DOS

Word size is 16 bits (32 in versions running on some newer IBM personal computers), and text byte size is 8 bits. Text is coded as 8-bit ("extended") ASCII. End-of-line is marked by a carriage-return and a line-feed. An accurate byte count of file size is maintained in the directory for marking the end of file. Some applications mark the end of file with a CTRL-Z (a holdover from CP/M days).

7.6   Macintosh

Word size is 32 bits , and text byte size is 8 bits. Text is coded as 8-bit ("extended") ASCII. End-of-line is marked by a carriage-return. An accurate byte count of file size is maintained in the directory for marking the end of file.

7.7   DEC PDP-11/RT-11

Word size is 16 bits, and text byte size is 8 bits. Text is coded as 7-bit ASCII, with the 8th (highest order) bit generally set to 0. End-of-line is marked by a carriage-return and a line-feed. The directory knows the file size to the nearest block. The final block of a file is padded to the end with NULs. Files are stored contiguously.

7.8   DECSYSTEM-10 and DECSYSTEM-20

Word size is 36 bits, and text byte size is 7 bits. Text files are packed as five 7-bit bytes into a word (leaving one bit unused). Text is coded as 7-bit ASCII. End-of-line is marked by a carriage-return and a line-feed. In DECSYSTEM-20, an accurate byte count of file size is maintained in the directory.

7.9   PRIME 50 series—PRIMOS

Word size is 16 bits, and text byte size is eight bits. Text is coded as 7-bit ASCII, but unlike most systems the eighth (high-order) bit is set to 1 rather than 0 (*very* annoying). Text files are stored compressed (with respect to blanks). Compression lead-in characters, and print control characters embedded in the file, have high-order bits set to 0 instead of 1. End-of-line is marked by a line-feed. The directory knows a file's size to the nearest word.

7.10   UCSD p System

Word size is 16 bits, and text byte size is 8 bits. Text is coded as 7-bit ASCII, with the eighth (high-order) bit generally set to 0. End-of-line is marked by a carriage-return. The directory maintains an accurate byte count of file size to mark the end-of-file. Files are stored contiguously.

7.11   CDC Cyber Systems—NOS

CDC Cyber computer systems vary greatly in their parameters. Word size is generally 64 bits, and text byte size is 6 or 12 bits. Text can be coded as 7-bit ASCII, with the eighth (high-order) bit generally set to 0. Text can also be coded with some 6-bit coding schemes that do not allow for lowercase letters. End-of-line is marked by a special word with at least 12 zero bits in the lowest-order positions. End-of-file is marked by a zero-word.

7.12   CP/M-80

Word size is 8 bits, and text byte size is 8 bits. Text is coded as 7-bit ASCII, with the eighth (high-order) bit generally set to 0. End-of-line is marked by a carriage-return and a line-feed. End-of-file is marked by a CTRL-Z. Files are stored in 128-byte blocks, and the directory knows the file size to the nearest block.

2

Data Communications
and File Transfer

In this section we have brought together a variety of useful information in the area of data communications, to aid the user who has occasion to work on many different types of computers. Chapter 8 begins with a summary of several major physical interface standards, including RS-232, RS-422, Centronics, SCSI, and IEEE 488. The chapter shows how to make simple null modems, and provides a reasonably extensive presentation of tables for connecting together Macintoshes and IBM-style PC's. The chapter also covers modems, and surveys the communication characteristics of major computers and operating systems. Chapter 9 provides information on public worldwide networks through which the user may communicate with counterparts everywhere on earth. Chapters 10 and 11 succinctly cover the basics of file transfer with Kermit and FTP.

Throughout the chapters in this part of the book, references are made to important standards. These standards, and the organizations which develop them, are listed and discussed in Section 3.

Interfaces, Connections, and Modems

8.1 RS-232 Serial Interface

8.1.1 Generalities

One of the best-known computer standards in the world is the EIA RS-232 serial interface.   It is used for serial communications between all types of computers and peripherals.   RS stands for "recommended standard." The standard has gone through several revisions, the last one in 1987, when it was issued by EIA as Recommended Standard 232-D. The RS-232 interface is compatible with that described by CCITT Recommendation V.24, and by ISO 2110. RS-232 is usually (but not always—see Sec. 8.1.5) used with a DB-25 connector, whose pin numbering scheme is shown in Fig. 8.1. RS-232 is effective for transmission rates of 0–20 kilobits per s, and ranges of about 15 m.   Table 8.1 lists the RS-232 signal assignments, along with their commonly used abbreviations and their EIA and CCITT designations.   The table also indicates differences between RS-232 and the Bell 113B/208A specifications.

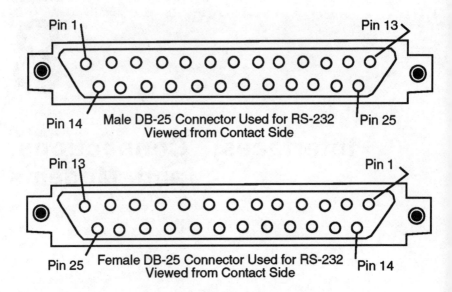

Fig. 8.1   Pin numbering for a DB-25 connector.

RS-232 voltage levels are as follows:

−15 to −5 V	Mark, logic 1
−5 to −3 V	Noise margin
−3 to +3 V	Transition region
+3 to +5 V	Noise margin
+5 to +15 V	Space, logic 0

8.1.2   Useful Subsets of RS-232

Some useful subsets of the RS-232 interface for various functions are as follows:

Four-way cable for dumb terminals   Use pins 1, 2, 3, and 7; jumper pins 8 and 20

Nine-way cable for asynchronous communications
                                               Use pins 1–8 and 20

Fifteen-way cable for synchronous communications
                                               Use pins 1–8, 13, 15, 17, 20, 22, and 24

TABLE 8.1 RS-232 (EIA 232)/CCITT V24 Pin Assignment

Circuit Pin No.	Abbrev.	Direction	CCITT	EIA	Function
1	FG	-	101	AA	Frame ground
2	TD	To DCE	103	BA	Transmitted Data
3	RD	To DTE	104	BB	Received Data
4	RTS	To DCE	105	CA	Request to Send
5	CTS	To DTE	106	CB	Clear to Send
6	DSR	To DTE	107	CC	Data set Ready
7	SG	-	102	AB	Signal ground
8	DCD	To DTE	109	CF	Data Carrier Detect
9		To DTE			Positive dc test voltage
10		To DTE			Negative dc test voltage
11	*QM*	*To DTE*	*Note 1*		*Equalizer mode*
12	SDCD	To DTE	122	SCF	Secondary Data Carrier Detect
13	SCTS	To DTE	121	SCB	Secondary Clear to Send
14	STD	To DCE	118	SBA	Secondary Transmitted Data
14	*NS*	*To DCE*	*Note 1*		*New Synchronization*
15	TC	To DTE	114	DB	Transmitter Clock
16	SRD	To DTE	119	SBB	Secondary Received Data
16	*DCT*	*To DTE*	*Note 1*		*Divided Clock Transmitter*
17	RC	To DTE	115	DD	Receiver Clock
18	*DCR*	*To DCE*	*Note 1*		*Divided Clock Receiver*
19	SRTS	To DCE	120	DCA	Secondary Request to Send
20	DTR	To DCE	108.2	CD	Data Terminal Ready
21	SQ	To DTE	110	CG	Signal Quality Detect
22	RI	To DTE	125	CE	Ring Indicator
23		To DCE	111	CH	Data Rate Selector
		To DCE	112	CI	Data Rate Selector
24	TC	To DCE	113	DA	External Transmitter Clock
25		*To DCE*	*Note 2*		*Busy*

Notes: 1. Bell 208A (pins 11 and 18 not specified by RS-232)
2. Bell 113B (pin 25 not specified by RS-232)
Italics indicate Bell Specification, not RS-232
DTE = Data terminal equipment (e.g., a terminal or microcomputer)
DCE = Data communications equipment, or data circuit terminating equipment (e.g., a modem)

8.1.3 Remarks on Connecting Computers to Modems

To make the pin listings of Table 8.1 somewhat less abstract, consider the concrete example of connecting a computer with a

modem (Sec. 8.7). Assume that the computer is configured as data
terminal equipment (DTE) and the modem is configured as data
communications equipment (DCE; now referred to as "data circuit–
terminating equipment"). The following pins are used for control
purposes:

Pin 4   RTS, Request to Send. The computer signals the modem that it
               is ready to send data to the modem.

Pin 5   CTS, Clear to Send. The modem signals the computer that it is
               ready to accept data.

Pin 6   DSR, Data Set Ready. The modem (= the "data set" in this
               case) signals the computer that it is connected to the telephone
               line.

Pin 8   DCD, Data Carrier Detect. The modem tells the computer that it
               has gone on line and the computer can receive data.

Pin 20   DTR, Data Terminal Ready. The computer (= the "data
               terminal" in this case) signals the modem that it (the computer)
               is powered up.

Pin 22   RI, Ring Indicator. The modem tells the computer thau une
               telephone on the other end is ringing.

Actual data transmission occurs over pins 2 and 3:

Pin 2   TD, Transmitted Data. The computer transmits data to the
               modem on this pin. The modem receives data from the
               computer on this pin.

Pin 3   RD, Received Data. The computer receives data from the
               modem on this pin. The modem sends data to the computer on
               this pin.

In addition, pin 1 acts as a protective frame ground (FG) and pin 7
acts as a signal ground (SG, the reference point for other voltages in
the interface).

8.1.4 Typical Connection for Two Computers

There are a number of ways to connect two computers each of which
has an RS-232 port and is configured as data terminal equipment
(DTE). The cable connecting two such computers is often referred to
as a "null modem." A possible arrangement is shown in Table 8.2.
Note that pin 6 of each computer is connected to pin 20 of the other
computer. The purpose of this is to "fool" each computer into
"thinking" that it is properly connected to a modem that has
established a connection with another computer. Pins 8 and 6 are
jumpered together on each computer. This is done to simulate a

carrier signal. If pins 6 and 8 are not jumpered together, the communications software on each computer may think that the carrier has been lost, and disconnect as a result. The voltage from pin 20 (Data Terminal Ready) sets pins 6 (Data Set Ready) and 8 (Data Carrier Detect) to a level such that they appear to indicate to the host system that a proper connection has been established. Note that the null modem described in Table 8.2 is for use between systems that fully honor DTE/DCE signaling conventions. Other configurations are possible, and may be required depending on the situation.

TABLE 8.2 Possible RS-232 Connection of Two Computers Both Configured as DTE

Computer 1			Computer 2	
Function	Pin No.		Pin No.	Function
Frame ground	1	-------------------	1	Frame ground
Transmitted Data	2	-------------------	3	Received Data
Received Data	3	-------------------	2	Transmitted Data
Request to Send	4	-------------------	5	Clear to Send
Clear to Send	5	-------------------	4	Request to Send
Data Set Ready	6	-------------------	20	Data Terminal Ready
Signal ground	7	-------------------	7	Signal ground
Data Carrier Detect	8	-------------------	20	Data Terminal Ready
Data Terminal Ready	20	-------------------	6	Data Set Ready
Data Terminal Ready	20	-------------------	8	Data Carrier Detect

Note: On each computer, pins 8 and 6 are jumped together and connected to pin 20 of the other computer.

8.1.5 RS-232 Implemented with a 9-Pin Connector

Although the standard specifies 25 pins, not all of these always need to be used. Pins 1–8 and 20 are actually sufficient for most applications. Some RS-232 ports thus do not use a full 25-pin connector. The IBM-PC/AT, for example, uses a 9-pin D connector (DB-9). The pin numbering scheme of the DB-9 connector is shown in Fig. 8.2.

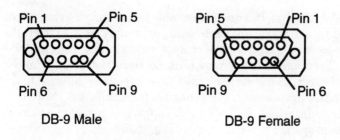

DB-9 Male   DB-9 Female

Viewed from Contact Side

Fig. 8.2   Pin numbering for a DB-9 connector.

An adapter from the AT's DB-9 to a conventional DB-25 can be made by connecting the pins as shown in Table 8.3. Tables 8.4 and 8.5 show possible configurations for null modems between computers configured as DTE.

TABLE 8.3   Making an Adapter Cable from PC/AT DB-9 to PC DB-25

PC/AT DB-9 Female			PC DB-25 Male	
Function	Pin No.		Pin No.	Function
Carrier Detect	1	-----------------------	8	Carrier Detect
Received Data	2	-----------------------	3	Received Data
Transmitted Data	3	-----------------------	2	Transmitted Data
Data Terminal Ready	4	-----------------------	20	Data Terminal Ready
Ground	5	-----------------------	7	Ground
Data Set Ready	6	-----------------------	6	Data Set Ready
Request to Send	7	-----------------------	4	Request to Send
Clear to Send	8	-----------------------	5	Clear to Send
Ring Indicate	9	-----------------------	22	Ring Indicate

TABLE 8.4 Making an RS-232 Null Modem when One Port is a DB-9 and the Other is a DB-25

DB-9 Function	Pin No.		DB-25 Pin No.	Function
Received Data	2	-------------------	2	Transmitted Data
Transmitted Data	3	-------------------	3	Received Data
Data Terminal Ready	4	-------------------	6	Data Set Ready
Ground	5	-------------------	7	Ground
Data Set Ready	6	-------------------	20	Data Terminal Ready
Request to Send	7	-------------------	5	Clear to Send
Clear to Send	8	-------------------	4	Request to Send

Note: On DB-9, pins 1 and 6 are jumpered together. On DB-25, Pins 6 and 8 are jumpered together.

TABLE 8.5 Making an RS-232 Null Modem when Both Ports are DB-9

DB-9 Function	Pin No.		DB-25 Pin No.	Function
Received Data	2	-------------------	3	Transmitted Data
Transmitted Data	3	-------------------	2	Received Data
Data Terminal Ready	4	-------------------	6	Data Set Ready
Ground	5	-------------------	5	Ground
Data Set Ready	6	-------------------	4	Data Terminal Ready
Request to Send	7	-------------------	8	Clear to Send
Clear to Send	8	-------------------	7	Request to Send

Note: On each computer, pins 1 and 6 are jumpered together.

8.2 RS-422 Serial Interface

RS-422 supports potentially far higher data rates than RS-232: it is capable of up to 10 megabits per s. RS-422 defines a balanced interface using differential signal lines. Whereas an RS-232 transmitter modulates signals with respect to a common ground, an RS-422 transmitter modulates a signal with respect to an inverted copy of the same signal. An RS-232 receiver must sense whether an incoming signal is negative enough (with respect to ground) to represent a mark; an RS-422 receiver must only sense which line is more negative than the other. This is the reason for RS-422's greater immunity to noise, and lower attenuation with distance. The voltage levels in RS-422 are as follows:

–6 to –2 V	Mark, logic 1
–2 to –0.2 V	Noise margin
–0.2 to +0.2 V	Transition region
+0.2 to +2 V	Noise margin
+2 to +6 V	Space, logic 0

The standard does not specify a physical connector. Some manufacturers use a DB-9, others use a DB-25 with nonstandard pinning, and still others use a DB-25 following RS-530. A DB-37 following RS-449 is also used sometimes.

RS-422 is the interface employed in the Apple Macintosh series of computers. The older Macintoshes use a DB-9, while the newer ones (starting with the Mac Plus) use a Mini-DIN 8-pin connector. The pin numbering scheme on the DB-9 is shown in Fig. 8.2, and that of the Mini-DIN is shown in Fig. 8.3.

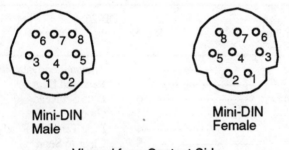

Mini-DIN
Male

Mini-DIN
Female

Viewed from Contact Side

Fig. 8.3 Pin assignments on the Macintosh Mini-DIN connector.

An adapter between DB-9 and Mini-DIN connectors can be made by connecting the pins as shown in Table 8.6.

TABLE 8.6 Making an Adapter Cable from Macintosh DB-9 to Mini-DIN

DB-9 Pin No.		Mini-DIN Pin No.
3	------------------	4
4	------------------	6
5	------------------	3
7	------------------	2
8	------------------	8
9	------------------	5

Tables 8.7 to 8.9 show the pin assignments for RS-422 interfaces on various Macintosh computers.

TABLE 8.7 Pin Assignments for Macintosh SE and II Serial Interfaces (Mini-DIN Connector)

Pin No.	Abbrev.	Function
1	DTR	Data Terminal Ready
2	CTS	Clear to Send
3	TD–	Transmitted Data
4	SG	Signal ground
5	RD–	Received Data
6	TD+	Transmitted Data/Balanced
7	DCD	Data Carrier Detect
8	RD+	Received Data/Balanced
Connector shell		Frame ground

TABLE 8.8 Pin Assignments for Macintosh Plus Serial Interface (Mini-DIN Connector)

Pin No.	Abbrev.	Function
1	DTR	Data Terminal Ready
2	CTS	Clear to Send
3	TD–	Transmitted Data
4	SG	Signal ground
5	RD–	Received Data
6	TD+	Transmitted Data/Balanced
8	RD+	Received Data/Balanced
Connector shell		Frame ground

TABLE 8.9 Pin Assignments for Macintosh 512K Serial Interface (DB-9 Connector)

Pin No.	Abbrev.	Function
1 and connector shell		Frame ground
3	SG	Signal ground
4	TD+	Transmitted Data/Balanced
5	TD–	Transmitted Data
7	CTS	Clear to Send
8	RD+	Received Data/Balanced
9	RD–	Received Data

8.3   Interconnecting Macintoshes, IBM-PC's, and Other Computers

Tables 8.10 to 8.20 give information for connecting together various types of computers in the IBM-PC and Apple Macintosh families, and connecting these computers to some peripherals. The information is adapted from Lu (1988). Computers are all assumed to be wired as DTE. The reader should exercise caution as many variations are possible in different system setups. The tables below, and others in this chapter, should be treated as starting points and not taken as gospel!

TABLE 8.10 Connecting a Macintosh 512K to an IBM-PC

Macintosh DB-9			PC DB-25	
Function	Pin No.		Pin No.	Function
Ground	3	----------------------	7	Ground
Transmit Data	5	----------------------	3	Receive Data
Receive Data	9	----------------------	2	Transmit Data

Notes: 1. On PC, pins 4 and 5 should be jumpered together.
2. On PC, pins 6, 8, and 20 should be jumpered together.

TABLE 8.11 Connecting a Macintosh Plus, SE, or II to an IBM-PC

Macintosh Mini-DIN			PC DB-25	
Function	Pin No.		Pin No.	Function
Ground	4	----------------------	7	Ground
Transmit Data	3	----------------------	3	Receive Data
Receive Data	5	----------------------	2	Transmit Data
Data Terminal Ready	1	----------------------	6	Data Set Ready

Notes: 1. On PC, pins 4 and 5 should be jumpered together.
2. On PC, pins 6, 8, and 20 should be jumpered together.

TABLE 8.12 Connecting a Macintosh 512K to an IBM-PC/AT, PS/2, or Similar Model Using a DB-9 Connector

Macintosh DB-9			PC DB-9	
Function	Pin No.		Pin No.	Function
Ground	3	----------------------	5	Ground
Transmit Data	5	----------------------	2	Receive Data
Receive Data	9	----------------------	3	Transmit Data

Notes: 1. On PC, pins 6 and 1 should be jumpered together.
2. On PC, pins 7 and 8 should be jumpered together.

TABLE 8.13 Connecting a Macintosh Plus, SE, or II to an IBM-PC/AT, PS/2, or Similar Model Using a DB-9 Connector

Macintosh Mini-DIN		PC DB-9	
Function	Pin No.	Pin No.	Function
Ground	4	5	Ground
Transmit Data	3	2	Receive Data
Receive Data	5	3	Transmit Data
Data Terminal Ready	1	6	Data Set Ready

Notes: 1. On PC, Pins 6 and 1 should be jumpered together.
2. On PC, Pins 7 and 8 should be jumpered together.

TABLE 8.14 Connecting a Macintosh 512K to a Tandy Model 100 Laptop, or to an Apple Imagewriter

Macintosh DB-9		DB-25	
Function	Pin No.	Pin No.	Function
Ground, Balanced Line	3, 8	7	Ground
Transmit Data	5	3	Receive Data
Receive Data	9	2	Transmit Data
Clear to Send	7	20	Data Terminal Ready

TABLE 8.15 Connecting a Macintosh Plus, SE, or II to a Tandy Model 100 Laptop, or to an Apple Imagewriter

Macintosh Mini-DIN		DB-25	
Function	Pin No.	Pin No.	Function
Ground, Balanced Line	4, 8	7	Ground
Transmit Data	3	3	Receive Data
Receive Data	5	2	Transmit Data
Clear to Send	2	20	Data Terminal Ready

TABLE 8.16 Connecting a Macintosh 512K to a Hayes Modem

Macintosh DB-9			DB-25	
Function	Pin No.		Pin No.	Function
Signal ground	3	---------------------	7	Signal ground
Transmit Data	5	---------------------	2	Transmit Data
Clear to Send	7	---------------------	5	Clear to Send
Receive Data	9	---------------------	3	Receive Data
Frame ground	1	---------------------	1	Frame ground

TABLE 8.17 Connecting a Macintosh Plus, SE, or II to a Hayes Modem

Macintosh Mini DIN			DB-25	
Function	Pin No.		Pin No.	Function
Signal ground	4	---------------------	7	Signal ground
Transmit Data	3	---------------------	2	Transmit Data
Clear to Send	2	---------------------	5	Clear to Send
Receive Data	5	---------------------	3	Receive Data
Frame ground	Shell	---------------------	1	Frame ground

TABLE 8.18 Connecting a Macintosh 512K to a Macintosh Plus, SE, or II

Macintosh DB-9			Macintosh Mini DIN	
Function	Pin No.		Pin No.	Function
Signal ground	3	---------------------	4	Signal ground
Transmit Data / Bal.	4	---------------------	8	Receive Data / Bal.
Transmit Data	5	---------------------	5	Receive Data
Receive Data / Bal.	8	---------------------	6	Transmit Data / Bal.
Receive Data	9	---------------------	3	Transmit Data

TABLE 8.19 Connecting Together Two Macintosh 512K's

Macintosh DB-9 Function	Pin No.		Pin No.	Macintosh DB-9 Function
Signal ground	3	-----------------	3	Signal ground
Transmit Data / Bal.	4	-----------------	8	Receive Data / Bal.
Transmit Data	5	-----------------	9	Receive Data
Receive Data / Bal.	8	-----------------	4	Transmit Data / Bal.
Receive Data	9	-----------------	5	Transmit Data

TABLE 8.20 Connecting Together Two Macintosh Plus, SE, or II's

Macintosh Mini DIN Function	Pin No.		Pin No.	Macintosh Mini DIN Function
Signal ground	4	-----------------	4	Signal ground
Transmit Data / Bal.	6	-----------------	8	Receive Data / Bal.
Transmit Data	3	-----------------	5	Receive Data
Receive Data / Bal.	8	-----------------	6	Transmit Data / Bal.
Receive Data	5	-----------------	3	Transmit Data
Data Terminal Ready	1	-----------------	2	Clear to Send
Clear to Send	2	-----------------	1	Data Terminal Ready

8.4   Centronics Parallel Printer Interface

The Centronics interface is a *de facto* standard for parallel data communication between a microcomputer and a printer. The connector used is a 36-pin Amphenol connector, whose pin-numbering scheme is shown in Fig. 8.4 below.

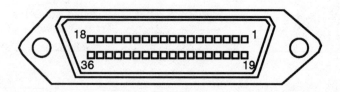

Fig. 8.4 Pin assignments for the Centronics parallel interface connector.

Table 8.21 shows the pin assignment for the interface. The pins as shown in the table are typically those found on the printer. The microcomputer may use another type of connector, for example a DB-25.

TABLE 8.21 Pin Assignment of Centronics Interface

Pin	Abbreviation	Function
1	STROBE	Signal for parallel data to be sent to printer buffer
2	DATA 1	Data line 1
3	DATA 2	Data line 2
4	DATA 3	Data line 3
5	DATA 4	Data line 4
6	DATA 5	Data line 5
7	DATA 6	Data line 6
8	DATA 7	Data line 7
9	DATA 8	Data line 8
10	ACKNLG	Acknowledge; indicate data has been received
11	BUSY	Busy (because printer is printing, printer is off-line, error occurs, or data are being entered)
12	PE	Paper End; printer out of paper
13	SLCT	Select
14	AUTO FEED XT	Automatic line feed after printing
15		Not used
16	0V	Logic ground
17	CHASSIS GND	Chassis ground
18		Not used
19–30	GND	Signal ground for pins 1–12
31	INIT	Initialize; reset printer controller
32	ERROR	Error due to paper end, off-line, or other
33	GND	Signal ground
34		Not used
35	LOGIC 1	Logic 1
36	SLCT IN	Select input

8.5 IEEE 488

The IEEE 488 bus [ANSI/IEEE 488.1, 488.2 (1987)] uses 8 bi-directional data lines, five bus management lines, and three handshake lines. The 24-pin connector used for the IEEE 488 bus is shown schematically in Fig. 8.5, and the pin assignments are given in Table 8.22.

Fig. 8.5   Pin assignments for the IEEE 488 interface connector.

TABLE 8.22 Pin Assignment of IEEE 488 Bus Connector

Pin	Abbreviation	Function
1	D101	Data line 1
2	D102	Data line 2
3	D103	Data line 3
4	D104	Data line 4
5	EOI	End or Identify; signals that data transfer is complete
6	DAV	Data Valid; signals that valid data has been placed on the bus
7	NRFD	Not Ready for Data
8	NDAC	Not Data Accepted
9	IPC	Interface Clear
10	SRQ	Request for service; issued to gain attention of controller
11	ATN	Attention; issued by controller when placing a command on the bus.
12	SHIELD	Shield
13	D105	Data line 5
14	D106	Data line 6
15	D107	Data line 7
16	D108	Data line 8
17	REN	Remote Enable; enable or disable bus control
18–24	GND	Ground

8.6   SCSI Interface on Apple Macintosh Computers

The small computer systems interface (SCSI, pronounced "Scuzzy") is specified by ANSI X3.131 (1986) [endorsed by the ISO, as ISO 9316

(1989)]. Like others mentioned in this chapter, the standard is listed in Chap. 17. The SCSI interface is used for high-speed parallel data transfer between computers and peripherals. It is commonly used for hard disks. Later-model Apple Macintoshes (beginning with the Mac Plus) all have SCSI ports. Table 8.23 shows the signal assignments of the internal 50-pin flat-ribbon SCSI connector used in the Macintosh, and fig. 8.6 shows its pin numbering.

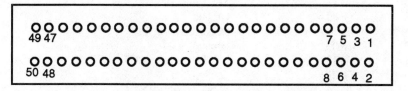

Fig. 8.6   Pin assignments for the internal SCSI connector on Macintosh computers.

TABLE 8.23 Pin Assignment of the Internal SCSI Interface on Macintosh Computers

Pin	Abbreviation	Function
1	GND	Ground
2	/DB0	SCSI data bus, bit 0
3	GND	Ground
4	/DB1	SCSI data bus, bit 1
5	GND	Ground
6	/DB2	SCSI data bus, bit 2
7	GND	Ground
8	/DB3	SCSI data bus, bit 3
9	GND	Ground
10	/DB4	SCSI data bus, bit 4
11	GND	Ground
12	/DB5	SCSI data bus, bit 5
13	GND	Ground
14	/DB6	SCSI data bus, bit 6
15	GND	Ground
16	/DB7	SCSI data bus, bit 7
17	GND	Ground
18	/DBP	SCSI data bus, parity bit
19	GND	Ground
20		Not connected
21	GND	Ground
22		Not connected
23	GND	Ground
24		Not connected
25	GND	Ground

TABLE 8.23 Pin Assignment of the Internal SCSI Interface on Macintosh Computers (continued)

Pin	Abbreviation	Function
26	TPWR	+5-V termination power
27	GND	Ground
28		Not connected
29	GND	Ground
30		Not connected
31	GND	Ground
32	/ATN	Indicates an Attention condition
33	GND	Ground
34		Not connected
35	GND	Ground
36	/BSY	Indicates whether SCSI data bus is busy
37	GND	Ground
38	/ACK	Acknowledge for a REQ/ACK data transfer handshake
39	GND	Ground
40	/RST	SCSI data bus Reset
41	GND	Ground
42	/MSG	Indicates the Message Phase
43	GND	Ground
44	/SEL	Selects a target or initiator
45	GND	Ground
46	/C/D	Indicates whether control or data is on SCSI bus
47	GND	Ground
48	/REQ	Request for a REQ/ACK data transfer handshake
49	GND	Ground
50	/I/O	Controls direction of data movement

The Macintosh uses a different SCSI connector externally than it does internally. Devices do not plug directly into the flat-ribbon connector, but into a 25-pin DB-25, such as is commonly used for RS-232. An RS-232 device should *never* be plugged into a Macintosh external SCSI port; RS-232 uses higher voltage levels, which can cause damage. The external Macintosh connector has the pin assignments shown in Table 8.24.

TABLE 8.24 Pin Assignment of External SCSI Connector on Macintosh Computers

Pin	Abbreviation	Function
1	/REQ	Request for a REQ/ACK data transfer handshake
2	/MSG	Indicates the Message Phase
3	/I/O	Controls the direction of data movement
4	/RST	SCSI data bus Reset
5	/ACK	Acknowledge for a REQ/ACK data transfer handshake
6	/BSY	Indicates whether SCSI data bus is busy
7	GND	Ground
8	/DB0	SCSI data bus, bit 0
9	GND	Ground
10	/DB3	SCSI data bus, bit 3
11	/DB5	SCSI data bus, bit 5
12	/DB6	SCSI data bus, bit 6
13	/DB7	SCSI data bus, bit 7
14	GND	Ground
15	/C/D	Indicates whether control or data is on the SCSI bus
16	GND	Ground
17	/ATN	Indicates an Attention condition
18	GND	Ground
19	/SEL	Selects a target or an initiator
20	/DBP	SCSI data bus, parity bit
21	/DB1	SCSI data bus, bit 1
22	/DB2	SCSI data bus, bit 2
23	/DB4	SCSI data bus, bit 4
24	GND	Ground
25	TPWR	+5-V terminator power

8.7 Modem Topics

A modem (*mo*dulator–*dem*odulator) translates digital signals into a form suitable for transmission over voice-band telephone lines. It is quite possible that sometime in the future, if integrated services digital networks (ISDNs) become widespread, modems may become obsolete. Their *raison d'être*—that telephone lines were designed with voice traffic and not digital transmission in mind—will no longer be relevant. For the time being, however, modems are important to the computer user.

8.7.1   Modem Standards

De jure modem standards are issued as CCITT V-series recommendations (listed in Chap. 17). For many years, however, modem standards in the United States were set, *de facto*, by AT&T (the Bell 100 and 200 series standards). The Bell standards resembled CCITT recommendations, but did not match them exactly. When Vadic, Inc. introduced the VA3400, the world's first 1200-bps full duplex modem, AT&T's dominance was challenged, and as a result CCITT recommendations began to be more influential, particularly in Europe. The essential parameters of the Bell modems and the CCITT V-Series modems are summarized in Tables 8.25 and 8.26 below. Speeds are in bits per second (bps).

TABLE 8.25   AT&T Bell Series Modems

Bell No	Speed (bps)	Synchronous/ Asynchronous[1]	Modulation[2]	Duplex[3]	Wire[4]
103A	300	A	FSK	H,F	2
103E	300	A	FSK	H,F	2
103F	300	A	FSK	H,F	4
201B	2400	S	PSK	H,F	4
201C	2400	S	PSK	H,F	2
202C	1200	A	FSK	H	2
202S	1200	A	FSK	H	2
202D/R	1800	A	FSK	H,F	4
202T	1800	A	FSK	H,F	4
208A	4800	S	PSK	H,F	4
208B	4800	S	PSK	H	2
209A	9600	S	QAM	F	4
212	0-300	A	FSK	H,F	2
212	1200	A,S	PSK	H,F	2

Notes: 1. A=asynchronous
　　　　　　　S=synchronous
　　　　2. FSK=frequency shift keying
　　　　　　　PSK = phase shift keying
　　　　　　　QAM=quadrature amplitude modulation
　　　　3. H = half duplex; 2-way nonsimultaneous data transfer
　　　　　　　F = full duplex; 2-way simultaneous data transfer
　　　　4. 2 = 2-wire switched line
　　　　　　　4 = 4-wire leased line

TABLE 8.26 CCITT V-Series Modems

CCITT. Recom.	Speed (bps)	Synchronous/ Asynchronous[1]	Modulation[2]	Duplex[3]	Wire[4]
V.21	300	A	FSK	H,F	2
V.22	600	A	PSK	H,F	2,4
V.22	1200	A,S	PSK	H,F	2,4
V.22bis	2400	A	QAM	H,F	2
V.23	600	A,S	FSK	H,F	2
V.23	1200	A,S	FSK	H,F	2
V.26	2400	S	PSK	H,F	4
V.26	1200	S	PSK	H	2
V.26bis	2400	S	PSK	H	2
V.26ter	2400	S	PSK	H,F	2
V.29	9600	S	QAM	H,F	4
V.32	9600	A	TCM/QAM	H,F	2
V.33	14,400	S	TCM	H,F	4

Notes: 1. A=asynchronous
S=synchronous
2. FSK=frequency shift keying
PSK = phase shift keying
QAM=quadrature amplitude modulation
TCM=trellis coded modulation
3. H = half duplex; 2-way nonsimultaneous data transfer
F = full duplex; 2-way simultaneous data transfer
4. 2 = 2-wire switched line
4 = 4-wire leased line

TABLE 8.27 Modem Signal Frequencies (in kHz)

Modem	Transmit space (0)	Transmit mark (1)	Receive space (0)	Receive mark (1)	Answer tone
Bell 103 Originate	1.070	1.270	2.025	2.225	
Bell 103 Answer	2.025	2.225	1.070	1.270	2.225
CCITT V.21 Originate	1.180	0.980	1.850	1.650	
CCITT V.21 Answer	1.850	1.650	1.180	0.980	2.100
CCITT V.23 Mode 1	1.700	1.300	1.700	1.300	2.100
CCITT V.23 Mode 2	2.100	1.300	2.100	1.300	2.100
Bell 202	2.200	1.200	2.200	1.200	2.025

TABLE 8.28 Frequencies for Telephone Touch-Tone Dialing

Digit	Low-band frequency (kHz)	High-band frequency (kHz)
1	0.697	1.209
2	0.697	1.336
3	0.697	1.477
4	0.770	1.209
5	0.770	1.336
6	0.770	1.477
7	0.852	1.209
8	0.852	1.336
9	0.852	1.477
0	0.941	1.336
*	0.941	1.209
#	0.941	1.477

Note: A digit is represented by signaling its high-band frequency and low-band frequency simultaneously.

8.7.2   Smart Modems

The main function of a modem is to modulate and demodulate a signal, and allow computers to interact successfully with telephone lines. However, a modem that fulfills only these traditional tasks is almost universally known as a "dumb" modem. A "smart" modem provides additional services to the user, by automating such functions as dialing, and switching to data mode, that require manual intervention in the case of a dumb modem. In the area of "smart" modems, a *de facto* standard has emerged: the Hayes standard. The AT command in particular (which tells to modem to request a dial tone) seems destined for complete acceptance. Tables 8.29 and 8.30 summarize the command set and result codes for the Hayes Smartmodem 1200™.

TABLE 8.29 Hayes Smartmodem 1200™ Commands

Command	Description
AT	Attention prefix: precedes all command lines except + + + and A/
A/	Repeat last command line (do not follow with carriage return)
+ + +	Escape code: go from on-line state to command state (one second pause before and after escape code entry; do not follow with carriage return)
D	Dial
P	Set dialing method to pulse dialing (do this before issuing dial command)
T	Set dialing method to touch-tone dialing (do this before issuing dial command)
,	Pause
!	Flash
/	Wait for 1/8 second
@	Wait for silence
W	Wait for second dial tone
;	Return to command state after dialing
R	Reverse mode (to call originate-only-modem)

TABLE 8.30 Hayes Smartmodem 1200™ Result Codes

Code	Word code	Description
0	OK	Command executed.
1	CONNECT	Connected at 300 or 1200 bps.
2	RING	Ringing signal detected.
3	NO CARRIER	Carrier signal not detected or lost.
4	ERROR	Possibilities: •Illegal command •Error in command line •Command line exceeds buffer (40 characters, including punctuation) •Cannot operate at 300 bps in CCITT V.22 mode •Invalid character format at 1200 bps •Invalid checksum
5	CONNECT 1200	Connected at 1200 bps.
6	NO DIALTONE	Dial tone not detected and subsequent commands not processed.
7	BUSY	Busy signal detected and subsequent commands not processed.
8	NO ANSWER	Silence not detected and subsequent commands not processed. Results from @ command only.

8.7.3 Transmission Speed

A point of confusion concerns the term "baud." It seems that almost everyone uses the term as if it were synonymous with "bits per second." In fact, baud refers to the number of *signal changes per second*. Depending on the modulation method used, baud may equal bit rate, or it may not.

In the Bell 103 standard, transmission occurs via frequency shift keying. A 1 and a 0 are represented by different tone frequencies. Thus one signal change along the phone line represents one bit, and one baud is one bit per second. Bell 103 has a speed of 300 baud, or 300 bits per second. The Bell 212A modem standard, however, uses a modulation method known as phase shift keying. In this method, one signal change represents one dibit (among the four possibilities of 00, 01, 10, 11). The standard achieves 600 baud, but 1200 bps. The CCITT V.22*bis* modem uses quadrature amplitude modulation, a scheme wherein one signal change transmits two dibits of information. CCITT V.22*bis* is 600 baud, but 2400 bps. More information on modulation methods can be found in Brewster (1989).

Using ever more ingenious techniques, modem manufacturers have achieved ever higher transmission speeds (up to 19,200 bps) over the very bandlimited phone system. What is the ultimate achievable transmission speed? The fundamental work of Nyquist related the baud rate B to the bandwidth W as follows:

$B \leq 2W$.

The maximum possible baud rate is twice the bandwidth of the channel. A conventional telephone channel has a bandwidth of 3 kHz, stretching from 300 to 3300 Hz. This means that the maximum possible baud rate over a telephone channel is 6 kbaud. However, as we have noted above, the baud rate is not necessarily the same as the actual rate of information transfer in bits per second. Modem designers can achieve high bps rates by packing more information into each signal change. The maximum possible rate C (channel capacity) in bps can be computed using Shannon's law:

$C = W \log_2 (1 + S/N)$

where W is bandwidth, S is signal power, and N is noise power. Assuming a very high signal-to-noise ratio of 1024 ($=2^{10}$), this gives a maximum bit rate of roughly 30 kbps. If the signal-to-noise ratio is 128 (2^7), then the maximum bit rate is 21 kbps. Thus improvement is still possible over the current maximum of 19.2 kbps, provided the line is not too noisy.

Table 8.31 gives some data transfer times for various quantities of data at various speeds. Although the calculation is trivial, the table may still be useful to the reader because it quickly gives him a concrete feeling for how long a typical transfer might take. One important *caveat* in evaluating the table is that the data are assumed to flow in an uninterrupted stream. No allowance is made for such factors as splitting the data into packets, protocol overhead, etc. For example, a Kermit file transfer of the quantities in the table will take considerably longer than indicated. The table does assume that each character transmitted requires the sending of 10 bits: 8 data bits, one start bit, and one stop bit.

TABLE 8.31 Illustration of Data Transfer Rates

Quantity of data	Data Transfer Time, at:			
	300 bps	1200 bps	9600 bps	19,200 bps
Typical page in this book (c. 1500 char.)	50 s	12.5 s	1.6 s	0.8 s
Typical chapter in this book (c. 20,000 char.)	11 min, 7 s	2 min, 47 s	21 s	10 s
This whole book (c. 350,000 char.)	3 h, 14 min, 27 s	48 min, 37 s	6 min, 5 s	3 min, 2 s

Notes: Assume 10 bits transmitted per character. Data transfer rates are in bits per second (bps). Data are assumed to flow in an uninterrupted stream. No allowance is made for overhead in file transfer protocols.

8.7.4 Communication Characteristics of Some Systems

Table 8.32, adapted from daCruz (1987), gives some communication characteristics for several important computer/operating system combinations. The table is not exhaustive. Note that *full duplex* means that data can travel in both directions simultaneously, whereas *half duplex* means that data can travel in both directions, but not simultaneously. *Even parity* means that each character must have an even number of bits set to logic 1 (including the parity bit). Recall that an ASCII byte uses only seven bits for character encoding, and that the eighth bit can be used for parity if desired (see Chap. 13). *Odd parity* means that each character must have an odd number of bits set to logic 1 (including the parity bit). *Mark parity* means that the parity bit is always set to logic 1. *Space parity* means that the parity bit is always set to logic 0. *No parity* means that the eighth bit is left alone (or perhaps used for additional encoding).

Flow control refers to the method used to ensure that the receiver always has a place to put data sent by the transmitter. That is, flow control ensures that transmission rates match processing capabilities and buffer capacities at both ends of the link . In XON flow control, also known as half-duplex handshaking, the transmitter over a half-duplex channel concludes each message with an XON code (e.g., an ASCII CTRL-Q). The receiver is not supposed to transmit back unless it has seen the XON code. In

XON/XOFF flow control for full-duplex channels, the receiver stops the transmitter from sending data if necessary by sending an XOFF code (e.g., an ASCII CTRL-S). The transmitter will not resume sending data until the receiver sends out an XON code (e.g., an ASCII CTRL-Q). In ENQ/ACK flow control, the transmitter requests permission to transmit by issuing an ENQ code (e.g., an ASCII CTRL-E). The receiver responds with an ACK code (e.g., an ASCII CTRL-F) when it has allocated (or thinks it has allocated) enough buffer space to receive the data. The ENQ/ACK method can operate over full- or half-duplex channels.

TABLE 8.32 Communication Characteristics of Various Systems

System	Parity	Duplex	Flow control
DEC VAX, VMS	None	Full	XON/XOFF
DEC PDP-11	None	Full	XON/XOFF
DEC-20, TOPS-20	None	Full	XON/XOFF
IBM mainframe (line mode)	Mark	Half	XON Handshake
IBM mainframe (full screen)	Even	Full	XON/XOFF
PRIME, PRIMOS	Mark	Full	XON/XOFF
Sperry 1100, OS 1100	Odd	Full	XON/XOFF
Honeywell DPS8, GCOS	None	Half	XON
HP-1000 RTE-6/VM	None	Full	ENQ/ACK
HP-3000 MPE	None	Half	XON
IBM-PC/AT	None	Full	Depends on comm. program
Apple Macintosh	None	Full	Depends on comm. program

8.8 Bibliography

Bingham, J. A. C. (1988), *The Theory and Practice of Modem Design*, John Wiley, New York, New York.

Black, U. (1988), *Physical Level Interfaces and Protocols*, Institute of Electrical and Electronics Engineers Computer Society Press, Los Angeles, California.

Brewster, R. L. (1989), *Data Communications and Networks 2*, Peter Peregrinus (on behalf of the Institution of Electrical Engineers), London, United Kingdom.

Curtis, C. and D. L. Majhor (1985), *Modem Connections Bible*, Sams, Indianapolis, Indiana.

da Cruz, F. (1987), *Kermit, a File Transfer Protocol*, Digital Press, Bedford, Massachusetts.

Harb, M. (1989), *Modern Telephony*, Prentice-Hall, Englewood Cliffs, New Jersey.

Held, G. (1991), *The Complete Modem Reference*, John Wiley, New York, New York.

Lu, C. (1988), *The Apple Macintosh Book*, Third Edition, Microsoft Press, Redmond, Washington.

McNamara, J. E. (1988), *Technical Aspects of Data Communication*, Third Edition, Digital Press, Bedford, Massachusetts.

Schweber, W. L. (1988), *Data Communications*, McGraw-Hill, San Francisco, California.

Seyer, M. D. (1984), *RS-232 Made Easy*, Prentice-Hall, Englewood Cliffs, New Jersey.

Seyer, M. D. (1988), *The Complete Guide to RS-232 and Parallel Connections*, Prentice-Hall, Englewood Cliffs, New Jersey.

Sherman, K. (1990), *Data Communications, A User's Guide*, Third Edition, Prentice-Hall, Englewood Cliffs, New Jersey.

9

Worldwide Networks

Computer scientists, engineers, scientists, students (and, increasingly, ordinary users), can now communicate and transfer files throughout the world, using the infrastructure of worldwide computer networks that has been built up over the last 20 years and is still expanding rapidly. In this chapter, we provide some information on some of these worldwide networks.

9.1 Descriptions of Important Networks

9.1.1 The Internet

An internet, usually spelled with a lowercase i, is any set of networks linked together with common protocols. *The* Internet (spelled with an uppercase I), refers to a specific set of worldwide networks now using the TCP/IP protocols (Chap. 15). There are many names in common use to describe the Internet: it has been known variously as the ARPANET, the ARPA Internet, the DARPA Internet, and the TCP/IP Internet. While ARPANET is a name still commonly applied to the Internet, it should be noted that the present Internet is a different and far more extensive entity than the ARPANET that originated in 1969 under the auspices of the U.S. Defense Advanced Research Projects Agency (DARPA, formerly ARPA). The ARPANET was essentially the first network in what is today the Internet. The original ARPANET was split into two parts in 1983: one part was a research network and retained the name ARPANET; the other was an unclassified military network known as the MILNET. In 1989 the original ARPANET began being phased out (with most members switching to the NSFNET, also part of the Internet—see below). Still the name "ARPANET" remains in the vernacular as a virtual synonym for the Internet.

Today, the Internet links over 2000 networks and upwards of 100,000 computers worldwide. Of the networks linked by the Internet, several are large wide-area networks:

CSNET	Computer Science Research Network (CREN CSNET). Links academic and research sites in North American, Australia, Europe, and Asia (Japan).
NSFNET	National Science Foundation Network, consisting of a "backbone," several independently administered mid-level networks, and campus networks. The NSFNET has existed since 1986. The following mid-level networks are among those connected to the NSFNET backbone:

BARRNet	Bay Area Regional Research Network, centered in California.
Merit	Michigan Educational Research Network, centered in Michigan.
MIDnet	Midwestern States Network, centered in Nebraska.
NorthWestNet	Northwestern States Network, centered in Washington State.
Westnet	Western States Network, centered in Utah.
USAN	University Satellite Network, centered in Colorado.
Sesquinet	Texas Sesquicentennial Network, centered in Texas.
SURANet	Southeastern Universities Research Association Network, centered in Maryland.

DDN	Defense Data Network, known also as MILNET (U.S., Europe, Japan)
Los Nettos	A high speed regional network linking southern-California institutions, including Caltech, UCLA, and USC.
NSN	NASA Science Network, managed from NASA Ames Research Center, California. Extends to United States, Europe, Japan, Australia, New Zealand.

Transmission speeds vary greatly within the Internet. Most of the MILNET long-distance lines have speeds of 56 kbps, while NSFNET has T1 1.5-Mbps links.

9.1.2   BITNET

BITNET stands for Because It's Time Network. BITNET is a "cooperative" network. This means that it is not administered by an outside agency, but by its users or some subset thereof. Funding for cooperative networks comes mostly from the membership. BITNET began in 1981 as a small IBM mainframe network centered at the City University of New York, and is today an international network with a membership of at least 500 research centers and academic institutions. BITNET uses IBM's Network Job Entry/Network Job Interface (NJE/NJI) protocols. Usually, BITNET nodes are connected by 9600-bps leased lines, so speeds are generally slow compared to the Internet. Efforts are under way to add TCP/IP protocols.

"BITNET" once referred only to the U.S.-centered cooperative network, but now includes the Canadian NetNorth and the European Academic Research Network (EARN), the latter of which is an important network connecting hosts throughout Europe, and some in the Middle East and North Africa.

In 1988, the controlling entities of BITNET and CSNET decided to merge the two networks. In 1989, BITNET, Inc. became CREN (Corporation for Regional and Educational Networking).

9.1.3   DECnet Internet

This is an internet of networks using Digital Equipment Corporation's DECnet protocols (Ethernet 2.0, CCITT X.25). Important networks in the DECnet internet include:

HEPnet   High Energy Physics Network, consisting of nodes at universities and national laboratories throughout the U. S.

SPAN   Space Physics Analysis Network, linking nodes in North America, Europe, and Japan, supported in the U. S. by NASA and in Europe by the European Space Agency (ESA).

THEnet   Texas Higher Education Network (also in the Internet).

9.1.4   UUCP

The UUCP network is named after the acronym for its transport protocol, the UNIX-to-UNIX Copy Program. The UUCP net is very decentralized, and operates largely via dial-up over RS-232 links in North America and Europe. In Europe it is occasionally used over X.25. Speeds range from 1200 to 11,000 bps.

9.1.5   USENET

USENET is a cooperative network that has been in existence since 1979. USENET supports a news and conferencing service, and not much else. Anyone can join USENET—and by "anyone" we mean individuals as well as organizations. Speeds range from 2400 bps to 11,000 bps. USENET has nodes all over the world, with most lying in the United States.

9.1.6   JANET

The Joint Academic Network (JANET) is the national research network of the U.K., linking academic and research institutions within the country and providing connections to the outside world. It is funded by the Computer Board for Universities and Research Councils. Local networks connected to JANET tend to follow either CCITT X.25 or Ethernet. Line speeds vary from 9600 bps to 512 kbps.

9.1.7   JUNET

The Japanese UNIX Network (JUNET) is a cooperative network linking research institutions in Japan. It began using UUCP as the common protocol, but has been gradually changing over to TCP/IP.

9.1.8   EUnet

The European UNIX Network (EUnet) is a cooperative network linking research institutions throughout Europe (mostly the EEC and Scandinavia). The network uses UUCP as the common protocol.

9.2   Important Computers

Quarterman (1990) makes the point that inter-internet traffic, that is, traffic between large internets like the Internet or the BITNET, is carried by surprisingly few computers. He calls these machines the "backbone of the world." He gives a partial list of some of these important computers, from which we draw the even smaller list below:

relay.cs.net The central CSNET machine, located at Bolt, Beranek, and Newman, Cambridge, Massachusetts.

psuvax1 A major gateway between BITNET and UUCP, located at Pennsylvania State University.

berkeley.edu Important gateway between the Internet and USENET news groups. Known also as ucbvax.

UUNET Center of the UUCP network. A Sequent Symmetry multiprocessor [at the time Quarterman (1990) was printed] located in Arlington Virginia. Connects UUCP and the Internet, and also connects to the Japanese JUNET, the European EUnet, and other networks outside the U.S. Known as uunet on the UUCP network, and as uunet.uu.net on the Internet.

cwi.nl Also known as mcvax, this is the center of the EUnet. Connects to EARN, BITNET, the Internet, and JUNET, among others. Located in Amsterdam, the Netherlands.

munnari.oz.au Connects Australia to UUCP, JUNET, and EUnet. Located in Melbourne, Australia.

u-tokyo Also known as ccut.cc.u-tokyo.junet. This is an important JUNET machine located at the University of Tokyo, Japan. It is the Japanese CSNET link, and connects also to UUNET

cunyvm.cuny.edu Also known as CUNYVM. This is the primary BITNET gateway to the Internet. Located at the City University of New York.

FRMOP22 Located at CERN (the European Nuclear Research Center) in Geneva, Switzerland. This is a primary EARN node, with a 56-kbps link to the U.S. This is the primary connection between EARN and BITNET (U.S.), and also the primary connection between EARN and the Internet.

9.3 Electronic Mail Addresses

Unfortunately, sending electronic mail across the worldwide networks is not always straightforward. There is no standard address syntax. Some addresses begin with the user's name (or alias) and then specify the computer the user is on, the institution to which the computer belongs, etc. This is roughly how it is done on the Internet. Some addresses, however, are "backwards," with the user coming last (e.g., on the UUCP network). Some addresses use a "@" as a delimiter between fields; others use a "::" and still others (again, the UUCP) use a "!"   Quarterman (1990) discusses the problem of address syntax in depth.   It would be difficult for us to give here an exhaustive list of address syntaxes for connecting between networks.   Quarterman (1990) and LaQuey (1990) have made brave attempts to do so, but even their considerable efforts cannot be guaranteed accurate (or unchanging).   In Table 9.1 we show some common address types for general reference.

TABLE 9.1   Some Common E-Mail Address Formats

Network	Format	Example (NOT real addresses)
BITNET	user@host(.bitnet)	msv@tacos.machilvich.bitnet
CSNET	user@host	msv@tacos
EARN	user@host(.earn)	msv@tacos.vx1.earn
Internet	user@machine(.subnet).campus.domain	
		msv@tacos.myuniv.edu
JANET	user@domain.campus(.subnet).machine	
		msv@uk.ns.myuniv.tacos
NSN	user::host	msv::tacos.nasa.gov
SPAN	host::site::user	tacos::cit::msv
UUCP	host1!host2!...host!user	phobos!deimos!tacos!msv
USENET	host1!host2!...host!user	phobos!deimos!tacos!msv

Notes: Items in parentheses are optional. They may be required to ensure satisfactory connectivity between networks.

9.4   Obtaining Internet Information

Many networks have special information services to which users can connect, to obtain data about hosts, procedures, etc. One such service, for the Internet, can be accessed by connecting to NIC.DDN.MIL. Since TCP/IP-based machines on the Internet generally run the Telnet remote-login utility, you should be able to connect to NIC.DDN.MIL by simply issuing the command

```
telnet nic.ddn.mil
```

You will then be remotely logged on to the information service. The service will respond with several announcements, and a @ prompt. For general information you may issue the command

```
nic
```

For news, you may issue the command

```
tacnews
```

A useful command is whois. This allows you to obtain complete data on machines connected to the Internet. For example,

whois tacos.myuniv.edu

will give you the full and formal name of the tacos computer, its numerical network address, what type of computer it is and what operating system it is running, the name and telephone number of the system coordinator, and when the information was last updated.

9.5 Bibliography

The book by Quarterman (1990) is absolutely indispensible. LaQuey (1990), which presents an extensive list of hosts, is also very useful. An earlier article by Quarterman and Hoskins (1986) is informative, but already somewhat outdated because of the rapid pace of change in this field. Quarterman and Hoskins (1986) has been reprinted in Denning (1990), which focuses on computer and network security but also has a wealth of fundamental information about worldwide networks.

Denning, P. J. (ed.) (1990) , *Computers Under Attack: Intruders, Worms and Viruses*, ACM Press and Addison-Wesley, New York, New York.

LaQuey, T. L. (1990), *The User's Directory of Computer Networks*, Digital Press, Bedford, Massachusetts.

Quarterman, J. S. (1990), *The Matrix: Computer and Conferencing Systems Worldwide*, Digital Press, Bedford, Massachusetts.

Quarterman, J. S., and J. C. Hoskins (1986), "Notable Computer Networks," *Communications of the ACM* 29, 932–971. [Reprinted in Denning (1990), 20–96.]

10

Kermit

It is often necessary to transfer files between computers—for example, between microcomputers and mainframes, or microcomputers and minicomputers—and this can be a confusing process. Several different file transfer protocols have been developed over the years. As a rule of thumb, when all else fails, try Kermit! Kermit is a file transfer protocol developed at Columbia University in the early 1980's and described in detail by one of its developers, Frank da Cruz, in an excellent book dedicated to the topic (1987). It has enjoyed a huge popularity, for several reasons. One is simply that it performs its task effectively. Another is that the developers generously decided to leave it in the public domain, and encourage other authors to improve it and make it available on a very wide variety of machines. Kermit is not fancy. If your computer is already in a network, you may never need it; but the day may well come when you need to transfer a file to a computer not on any notable network, and then you may have to turn to Kermit!

10.1 A Sample Kermit Session

Below, we show a sample session using Kermit. In this example, an IBM-PC is linked directly to a DEC VAX computer via a 9600-baud capacity line. In the session, we transfer the binary file file.dat from the PC to the VAX. > indicates the IBM-PC MS-DOS prompt, and $ indicates the VAX-VMS prompt. The prompt when Kermit is

running on the PC is, in this example, `kermit-86>`, while the
prompt when Kermit is running on the VAX is `kermit-32>`.

1. `> kermit`
   (Run the Kermit program on the PC.)
2. `kermit-86>` **`set baud 9600`**
   (Set the transmission speed to 9600 baud.)
3. `kermit-86>` **`connect`**
   (Connect to the VAX.)
4. `username:` **`XXX`**
   `password:` **`YYY`**
   (Log onto the VAX, after which it may type various notices, etc.)
5. `$   run   sys$system:kermit`
   (Run the Kermit program on the VAX.)
6. `kermit-32>` **`set file type binary`**
   (Let Kermit know that the file is in binary format.)
7. `kermit-32>` **`server`**
   [Tell the VAX Kermit to become a server (see below) of the IBM-PC Kermit.]
8. `kermit-32>` **`CTRL-]`**
   (Type an escape character sequence to get back to the PC. The particular characters may vary.) Kermit will then say something like:
   `(back at micro)`
9. `kermit-86>` **`send b:file.dat`**
   (Send the file `file.dat` *on drive* b: *to the VAX.)*
10. `kermit-86>` **`finish`**
11. `kermit-86>` **`connect`**
    (Reconnect to VAX so you can log out if desired, or conduct other business.)
11. `$` **`logout`**
12. **`CTRL-]`**
    (Escape back to PC.)
    `(back at micro)`
13. `kermit-86>` **`exit`**
14. `>`

Notice that there are two Kermit programs running, one on the
VAX (the remote Kermit) and one on the PC (the local Kermit).
Notice also that in this example, the VAX Kermit is operating as a
server to the PC Kermit. The `server` command typed in line 7 tells
the VAX Kermit to stop taking commands from the keyboard and to
take all further instructions in the form of Kermit packets from the

PC Kermit program. Let us stylize the above session, so that it is not so specific to the IBM PC and VAX hardware and software systems. In essence, what is happening above is as follows:

    run Kermit on microcomputer
    set needed parameters
    connect to remote computer
    log in to remote computer
    run Kermit on remote computer
    set needed parameters
    tell remote computer to act as a server
    escape back to microcomputer
    send file(s)
    finish
    connect back to remote computer
    do business on remote computer if desired
    log off remote computer
    escape back to microcomputer
    exit from Kermit

The above sequence is appropriate for a situation when a microcomputer is communicating with a remote server. Below, we show a sequence appropriate for a microcomputer communicating with a remote host computer that is not acting as a server. In this case, the files are moving from the host computer to the microcomputer.

    run Kermit on microcomputer
    set needed parameters
    connect to remote computer
    log in to remote computer
    run Kermit on remote computer
    set needed parameters
    send file(s)
    escape back to microcomputer
    receive files on microcomputer
    connect back to remote computer
    exit from Kermit on remote computer
    log off remote computer
    escape back to microcomputer
    exit from Kermit on microcomputer

Note that when the host is not acting as a server, a send command alone is not enough. We must issue a receive command to accept the files which we sent using the send command.

When the host is an IBM mainframe, several parameters must be set correctly for communication to take place. Commonly, these are:

```
set local-echo on
set flow none
set duplex half
set handshake xon
set timer on
set parity mark
```

(see below for more on the set command).

Kermit may also be used to transfer files between PC's, provided there is an appropriate physical link between them. This can be done by using compatible modems on each end and establishing a telephone connection, provided the receiving modem can answer calls. Once the connection is established, the user wishing to receive files issues a receive command, after which the user wishing to send files issues the send command. Clearly, you will not be able to use the sequences above to transfer files in every situation you may encounter. However, it is very likely that your session will be quite similar to the ones above.

10.2 Remarks on Kermit Commands

Below, we explain some of Kermit's important commands more fully. Since there are many different Kermit programs, it is perhaps inevitable that there be slight syntactic variations in commands. What follows is a set of "typical" versions of common commands. For a complete discussion, see da Cruz (1987).

10.3 The connect Command

This command should be issued in local mode only. It establishes a connection to the remote system. Before issuing a connect, you may need several set commands, for example:

```
set baud 9600
set duplex half
connect
```

10.4 The set Command

This very important command sets various parameters essential to Kermit operation. It is typically augmented by at least another keyword, indicating the parameter to be set (for example, set baud, set file, etc.)

10.4.1 set baud

Sometimes denoted set speed.
  Example:
    set baud 1200

10.4.2 set delay

You may need this if you are running the remote Kermit and you are sending data back to the local Kermit. If the remote Kermit is not a server, for example, you may issue a send command from the remote Kermit, and then need time to escape back to the local Kermit and issue a receive command before the file starts to arrive. The default delay is 5 seconds, but you may need 20 seconds, in which case you would issue:
    set delay 20

10.4.3 set duplex

The choices are set duplex full and set duplex half. Full duplex, which is the case in most systems, generally implies remote echo and XON/XOFF flow control. Half duplex, which is relevant when connecting to IBM mainframes, generally implies local echo and handshake (see Chap. 8, Sec. 8.7.4).

10.4.4 set escape

This sets the escape characters used to get back to the local Kermit from the remote Kermit. It is wise to choose something unusual, for example
    set escape CTRL-]
to avoid possibly disastrous confusion with the escape sequences of the particular computer system running the Kermit.

10.4.5 set file

There are many parameters for this command. Some important ones are

`set file type`
Examples:
```
set file type binary
set file type text (or set file type ascii)
```

`set file byte`
Examples:
```
set file byte 7
```
(Makes a 7-bit byte. You might use this if you are sending the output of some word processor that uses the eighth bit of a byte to indicate something the target system might not understand—e.g., italics, underscoring, etc.)

10.4.6 set flow

This command tells Kermit the system-level flow control method (See Chap. 8, Sec. 8.7.4).
Examples:
```
set flow none
set flow enq/ack
set flow xon/xoff
```
XON/XOFF is the most common type of flow control on full-duplex systems. If you are involved with a half-duplex system, use `set flow none`, and use `set handshake` instead.

10.4.7 set handshake

This is for half-duplex systems (like IBM mainframes). If you use this you should also issue `set flow none`. When a handshake is set, Kermit will wait for the half-duplex host to send the handshake character before sending out a packet.
Examples:
```
set handshake ESC
```
   (handshake is the escape character)
```
set handshake CR
```
   (handshake is the carriage return)
```
set handshake NONE
```
   (no handshake)

10.4.8 set IBM

This command is not available on all Kermit implementations. If it is, however, it provides a handy way to set all the parameters required for communication with an IBM mainframe in line mode. Generally, there are only two options:

```
set IBM on
```
and
```
set IBM off.
```
In some systems the command might be do IBM instead of set IBM. The parameters which might typically be set by this command are handshake xon, flow none, duplex half, parity mark, and timer on.

10.4.9 set parity

Examples (the default is none):
```
set parity even  (7 data bits with even overall parity)
set parity odd   (7 data bits with odd overall parity)
set parity mark  (7 data bits with parity bit set to 1)
set parity space (7 data bits with parity bit set to 0)
set parity none  (8 data bits, no parity bit)
```

10.5 The send Command

To send a single file:
```
send filename
```
or
```
send filename filename1
```
The second option will send the file filename with the new name filename1. Wild cards are also supported. Examples are:
```
send *.dat
send *.dat file5.dat
```
The first example will send all files whose names end with .dat. The second example will do the same, but starting with file5.dat.

If you are downloading files from a remote system that is not a server to a local system, you must issue the send from the remote system and then escape to the local system and issue a receive. If you are uploading files from a local system, usually a microcomputer, to a remote system, you must issue a receive command from the remote system before issuing a send from the local system. If the remote system can act as a server, you should issue a command for it to do so before issuing a send from the local system.

10.6 The receive Command

receive tells Kermit to await the arrival of a file. To upload files from a local system (usually a microcomputer) to a remote system (usually a minicomputer or a mainframe), issue a receive from the remote system before escaping back to the local system and issuing a send. To download files from a remote system to a local one, issue a send command from the remote system before issuing a receive from the local system.

The receive command cannot generally be used to download files from a Kermit server. To accomplish this, use the get command. Some Kermit programs do use

    receive filename

to download files from a remote server.

10.7 The get Command

This command can be issued only from a local Kermit to download files from a remote computer acting as a server. When using a get command, one does not need to issue a send from the server. One can simply say

    get filename

to get the file filename. In general, filename may contain wild cards to specify a group of files. The only constraint is that the file specification in filename be recognizable to the remote system.

10.8 Kermit Operation and Packet Format

Those wanting full details on the Kermit protocol should consult da Cruz (1987). Kermit operates basically by splitting files into packets. A packet may be a data packet, in which case it contains a portion of the file's data, as well as other information to enable transmission. It may also be a control packet, used to allow cooperating Kermit programs to work with each other. A Kermit packet contains the following fields:

MARK	Start of header, usually SOH or CTRL-A.
LEN	Length of packet excluding MARK and CHECK, in excess-32 notation, expressed as a character. Conversion function from integer to character is $char(x) = x + 32$.
SEQ	Modulo-64 packet sequence number, expressed as a character (same conversion function as LEN).
TYPE	The type of packet, some of which are:

	D	Data Packet (data field contains encoded file data)
	E	Error Packet (data field contains encoded error message)
	Y(ACK)	Acknowledgement packet (data field varies according to what type of packet is being acknowledged)

N(NAK)	Negative Acknowledgement (data field always empty)
S	Send-Initiate Packet (data field contains initialization string). Tells receiver to expect files.
F	File-Header Packet (data field contains encoded filename). Indicates that file data are about to arrive for named file.
Z	End-of-File (data field may contain D for discard)
B	Break Transmission

DATA   The contents of the packet, according to the packet type. Can be empty or contain up to 91 characters of data. ASCII control characters are preceded typically by #, and are modified to become printable ASCII characters using the function $ctl(x) = x \text{ XOR } 64$

CHECK   Block check on characters in the packet excluding MARK and CHECK itself. If SUM is the arithmetic sum of the ASCII characters,
CHECK=char((SUM + ((SUM AND 192)/64)) AND 63)

Thus it is clear that a packet—even a data packet—contains not only file data, but also a fair amount of overhead. Madron (1987) computes the percent overhead for Kermit and also for XMODEM and X.PC, two other asynchronous file transfer protocols. For a full data packet, the overhead percentages are 24.0%, 22.4%, and 22.4% for Kermit, XMODEM, and X.PC, respectively. For a "minimum" packet (one that contains the minimum amount of data transmittable by the protocol), the overhead percentages are, respectively, 86.7%, 99.4%, and 88.6%.

There are a variety of Kermit transactions that can take place between sender and receiver, with a variety of control packets sent back and forth. A typical transaction might occur as follows: The sender issues an S (Send-Initiate) packet, which is acknowledged by the receiver via a Y(ACK) packet. The sender then issues an F (File-Header) packet, also acknowledged by an appropriate Y(ACK). The sender then transmits the file as a series of D (Data) packets, each acknowledged by appropriate Y's. When transfer is complete, the sender issues a Z (End-of-File) packet, acknowledged by the appropriate Y(ACK). A variety of mechanisms exist in the Kermit protocol to deal with packets which are not transmitted, or transmitted in corrupted form. For example, the receiver may issue a negative acknowledgement N(NAK). The NAK will contain the same packet number as the corrupt packet, and the packet will be retransmitted by the sender.

10.9 Bibliography

da Cruz, F. (1987), *Kermit, a File Transfer Protocol*, Digital Press, Bedford, Massachusetts.

Gianone, C. (1990), *Using MS-DOS Kermit*, Digital Press, Bedford, Massachusetts.

Madrone, T. W. (1987), *Micro-Mainframe Connection*, Hayden Books, Indianapolis, Indiana.

FTP

For those who work on computers connected to the Internet, there is a much faster way to transfer files than using Kermit. Most TCP/IP nodes (see Chap. 15) will have an application called FTP (file transfer protocol). FTP is very easy to use, and one can operate it effectively with a small subset of commands.

11.1 A Sample FTP Session

Below, we show a sample session using FTP. In this example, the user msv is on a computer connected to the Internet, and is transferring files between his computer and another node, called tacos.myuniv.edu, with which he has an account. Commands typed by the user are in bold, and our annotations are in italics.

First, msv issues the command ftp to connect to the remote node tacos.myuniv.edu:

ftp   tacos.myuniv.edu

Now ftp first responds that it is attempting to connect to tacos.myuniv.edu, and then informs msv that the connection has been made:

```
FTP-I-ATTEMPTING, Attempting to connect to host
TACOS.MYUNIV.EDU
220 TACOS.MYUNIV.EDU MultiNet FTP Server Process
2.1(8) at Tue 19-Mar-91 11:10P
```

The prompt is now ftp (it may vary depending on the version of FTP being used). User msv issues the command to log in to the remote node tacos.myuniv.edu. Some versions of FTP may not require a user to issue a login command—they may simply ask for the user name immediately.

    FTP> **login**

FTP now prompts msv for his user name:

    _Username: **msv**

FTP now prompts msv for the user account number. The operating system on the remote node does not use account numbers, so msv simply enters a carriage-return. Some FTP versions may not ask for the user account.

    _USER_ACCT:

FTP now prompts msv for the password:

    331 User name (MSV) ok. Password, please.
    Password: **mypassword**

FTP now informs msv that he has logged in successfully:

    230 User MSV logged into USER:[MSV] at Tue 19-Mar-91
    23:10, job c6a.

msv issues a command to copy a file named test.txt from the original node to the remote node:

    FTP> **put test.txt**

FTP now informs msv of the progress of his file transfer:

    200 Port 191.0 at Host 130.50.7.8 accepted.
    150 ASCII Store of USER:[MSV]TEST.TXT;1 started.
    226 Transfer completed. 51975 (8) bytes
    transferred.
    %FTP-I-DATA_RATE, Transferred 51975 bytes in
    00:00:11.03 = 4712 bytes/Second

msv issues a command to copy a file named an0319.91 from the remote node back to the original node:

    FTP> **get an0319.91**

Once again, FTP informs msv of the progress of the file transfer:

    200 Port 191.1 at Host 130.50.7.8 accepted.
    150 ASCII retrieve of USER:[MSV]AN0319.91;1 started.
    226 Transfer completed. 3465 (8) bytes transferred.
    %FTP-I-DATA_RATE, Transferred 3465 bytes in
    00:00:01.47 = 2357 bytes/Second

Until now, msv has been transferring ASCII files, the default type. At this time, msv wishes to transfer an executable file, so he sets the parameter type to the appropriate value, image:

    FTP> **set type image**
    200 Type I ok.

msv issues a get command to copy the executable file prog.exe from the remote node back to the original node:

```
FTP> get prog.exe
```
FTP now informs msv of the progress of his file transfer:
```
200 Port 191.2 at Host 130.50.7.8 accepted.
150 IMAGE retrieve of USER:[MSV]PROG.EXE;2 started.
226 Transfer completed.  8192 (8) bytes transferred.
%FTP-I-DATA_RATE, Transferred 8192 bytes in
00:00:01.94 = 4222 bytes/Second
```
msv has finished his business and terminates the FTP session:
```
FTP> quit
221 QUIT command received. Goodbye.
%FTP-I-CLOSING, Connection Closing
```

11.2   A Subset of Essential FTP commands

As we noted above, it is possible to use FTP very effectively knowing only a subset of important commands. The essential ones are:

HELP	To get a listing of available commands, and the option to ask for more information on them.
LOGIN	Sign on to remote computer. FTP will prompt for user name, password, etc.
PUT FILENAME	Transfer a copy of the file with the name FILENAME from the originating computer to the remote computer.
GET FILENAME	Transfer a copy of the file with the name FILENAME from the remote computer to the originating computer.
SET	Used to set various parameters, An essential variant of this command is SET TYPE, to specify the character encoding used in the file. ASCII is the default. SET TYPE EBCDIC changes the assumed encoding to EBCDIC; SET TYPE ASCII changes it back to ASCII. For executable files, use SET TYPE IMAGE. SET LOCAL_DEFAULT DIRNAME is used to set the directory DIRNAME as the default directory on the originating computer.
DIR	List out directory contents on the remote computer.
CD DIRNAME	Change to a different directory (specified by DIRNAME) in the hierarchical file system of the remote computer. DIRNAME should be specified in a manner recognizable to the operating system of the remote machine.

Section

3

Standards

Many computer users do not like standards. They feel that standards serve to stifle the normally rapid creative pace of information technology. Standards to these individuals represent, in some measure, a looming "establishment" to be distrusted. While these people do have a point, it is undeniable that standards also fulfill some necessary functions. Incompatibility of systems, hardware, and languages can be a source of great frustration. Well-chosen standards are necessary to prevent a state of anarchy, particularly in the field of data communications.

As important as standards are, most computer professionals and computer users have very little idea of what standards exist, of who formulates them, and of where the standards can be obtained. It is our aim to remedy this situation by providing a broad overview of standards organizations and procedures in Chap. 12. Chapters 13 through 16 discuss certain categories of information technology standards in detail.

In Chaps. 12 to 16 the reader will find many useful tables. Chapter 13, on character codes, contains descriptions and tabulations of all the standard encoding methods such as ASCII and the ISO alphabets, as well as tabulations of deviations from those standards by major manufacturers. Chapter 13 also contains information and tables on digital typography, and tables of letter frequencies in various languages. Chapter 14 discusses the important IEEE standard for the representation of floating-point numbers. Chapter 15 discusses network standards, outlining the Open Systems Interconnection (OSI) model. The relationship between the IEEE standards for local area networks and OSI is also explored, as is the relationship of OSI to TCP/IP. Chapter 16 surveys programming language standards.

Chapter 17 provides a list of other information technology standards not covered in Chaps. 13 to 16 but still important for the programmer and computer user to keep in mind.

12

Standards Organizations and Procedures

In order to make sense of the myriad standards that now exist in information technology, one must have some understanding of the various standards organizations and their procedures. The situation is quite confusing, and the computer scientist can easily find himself lost in a veritable alphabet soup: ANSI, IEEE, AFNOR, BSI, CCITT, ITU, ISO, IEC, EIA, and so on. There are international standards organizations, national standards organizations, Pan-European standards organizations, industry standards bodies, and professional engineering organizations with standards boards. The organizations often interact with each other in complex ways. For example, it is fairly common for the Computer Society of IEEE (The Institute of Electrical and Electronics Engineers) to develop and publish a widely accepted and popular standard, which then becomes accepted by ANSI as an American National Standard. ANSI may then submit the standard to the ISO (the International Standards Organization), which may then modify the document before enshrining it as a worldwide standard. The modified standard may then be accepted by ANSI and the IEEE, which then issue their own printings of it. In the sections below, we examine all the major standards bodies, and also list their addresses. The glossary of acronyms in the back of the book should help the reader keep track of all the various organizations.

12.1   Standards Organizations

12.1.1   International Organizations

ISO and IEC

There are two major international standards bodies dealing with information technology: the International Organization for Standardization (ISO) and the International Electrotechnical Commission (IEC). IEC and ISO are composed of member bodies, like the American National Standards Institute (ANSI), which are the representative national standards bodies in their respective countries. IEC and ISO are on an equal footing, but IEC deals only with electronics engineering standards, whereas ISO deals with standards in every other industrial area, including computer science.

Since the barriers between information technology *per se* and electrical and electronic engineering have become less well delineated in recent years, there is some overlap now between the ISO and the IEC. There is an important Joint Technical Committee between the ISO and IEC, known as "Joint Technical Committee 1 (JTC1)," formed in 1987. JTC1 is now responsible for standardization in computer and information technology. The Secretariat of JTC1 lies with the United States, and is the responsibility of the American National Standards Institute (ANSI). JTC1 has many subcommittees (SCs), each responsible for a broad area. The subcommittees of JTC1 are (with the country acting as secretary for each subcommittee denoted in parentheses):

SC1	*Vocabulary* (France).
SC2	*Character Sets and Information Coding.* This subcommittee is also responsible for image coding, audio coding, facsimile, videotex, and teletext (France).
SC6	*Networking Services* (U.S.).
SC7	*Design and Documentation of Computer-Based Information Systems* (Canada).
SC11	*Flexible Magnetic Media* (U.S.).
SC14	*Representation of Data Elements* (Sweden).
SC15	*Labelling and File Structure* (Switzerland).
SC17	*Identification and Credit Cards* (U.K.).
SC18	*Text and Office Systems.* Document architecture, document interchange format, page description languages, fonts (U.S.).

SC21   *Open Systems Interconnection.* Apart from OSI, this
              subcommittee also covers data bases, operating systems, and
              file transfer protocols (U.S.).

SC22   *Programming Languages* (Canada).

SC23   *Optical Digital Data Disks* (Japan).

SC24   *Computer Graphics* (Germany).

SC25   *Interconnection and Information Technology* (Germany).

SC26   *Microprocessor Systems* (Japan).

SC27   *Security Techniques* (Germany).

The standards development process in the ISO and IEC is a
lengthy one. A standard begins as a New Work Item (NWI),
submitted to JTC1 for initial consideration by one of the
subcommittees or by a national standards body such as ANSI. The
member bodies of JTC1 must then vote to approve the NWI, and this
can take up to eight months. When the NWI is approved, the
appropriate JTC1 subcommittee then prepares a Working Draft
(WD). It generally takes between six months and two years to
produce a satisfactory WD. When the WD is complete, the
subcommittee involved registers it as a Draft Proposal (DP). At this
time the DP is assigned an official four- or five-digit ISO reference
number. The DP is then circulated for comment, approval, and
revision to national standards bodies. If substantial changes are
required, the DP must be reapproved by vote. The entire DP stage
can take a year or longer. When the DP is finally approved by the
subcommittee, it becomes a Draft International Standard (DIS), and
it is circulated by the Central ISO office to the national body
members of both JTC1 and the subcommittee in question. The DIS
stage can also take a year. After the DIS stage, if the document is
finally approved by both JTC1 and the subcommittee, the standard is
submitted to the ISO and the IEC for final acceptance and publication
as a standard.

ITU and CCITT
Another important international organization is the
International Telecommunications Union (ITU). This is different
from the ISO in that its membership consists not of national
standards bodies, but of national governments. The ITU is
concerned, as its name implies, with telecommunications. The
ITU has two consultative committees, the CCIR (Comité Consultatif
International de Radio, or International Radio Consultative
Committee) and the CCITT (Comité Consultatif International
Télégraphique et Téléphonique, or International Telegraph and

Telephone Consultative Committee). The CCITT is the important entity for information technology, since it issues recommendations in the area of data communications. CCITT recommendations are formulated by study groups composed of specialists from various countries, and a set of recommendations is issued every four years. The last set (the "blue books") was released in 1988. ISO/IEC JTC1 often cooperates with CCITT (ISO, 1988). CCITT has four study groups relevant to information technology:

SGVII	*Data Communications Networks* (issues the X-Series Recommendations).
SGVIII	*Terminal Equipment for Telematic Services* (issues the T-Series Recommendations).
SGXVII	*Data Transmission Over the Telephone Network* (issues the V-Series Recommendations).
SGXVIII	*Digital Networks Including ISDN* (issues the G- and I-Series Recommendations).

Of the above, the most important for information technology at the present time are probably the X-Series Recommendations issued by SGVII, and the V-Series Recommendations issued by SGXVII. A complete list of the X- and V-Series recommendations is provided in Chap. 17.

12.1.2   European Organizations

There are pan-European organizations similar in function to all three international organizations. The Comité Européen de Normalisation (CEN, European Committee for Standardization) corresponds roughly to the ISO; the Comité Européen de Normalisation Électrotechnique (CENELEC, European Committee for Electrical Standardization) corresponds to the IEC; and the Conférence Européenne des Administrations des Postes et Télécommunications (CEPT, European Conference of Postal and Telecommunications Administrations) corresponds roughly to the ITU. CEN is responsible for all areas of standardization, while CENELEC is responsible only for electrotechnology. Like the ISO and the IEC, they work closely together in the field of information technology. CEN is made up of the national standards bodies of the eighteen nations comprising the European Economic Community (EEC) and the European Free Trade Association (EFTA). CENELEC is composed of national committees on electrotechnology throughout Europe. CEN and CENELEC generally promote ISO and IEC standards, and do not consider it their mission to duplicate

other efforts. CEN and CENELEC attempt to achieve harmonization
of national standards throughout Europe.

In addition, there are two other organizations: The European
Telecommunications Standards Institute (ETSI), established in
1988; and the European Workshop on Open Systems (EWOS),
founded in 1987 with the support of the EEC and EFTA. The function
of EWOS is to act as a European agent for the development of profiles
for Open Systems Interconnection (OSI—see Chap. 15). ETSI has
taken over some of the functions previously belonging to CEPT,
specifically standards relating to Terminal Equipment, Signaling
Protocols and Switching, and Transmission and Multiplexing.

ETSI cooperates with CEPT to develop European
Telecommunications Standards (NETs). These often focus on
amplifying and adding specifications to CCITT recommendations.
Usually, ETSI develops recommendations, which are then approved
by CEPT's Technical Recommendations Application Committee
(TRAC). Some NETs are listed in Chap. 17.

12.1.3   National Organizations

ANSI (U.S.)

The American National Standards Institute (ANSI) is perhaps the
world's most important and influential national standards body.
As mentioned above, ANSI is the Secretary of ISO/IEC JTC1. ANSI
is composed of 900 industrial companies and 200 professional, trade,
and other organizations. ANSI does not develop standards, but
provides procedures to be followed by members and publishes the
resulting standards.

Most national standards bodies no longer follow extensive
procedures for standards development, but instead participate in the
ISO and IEC procedures. ANSI is an exception. The members of
ANSI generate very meaningful U.S. National Standards,
following procedures as complicated as those of the International
Organizations. The ISO and IEC often do nothing more than
endorse ANSI standards. The ANSI Technical Advisory Group
(TAG) responsible for information technology is X3.   X3
corresponds roughly to ISO/IEC JTC1. The subcommittees of X3
(and some of their own subcommittees) are:

X3A	*Recognition.* Includes X3A1, OCR and MICR.
X3B	*Media.* Includes X3B5, Digital Magnetic Tape; X3B6, Instrumentation Tape; X3B7, Magnetic Disks; X3B8, Flexible Disk Cartridges; X3B9, Paper Forms; X3B10, Credit and Identification Cards; and X3B11, Optical Digital Data Disks.
X3H	*Languages (1).* Includes X3H2, Data Base; X3H3, Computer Graphics; and X3H4, Information Resource and Dictionary.
X3J	*Languages (2).* Includes X3J1, PL/1; X3J2, BASIC; X3J3, FORTRAN; X3J4, COBOL; X3J9, PASCAL; X3J10, APL; X3J11, C; X3J12, DIBOL; and X3J13, Common LISP.
X3K	*Documentation.* Includes X3K1, Computer Documentation; X3K5, Vocabulary for Information Processing Standards.
X3L	*Data Representation.* Includes X3L2, Codes and Character Sets; X3L5, Labels and File Structure; X3L8, Data Representation.
X3S	*Communications.* Includes X3S3, Data Communications.
X3T	*Systems Technology (1).* Includes X3T1, Data Encryption; X3T2, Data Interchange; X3T5, Open Systems Interconnection; and X3T9, I/O Interface.
X3V	*Systems Technology (2).* Includes X3V1, Text, Office and Publishing Systems.

An ANSI standard begins as a project proposal (PP) developed by an appropriate X3 subcommittee. The PP is voted on by the entire X3 committee, and then passes into the stage of a Working Draft. The Working Draft is circulated among the members of the appropriate X3 subcommittee and comments are solicited. This often goes on for several years. When the subcommittee is satisfied that the Working Draft is reasonably complete and stable, the Working Draft becomes a Draft Proposal American National Standard (DPANS). The DPANS is circulated for public review outside the committee. There may be several public reviews, resulting in several revisions of the DPANS. When a reasonable consensus has finally been reached, the DPANS is submitted to the ANSI Board of Standards Review (BSR) for final acceptance. The BSR assures that all proper procedures were followed, and the DPANS is accepted as an American National Standard.

NIST (U.S.)

The National Institute of Standards and Technology (NIST), formerly known as the National Bureau of Standards (NBS), is part of the United States Government. ANSI standards, influential as they may be, are entirely voluntary, and are not backed in general by government authority. Some ANSI standards in information technology are adopted by NIST as Federal Information Processing Standards (FIPS). FIPS are mandatory for use by government agencies and their contractors.

JISC (Japan)

The Japanese Industrial Standards Committee (JISC) is the Japanese national standards body and the Japanese member of ISO and IEC. JISC is under the direction of the Agency of Industrial Science and Technology, which in turn is part of the extremely powerful Ministry of International Trade and Industry (MITI). MITI plays a dominant role in Japanese industry, much more pervasive than any part of the United States Government plays in American industry (with the possible exception of the Department of Defense in its relationships with defense contractors). Because of MITI's influence, JISC is extremely powerful, and the Japanese have an almost unparalleled ability to adopt and take advantage of standards, compared with other countries. The publishing arm of JISC is the Japanese Standards Association.

BSI (Britain) and Other National Bodies

The British Standards Institution (BSI) formerly worked to define British Standards in information technology, in a manner similar to ANSI. Increasingly, however, BSI has tended to adopt ISO standards. BSI publishes ISO Draft International Standards as its own Drafts for Development (DD), to encourage public comment on ISO standards in progress. The BSI has a committee for information technology, called IST/-, which is the British National Equivalent of ISO/IEC-JTC1.

Other influential national bodies which now work largely within ISO procedures for information technology standards are the German Deutsches Institut für Normung (DIN), the French Association Française de Normalisation (AFNOR), and the Dutch Nederlands Normalisatie Instituut (NNI).

12.1.4   Professional and Industry Organizations

National and international organizations are not the only producers of important standards in information technology. There are several influential industry organizations that produce their own standards, or play a leading role in the national and international standards bodies.

ECMA

The European Computer Manufacturers Association (ECMA) was established in the late 1950s and began standardizing information technology at a time when the national standards bodies were not yet taking an active role in the area. At present, ECMA produces drafts for consideration by organizations such as ISO/IEC JTC1, or CCITT. ECMA representatives sit on many JTC1 subcommittees.

IEEE

The Institute of Electrical and Electronics Engineers (IEEE) is an international professional organization, based in the United States, of engineers and scientists. The scope of the IEEE is very broad, and includes computer science and engineering. The IEEE is composed of several distinct societies, of which the Computer Society is one of the largest and most important. The IEEE Computer Society is active in the development of standards in information technology. The IEEE cooperates closely with ANSI. Many American standards are joint ANSI/IEEE standards.

EIA

The Electronic Industries Association (EIA), founded in 1924 as the Radio Manufacturers Association, takes a leading role in standards development in certain areas of information technology, particularly interfaces and data communications. EIA standards, like IEEE standards, are forwarded to ANSI for consideration as American National Standards. The EIA developed one of the best-known computer standards in the world: the RS-232 interface.

12.2 Addresses of Standards Organizations

12.2.1 International Organizations

International Electrotechnical Commission (IEC), 3, Rue de Varembé, 1211 Geneva 20, SWITZERLAND.

International Organization for Standardization (ISO), 1, Rue de Varembé, Geneva, SWITZERLAND.
Telephone: 41 22 341240

International Telecommunications Union (ITU), Place des Nations, CH-1211 Geneva, SWITZERLAND.
Telephone: 41 22 995111

12.2.2   European Organizations

European Committee for Standardization (CEN) Rue Brederode 2, 5-1000 Bruxelles, BELGIUM.
Telephone 32 25196811

12.2.3   National Organizations

Association Française de Normalization (AFNOR), Division Informatique, Tour Europe-Cedex 7, 92080 Paris La Defense, FRANCE.
Telephone: 33 1 42 91 57 06

American National Standards Institute (ANSI), 1430 Broadway, New York, New York 10018, U.S.A.
Telephone: (212) 642 4934

British Standards Institution (BSI), 2 Park St., London W1A 2BS, UNITED KINGDOM.
Telephone: 44 1 629 90 00

Deutsches Institut für Normung (DIN), Burggrafenstr. 6 – Postfach 11 07, 1000 Berlin 30, GERMANY.
Telephone: 49 3026011

Japanese Industrial Standards Committee (JISC), 1-24, Akaska 4, Minato-ku, Tokyo 107, JAPAN.

Nederlands Normalisatie Instituut (NNI), Kalfjeslann 2, Postfach 50 59, 2600 GB Delft, THE NETHERLANDS.
Telephone: 31 15 61 1061

Standards Association of Australia (SAA), Standards House, 80-86 Arthur St., North Sydney, New South Wales 2060, AUSTRALIA.
Telephone: 61 2 963 4111

Standards Council of Canada (SCC), International Standards Branch, 350 Sparks St., Suite 1200, Ottawa, Ontario K1P 7S8, Canada.
Telephone (613) 238-3222

12.2.4   Professional and Industry Organizations

Electronic Industries Association (EIA), Engineering Dept., 2001 Eye St., Washington, D. C. 20006, U.S.A.
Telephone: (202) 457-4966

European Computer Manufacturers' Association (ECMA), 114 Rue du Rhône, CH-1204 Geneva, SWITZERLAND.
Telephone 41 22 7353634

Institute of Electrical and Electronics Engineers (IEEE) (Headquarters), 345 E. 47th St. New York, New York 10017-2394, U.S.A.
Telephone: (212) 705-7900

Institute of Electrical and Electronics Engineers (IEEE) (Sales) 445 Hoes Lane, P.O. Box 1331, Piscataway, New Jersey 08855-1331, U.S.A.
Telephone: (201) 981-0060

12.3   Bibliography

Much useful information can be obtained from the ANSI catalog (published annually) and the catalog of IEEE standards (published quarterly). The IEEE also issues a quarterly newsletter, *The Standards Bearer,* which contains news on standardization activity. Those interested in delving into the structure of standards organizations and the theory and process of standardization may consult Cargill's (1989) book. Hill and Meek (1980) also present a considerable amount of useful information, although their book is now somewhat out of date. Arnold and Duce (1990) have written an excellent book about ISO Graphics Standards, and they include an in-depth discussion of standards organizations and the standards process as well. Macpherson (1990) and Wallenstein (1990) focus on international telecommunications standardization. Ruggles (1990) concentrates on the application of formal methods and specifications in information technology standardization. Many useful addresses can be found in Reference on Research (1989).

Arnold, D. B., and D. A. Duce (1990), *ISO Standards for Computer Graphics,* Computer Graphics Standards Series, Butterworths, Boston, Massachusetts.

Cargill, Carl F. (1989), *Information Technology Standardization: Theory, Processes, and Organizations*, Digital Press, Bedford, Massachusetts.

Hill, I. D., and B. L. Meek (1980), *Programming Language Standardisation*, Ellis Horwood, Chichester, United Kingdom (In U.S.: John Wiley, New York, New York).

ISO (1988), *Informal Guide for ISO/IEC JTC1 and CCITT Cooperation, ISO/IEC/JTC1 N303*, Geneva, Switzerland.

Macpherson, A. (1990), *International Telecommunications Standards Organizations*, Artech House, Boston, Massachusetts.

Reference on Research (1989), *European Sources of Scientific and Technical Information*, Eighth Edition, Longman, Harlow, Essex, United Kingdom (distributed in the U.S. and Canada by Gale Research Co., Detroit, Michigan).

Ruggles, C. L. N. (1990) (ed.), *Formal Methods in Standards, A Report from the BCS Working Group*, Springer Verlag, New York, New York.

Wallenstein, G. (1990), *Setting Global Telecommunications Standards*, Artech House, Boston, Massachusetts.

13

Character Codes and Typography

In this chapter we present tables and information pertaining to a large number of standard and quasi-standard character codes: the old Baudot code, ASCII, ISO standards, IBM's EBCDIC, and the "standards" of other manufacturers. It may be helpful to refer to Chap. 12, which introduces standards organizations. We also discuss here the topic of digital typography (Sec. 13.10).

13.1   ASCII

ASCII, the American National Standard for Information Interchange [ANSI X3.4 (1968)] is perhaps the world's best-known character set. It is very widely used. It is probably fair to say that ASCII is a *de facto* standard as well as a *de jure* one in the United States and many parts of the world. However, ASCII is also a very troublesome standard, because its code is only seven bits long (giving 128 possible characters), and no one is quite sure what to do with the eighth bit in the byte. For example, some systems use the eighth bit as a mark-parity bit, while others use it as a space-parity bit (see Sec. 8.7.4 and Chap. 7). There is also a great temptation to use the eighth bit to double the size of the character set to 256, and this many manufacturers have done. The problem is that since ASCII only specifies seven bits, they have all done it differently.

In any case, what many people erroneously call the "first half" of ASCII, the 128 characters actually specified by the standard, is agreed upon by almost everyone. Table 13.1 presents characters 0 through 127 (decimal), with their decimal (dec.), octal, binary, and hexadecimal (hex.) values. Table 13.1 also presents EBCDIC equivalents of ASCII characters (see below). Since EBCDIC defines more than 128 characters, a one-to-one map is not possible, and variations are bound to occur in the translation method; however, the values presented in Table 13.1 are commonly accepted. The first 32 characters of ASCII (0 to 31 dec.) are control characters and are generally nonprintable. Table 13.3 gives the meanings of these control characters, as well as keyboard entries to produce them. Although the control characters are normally nonprintable, ANSI has prescribed graphic representations of them [ANSI X3.32 (1973), endorsed by ISO 2047 (1975)]. These are shown in Table 13.5. Also shown in Table 13.5 are the graphical representations used in the IBM-PC character set—not the same as the ANSI specifications [note that the IBM-PC character set for positions 0 to 127 (dec.) conforms in every other respect to ANSI standards].

13.2   EBCDIC

Before moving to international standards based on ASCII, we digress and discuss EBCDIC. EBCDIC (extended binary coded decimal interchange code) is not a standard, but it is used by IBM in its large computers. Anything used by IBM automatically has the status of a competing standard (although this is less and less true as time goes on; even IBM uses ASCII in its personal computers).

EBCDIC is an eight-bit code, giving 256 possible characters. However, there are many unused positions. Note that EBCDIC is not an absolute "standard" even within the community that uses it. Implementations may vary; the one in Table 13.1 is a common one.

13.3   ISO 646 and International Versions of ASCII

Although it began as an American national standard, ASCII has been adopted internationally. The international standard ISO 646 is essentially an endorsement of ASCII. ISO 646 allows certain ASCII characters to be modified for national use by different countries. The ISO encourages those entities that do not need to make replacements to refrain from doing so, and to use the International Reference Version (IRV) specified by ISO 646. The IRV is identical to ASCII, with the following two exceptions: The universal currency sign ¤ is used in place of the dollar sign $ in position 24 (hex.); the IRV also assigns an overbar instead of a tilde to position 7E (hex.).

ISO 646 allows those countries that find the IRV unsuitable for their needs to make the following substitutions: position 23 (hex.) may be allocated either a pound sign # or a pound sterling sign £; position 24 (hex.) may be allocated either a dollar sign $ or a universal currency sign ¤; positions 40, 60, 5B through 5E inclusive, and 7B through 7E inclusive (all hex.) may be assigned to any alternative replacement characters, as needed.

Tables 13.6 through 13.13 give the replacement characters for the national versions of ISO 646 (the "national ASCIIs") for several languages: British English, German, Danish, Swedish, Norwegian, French, Spanish, and Italian.

13.4   The Eight-Bit Code ISO 6937

As we have discussed, ASCII's great deficiency is the fact that it is only a seven-bit code, and can represent a paltry 128 characters. The ISO has introduced several eight-bit codes, one of which is ISO 6937. ISO 6937/2 (ISO 6937/1 is a general introduction to the standard; ISO 6937/2 specifies the coding table) is presented in Table 13.14. The table only gives positions A0–FF (hex.). The first 128 (00–7F hex.) positions are the same as the International Reference Version of ISO 646 (i.e., virtually identical to ASCII). Positions 80–9F (hex.) do not contain printable characters, and positions A0–FF (hex.), shown in the table, contain accented letters and other graphic characters useful in various European languages. Note that some positions are reserved for future standardization.

ISO 6937 is not limited to the values shown in the table. ISO 6937 is intended to be an extendable code. The techniques of character-set extension to be applied to ISO 6937 are delineated in ISO 2022. ISO 2022 represents alternate character sets via the device of the single-shift character, which temporarily redefines the character immediately following it. ISO 6937 coupled with ISO 2022 is thus a variable-length code. Variable-length encoding can be inefficient for information processing; ISO 6937/2 was designed for information interchange only.

13.5   The Eight-Bit ISO Alphabets 8859/1 to 8859/9

More popular than ISO 6937/2 are the alphabets defined by ISO/IEC 8859, commonly referred to simply as ISO 8859 since early parts of the standard were issued under the ISO name alone. ISO 8859 was prepared by the European Computer Manufacturers Association (ECMA) as ECMA-128, and adopted by ISO/IEC Joint Technical Committee 1. ISO 8859 has nine parts, each defining an eight-bit code (256 characters). The most widely used is ISO 8859/1. known as Latin Alphabet No. 1. The code table of ISO 8859/1 exists also as an ANSI standard (ANSI X3.132.2) and as ECMA-94.

Each part of ISO 8859 is a table with FF (hex.) positions. Positions 00 through 7F (hex.) are filled with characters identical to those of ASCII. This is the "left side" of the table. In the right side of the table, positions 80–9F (hex.) do not contain printable characters, and positions A0–FF (hex.) contain accented letters and other characters useful in various languages. The right sides (A0–FF) of ISO 8859/1 through 8859/9 are shown in Tables 13.15 to 13.20.

The intended languages of application of ISO 8859/1 through 8859/9 are as follows:

ISO 8859/1 *Latin Alphabet No. 1*: Danish, Dutch, English, Faeroese, Finnish, French, Frisian, German, Icelandic, Irish, Italian, Norwegian, Portuguese, Spanish, and Swedish.

ISO 8859/2 *Latin Alphabet No. 2*: English, German, and certain Eastern European languages employing Latin-based alphabets, such as Albanian, Czech, Hungarian, Polish, Rumanian, Serbo-Croatian, Slovak, and Slovene.

ISO 8859/3 *Latin Alphabet No. 3:* Catalan, Esperanto, Galician, Maltese, and Turkish, as well as English, German, Italian, and Spanish.

ISO 8859/4 *Latin Alphabet No. 4:* Estonian, Greenlandic, Lappish, Latvian, and Lithuanian, in addition to English, Danish, Finnish, German, Norwegian, and Swedish.

ISO 8859/5 *Latin/Cyrillic Alphabet:* Bulgarian, Byelorussian, Macedonian, Russian, Serbo-Croatian, and Ukrainian, as well as English and other languages served by ASCII.

ISO 8859/6 *Latin/Arabic Alphabet:* Arabic, as well as English and other languages served by ASCII.

ISO 8859/7 *Latin/Greek Alphabet:* Greek, as well as English and other languages served by ASCII.

ISO 8859/8 *Latin/Hebrew Alphabet:* Hebrew, as well as English and other languages served by ASCII.

ISO/IEC 8859/9 *Latin Alphabet No. 5:* Various European languages using Latin-based alphabets.

13.6   Manufacturers' "Extended ASCII's"

As we mentioned in Sec. 13.1, the fact that ASCII leaves one bit in an eight-bit byte undefined has led to chaos, with various manufacturers assigning positions 80 through FF (hex.) as they have seen fit. ISO eight-bit standards did not enjoy wide acceptance when many manufacturers were deciding what to do with the second half of their code tables.

We do not present all manufacturers' code tables here. Tables 13.21 and 13.22 list the alphanumeric character sets of a few important ones, with ISO 8859/1 listed for purposes of comparison. The DEC Multinational character set is very similar to ISO 8859/1. Table 13.21 lists it, along with the "standard" Apple Macintosh character set. Table 13.22 lists characters in alphabetical order for many different versions of the IBM-PC character set; each version is referred to as a "code page" (CP). CP437 is the code page for the original IBM-PC. CP860 is specifically for Portugal and Brazil, CP863 for Quebec and the rest of French Canada, and CP865 for Norway. CP850 is IBM's multilingual code page, which is intended to be useful for a variety of European languages. It differs significantly from ISO 8859/1. (Note that the IBM code-page information was obtained from Gianone (1990), who has corrected errors in the manufacturer's tables.)

13.7   Accented Letters in ISO Alphabets and Manufacturers' "Extended ASCII's"

ISO standard alphabets, as well as many manufacturers' extended character sets, contain several accented letters useful in a large variety of languages. Rather than describe the various accents and diacritical marks verbally, we give examples of accented letters in Figure 13.1.

The reader will notice that each accented letter in Figure 13.1 is accompanied by an "ISO I.D." The ISO identification scheme for accented letters is delineated in Annex A to ISO 6937/1. All characters are identified by a four-position code.

The first (leftmost) position in the code is one of the following letters: L, indicating a Latin alphabetic character; C, indicating a control function; N, indicating a numeric graphic character; or S, indicating a special graphic character.

The second position depends on the first. If the first is an L, indicating that the character in question is a Latin alphabetic character, then the second position is simply one of the letters A to Z.

The third position (assuming we are dealing with a Latin alphabetic character) is one of the numbers 0 through 6. A 0 indicates a letter without a diacritical mark; a 1, 2, or 3 indicates a letter with a diacritical mark above it. A 4 indicates a letter with a diacritical mark below it. A 5 indicates a diphthong or ligature, and a 6 indicates a special form. The fourth position is an odd digit for lowercase letters, and an even digit for uppercase letters. The following are the combinations of third and fourth positions, which correspond to several accents:

Diacritical mark	Code for lowercase letter	Code for uppercase letter
None	01	02
Acute accent	11	12
Grave accent	13	14
Circumflex accent	15	16
Umlaut	17	18
Tilde	19	20
Caron	21	22
Breve	23	24
Double acute accent	25	26
Ping	27	28
Dot above	29	30
Macron	31	32
Cedilla	41	42
Ogonek	43	44
Diphthong or Digraph	51	52
Special form	61,63,...	62,64,...

Thus, LA11 indicates á, a lowercase "a" with an acute accent, LU18 indicates Ü, an uppercase "u" with an umlaut, etc.

The above applies to Latin alphabetic characters, which have L in the first (leftmost) position of the code. If the first position of the code is C, indicating a control character, then the second position is one of the following: E, indicating a code extension control function; F, indicating a format effector; P, indicating a presentation control function; or M, indicating some other control function. Positions 3 and 4 have no special meaning.

If the first position is N, indicating a numeric graphic character, then the second position is one of the following: D, indicating a decimal digit; F, indicating a fraction; or S, indicating a superscript. Positions 3 and 4 have no special meaning.

If the first position is S, indicating a special graphic character, then the second position is one of the following: A, indicating an arithmetic sign; C, indicating a currency sign; D, indicating a diacritical mark; P, indicating a punctuation mark; or M, indicating some other symbol. Positions 3 and 4 have no special meaning.

13.8   Character Code Tables

TABLE 13.1   ASCII and EBCDIC Table

	ASCII				EBCDIC
dec.	hex.	octal	binary	char.	hex.
0	00	000	00000000	NUL	00
1	01	001	00000001	SOH	01
2	02	002	00000010	STX	02
3	03	003	00000011	ETX	03
4	04	004	00000100	EOT	37
5	05	005	00000101	ENQ	2D
6	06	006	00000110	ACK	2E
7	07	007	00000111	BEL	2F
8	08	010	00001000	BS	16
9	09	011	00001001	HT	05
10	0A	012	00001010	LF	25
11	0B	013	00001011	VT	0B
12	0C	014	00001100	FF	0C
13	0D	015	00001101	CR	0D
14	0E	016	00001110	SO	0E
15	0F	017	00001111	SI	0F
16	10	020	00010000	DLE	10
17	11	021	00010001	DC1	11
18	12	022	00010010	DC2	12
19	13	023	00010011	DC3	13
20	14	024	00010100	DC4	3C
21	15	025	00010101	NAK	3D
22	16	026	00010110	SYN	32
23	17	027	00010111	ETB	26
24	18	030	00011000	CAN	18
25	19	031	00011001	EM	19
26	1A	032	00011010	SUB	3F
27	1B	033	00011011	ESC	27
28	1C	034	00011100	FS	1C
29	1D	035	00011101	GS	1D
30	1E	036	00011110	RS	1E
31	1F	037	00011111	US	1F
32	20	040	00100000	space	40
33	21	041	00100001	!	5A
34	22	042	00100010	"	7F
35	23	043	00100011	#	7B

TABLE 13.1 ASCII and EBCDIC Table (continued)

	ASCII				EBCDIC
dec.	hex.	octal	binary	char.	hex.
36	24	044	00100100	$	5B
37	25	045	00100101	%	6C
38	26	046	00100110	&	50
39	27	047	00100111	'	7D
40	28	050	00101000	(	4D
41	29	051	00101001	)	5D
42	2A	052	00101010	*	5C
43	2B	053	00101011	+	4E
44	2C	054	00101100	,	6B
45	2D	055	00101101	−	60
46	2E	056	00101110	.	4B
47	2F	057	00101111	/	61
48	30	060	00110000	0	F0
49	31	061	00110001	1	F1
50	32	062	00110010	2	F2
51	33	063	00110011	3	F3
52	34	064	00110100	4	F4
53	35	065	00110101	5	F5
54	36	066	00110110	6	F6
55	37	067	00110111	7	F7
56	38	070	00111000	8	F8
57	39	071	00111001	9	F9
58	3A	072	00111010	:	7A
59	3B	073	00111011	;	5E
60	3C	074	00111100	<	4C
61	3D	075	00111101	=	7E
62	3E	076	00111110	>	6E
63	3F	077	00111111	?	6F
64	40	100	01000000	@	7C
65	41	101	01000001	A	C1
66	42	102	01000010	B	C2
67	43	103	01000011	C	C3
68	44	104	01000100	D	C4
69	45	105	01000101	E	C5
70	46	106	01000110	F	C6

TABLE 13.1 ASCII and EBCDIC Table (continued)

ASCII					EBCDIC
dec.	hex.	octal	binary	char.	hex.
71	47	107	01000111	G	C7
72	48	110	01001000	H	C8
73	49	111	01001001	I	C9
74	4A	112	01001010	J	D1
75	4B	113	01001011	K	D2
76	4C	114	01001100	L	D3
77	4D	115	01001101	M	D4
78	4E	116	01001110	N	D5
79	4F	117	01001111	O	D6
80	50	120	01010000	P	D7
81	51	121	01010001	Q	D8
82	52	122	01010010	R	D9
83	53	123	01010011	S	E2
84	54	124	01010100	T	E3
85	55	125	01010101	U	E4
86	56	126	01010110	V	E5
87	57	127	01010111	W	E6
88	58	130	01011000	X	E7
89	59	131	01011001	Y	E8
90	5A	132	01011010	Z	E9
91	5B	133	01011011	[	AD
92	5C	134	01011100	\	E0
93	5D	135	01011101	]	BD
94	5E	136	01011110	^	5F
95	5F	137	01011111	_	6D
96	60	140	01100000	`	79
97	61	141	01100001	a	81
98	62	142	01100010	b	82
99	63	143	01100011	c	83
100	64	144	01100100	d	84
101	65	145	01100101	e	85
102	66	146	01100110	f	86
103	67	147	01100111	g	87
104	68	150	01101000	h	88
105	69	151	01101001	i	89

TABLE 13.1 ASCII and EBCDIC Table (continued)

dec.	hex.	octal	binary	char.	EBCDIC hex.
106	6A	152	01101010	j	91
107	6B	153	01101011	k	92
108	6C	154	01101100	l	93
109	6D	155	01101101	m	94
110	6E	156	01101110	n	95
111	6F	157	01101111	o	96
112	70	160	01110000	p	97
113	71	161	01110001	q	98
114	72	162	01110010	r	99
115	73	163	01110011	s	A2
116	74	164	01110100	t	A3
117	75	165	01110101	u	A4
118	76	166	01110110	v	A5
119	77	167	01110111	w	A6
120	78	170	01111000	x	A7
121	79	171	01111001	y	A8
122	7A	172	01111010	z	A9
123	7B	173	01111011	{	C0
124	7C	174	01111100			4F
125	7D	175	01111101	}	D0
126	7E	176	01111110	~	A1
127	7F	177	01111111	DEL	07

TABLE 13.2 Hexadecimal-to-Decimal Conversion

Hex.	Dec.	Hex.	Dec.	Hex.	Dec.	Hex.	Dec.
00	00	20	32	40	64	60	96
01	01	21	33	41	65	61	97
02	02	22	34	42	66	62	98
03	03	23	35	43	67	63	99
04	04	24	36	44	68	64	100
05	05	25	37	45	69	65	101
06	06	26	38	46	70	66	102
07	07	27	39	47	71	67	103
08	08	28	40	48	72	68	104
09	09	29	41	49	73	69	105
0A	10	2A	42	4A	74	6A	106
0B	11	2B	43	4B	75	6B	107
0C	12	2C	44	4C	76	6C	108
0D	13	2D	45	4D	77	6D	109
0E	14	2E	46	4E	78	6E	110
0F	15	2F	47	4F	79	6F	111
10	16	30	48	50	80	70	112
11	17	31	49	51	81	71	113
12	18	32	50	52	82	72	114
13	19	33	51	53	83	73	115
14	20	34	52	54	84	74	116
15	21	35	53	55	85	75	117
16	22	36	54	56	86	76	118
17	23	37	55	57	87	77	119
18	24	38	56	58	88	78	120
19	25	39	57	59	89	79	121
1A	26	3A	58	5A	90	7A	122
1B	27	3B	59	5B	91	7B	123
1C	28	3C	60	5C	92	7C	124
1D	29	3D	61	5D	93	7D	125
1E	30	3E	62	5E	94	7E	126
1F	31	3F	63	5F	95	7F	127

TABLE 13.2 Hexadecimal-to-Decimal Conversion (continued)

Hex.	Dec.	Hex.	Dec.	Hex.	Dec.	Hex.	Dec.
80	128	A0	160	C0	192	E0	224
81	129	A1	161	C1	193	E1	225
82	130	A2	162	C2	194	E2	226
83	131	A3	163	C3	195	E3	227
84	132	A4	164	C4	196	E4	228
85	133	A5	165	C5	197	E5	229
86	134	A6	166	C6	198	E6	230
87	135	A7	167	C7	199	E7	231
88	136	A8	168	C8	200	E8	232
89	137	A9	169	C9	201	E9	233
8A	138	AA	170	CA	202	EA	234
8B	139	AB	171	CB	203	EB	235
8C	140	AC	172	CC	204	EC	236
8D	141	AD	173	CD	205	ED	237
8E	142	AE	174	CE	206	EE	238
8F	143	AF	175	CF	207	EF	239
90	144	B0	176	D0	208	F0	240
91	145	B1	177	D1	209	F1	241
92	146	B2	178	D2	210	F2	242
93	147	B3	179	D3	211	F3	243
94	148	B4	180	D4	212	F4	244
95	149	B5	181	D5	213	F5	245
96	150	B6	182	D6	214	F6	246
97	151	B7	183	D7	215	F7	247
98	152	B8	184	D8	216	F8	248
99	153	B9	185	D9	217	F9	249
9A	154	BA	186	DA	218	FA	250
9B	155	BB	187	DB	219	FB	251
9C	156	BC	188	DC	220	FC	252
9D	157	BD	189	DD	221	FD	253
9E	158	BE	190	DE	222	FE	254
9F	159	BF	191	DF	223	FF	255

TABLE 13.3 ASCII and EBCDIC Nonprintable Control Characters

ASCII hex.	EBCDIC hex.	Char.	Meaning	Keyboard entry
00	00	NUL	Null	CTRL-@
01	01	SOH	Start of heading	CTRL-A
02	02	STX	Start of text	CTRL-B
03	03	ETX	End of text	CTRL-C
04	37	EOT	End of transmission	CTRL-D
05	2D	ENQ	Enquiry	CTRL-E
06	2E	ACK	Acknowledge	CTRL-F
07	2F	BEL	Bell	CTRL-G
08	16	BS	Backspace	CTRL-H
09	05	HT	Horizontal tab	CTRL-I
0A	25	LF	Line feed	CTRL-J
0B	0B	VT	Vertical tab	CTRL-K
0C	0C	FF	Form feed	CTRL-L
0D	0D	CR	Carriage return	CTRL-M
0E	0E	SO	Shift out	CTRL-N
0F	0F	SI	Shift in	CTRL-O
10	10	DLE	Data link escape	CTRL-P
11	11	DC1	Device control one	CTRL-Q
12	12	DC2	Device control two	CTRL-R
13	13	DC3	Device control three	CTRL-S
14	3C	DC4	Device control four	CTRL-T
15	3D	NAK	Negative acknowledge	CTRL-U
16	32	SYN	Synchronous idle	CTRL-V
17	26	ETB	End of transmission	CTRL-W
18	18	CAN	Cancel	CTRL-X
19	19	EM	End of medium	CTRL-Y
1A	3F	SUB	Substitute	CTRL-Z
1B	27	ESC	Escape	CTRL-[
1C	1C	FS (IFS)[1]	File separator	CTRL-\
1D	1D	GS (IGS)[1]	Group separator	CTRL-]
1E	1E	RS (IRS)[1]	Record separator	CTRL-^
1F	1F	US (IUS)[1]	Unit separator	CTRL-_

Note: 1. In EBCDIC, FS, GS, RS, and US are commonly referred to as IFS, IGS, IRS, and IUS, where the "I" stands for information. EBCDIC has another special character RS, which stands for Reader Stop, at position 35 hex.; EBCDIC also has an extra file separator FS at position 22 hex.

TABLE 13.4 EBCDIC Control Characters Without Direct ASCII Equivalents

Character	Meaning	EBCDIC value (hex.)
BYP	Bypass	24
FS[1]	File Separator	22
IL	Idle	17
LC	Lower Case	06
NL[2]	New Line	15
PF	Punch Off	04
PN	Punch On	34
RES	Restore	14
RS[3]	Reader Stop	35
SM	Start Message	2A
UC	Upper Case	36

Notes: 1. The ASCII FS is commonly taken to be equivalent to the EBCDIC IFS. The FS in this table is another file separator character in EBCDIC.
2. Not the same as ASCII line-feed LF. EBCDIC also has a line-feed LF.
3. Do not confuse with ASCII RS, Record Separator. ASCII RS is commonly taken to be equivalent to EBCDIC IRS.

TABLE 13.5   Graphical Representations of Normally Nonprintable ASCII Control Characters

ASCII hex.	Keyboard entry	Standard alphanumeric representation	Standard graphical representation	IBM-PC printable representation
00	CTRL-@	NU	▯	None
01	CTRL-A	SH	⌐	☺
02	CTRL-B	SX	⊥	☻
03	CTRL-C	EX	⌐	♥
04	CTRL-D	ET	⚡	♦
05	CTRL-E	EQ	⊠	♣
06	CTRL-F	AK	✓	♠
07	CTRL-G	BL	♪	●
08	CTRL-H	BS	↖	■
09	CTRL-I	HT	≫	○
0A	CTRL-J	LF	≡	◙
0B	CTRL-K	VT	⇊	♂
0C	CTRL-L	FF	⇊	♀
0D	CTRL-M	CR	⇐	♪
0E	CTRL-N	S0	⊗	♫
0F	CTRL-O	SI	⊙	☼
10	CTRL-P	DL	⊟	►
11	CTRL-Q	D1	⊕	◄
12	CTRL-R	D2	⊞	↕
13	CTRL-S	D3	⊙	‼
14	CTRL-T	D4	⊘	¶
15	CTRL-U	NK	✓	§
16	CTRL-V	SY	∏	▬
17	CTRL-W	EB	⊤	↨
18	CTRL-X	CN	⊠	↑
19	CTRL-Y	EM	♦	↓
1A	CTRL-Z	SB	ↄ	→
1B	CTRL-[	EC	⊖	←
1C	CTRL-\	FS	⊡	∟
1D	CTRL-]	GS	⊟	↔
1E	CTRL-^	RS	⊡	▲
1F	CTRL-_	US	⊡	▼
20	Space	SP	△	(space)
7F	Delete	DT	▨	⌂

ISO I.D.	LETTER	DESCRIPTION
LA11	á	a-acute
LA13	à	a-grave
LA15	â	a-circumflex
LA17	ä	a-umlaut
LC41	ç	c-cedilla
LN19	ñ	n-tilde
LS21	š	s-caron
LT61	ŧ	t-stroke

Fig. 13.1 Illustration of accented letters in ISO alphabets.

ISO I.D.	LETTER	DESCRIPTION
LA27	å	a-ring
LE43	ę	e-ogonek
LE12	É	E-acute
LD62	Đ	D-stroke
LA23	ă	a-breve
LZ29	Ż	z-dot
LU31	ū	u-macron
LO62	Ø	O-slash
LU25	ű	u-double acute

Fig. 13.1 Illustration of accented letters in ISO alphabets (continued).

TABLE 13.6   Replacement Characters for British Version of ASCII (Conforming to ISO 646)

Hex. value	Character	Hex. value	Character
23	£	5E	^
24	$	60	`
40	@	7B	{
5B	[	7C	|
5C	\	7D	}
5D	]	7E	~

TABLE 13.7   Replacement Characters for German Version of ASCII (Conforming to ISO 646)

Hex. value	Character	Hex. value	Character
23	#	5E	^
24	$	60	`
40	§	7B	ä
5B	Ä	7C	ö
5C	Ö	7D	ü
5D	Ü	7E	ß

TABLE 13.8   Replacement Characters for French Version of ASCII (Conforming to ISO 646)

Hex. value	Character	Hex. value	Character
23	£	5E	^
24	$	60	`
40	à	7B	é
5B	¤	7C	ù
5C	ç	7D	è
5D	§	7E	¨

TABLE 13.9   Replacement Characters for Italian Version of ASCII (Conforming to ISO 646)

Hex. value	Character	Hex. value	Character
23	£	5E	^
24	$	60	ù
40	§	7B	à
5B	¤	7C	ò
5C	ç	7D	è
5D	é	7E	ì

TABLE 13.10   Replacement Characters for Spanish Version of ASCII (Conforming to ISO 646)

Hex. value	Character	Hex. value	Character
23	£	5E	^
24	$	60	`
40	§	7B	¤
5B	¡	7C	ñ
5C	Ñ	7D	ç
5D	¿	7E	~

TABLE 13.11 Replacement Characters for Swedish Version of ASCII (Conforming to ISO 646)

Hex. value	Character	Hex. value	Character
23	#	5E	^
24	$	60	`
40	@	7B	ä
5B	Ä	7C	ö
5C	Ö	7D	å
5D	Å	7E	~

TABLE 13.12   Replacement Characters for Danish Version of
ASCII (Conforming to ISO 646)

Hex. value	Character	Hex. value	Character
23	#	5E	^
24	$	60	`
40	@	7B	æ
5B	Æ	7C	ø
5C	Ø	7D	å
5D	Å	7E	~

TABLE 13.13   Replacement Characters for Norwegian Version
of ASCII (Conforming to ISO 646)

Hex. value	Character	Hex. value	Character
23	#	5E	^
24	$	60	`
40	@	7B	æ
5B	Æ	7C	ö̊
5C	Ø	7D	å
5D	Å	7E	~

TABLE 13.14 ISO 6937/2 Character Set: Descriptive Listing of Additional Characters Beyond ISO 646

Hex.	Character	Hex.	Character	Hex.	Character
A0	*Not defined*	C0	*Reserved*[1]	E0	Ohm: Ω
A1	Inverted excl.: ¡	C1	Grave: `	E1	AE digraph: Æ
A2	Cent: ¢	C2	Acute: ´	E2	D-stroke: Đ
A3	Sterling: £	C3	Circumflex: ^	E3	Ordinal, fem.: ª
A4	Dollar: $	C4	Tilde: ~	E4	H-stroke: Ħ
A5	Yen: ¥	C5	Macron: ‾	E5	*Reserved*[1]
A6	*Reserved*[1]	C6	Breve: ˘	E6	IJ digraph: IJ
A7	Paragraph: §	C7	Dot above: ˙	E7	L-middle dot: L̇
A8	*Reserved*[1]	C8	Umlaut: ¨	E8	L-stroke: Ł
A9	L. single quote: '	C9	*Reserved*[1]	E9	O-slash: Ø
AA	L. double quote: "	CA	Ring: °	EA	OE digraph: Œ
AB	L. angle quote: «	CB	Cedilla: ¸	EB	Ordinal, masc.: º
AC	Arrow left: ←	CC	Underscore: _	EC	Icelandic Thorn: Þ
AD	Arrow up: ↑	CD	Double acute: ˝	ED	T-stroke: Ŧ
AE	Arrow right: →	CE	Ogonek: ˛	EE	Lappish Eng: Ŋ
AF	Arrow down: ↓	CF	Caron: ˇ	EF	Apostrophe-n: 'n
B0	Degree: °	D0	Dash: -	F0	kappa: κ
B1	Plus/minus: ±	D1	Super 1: [1]	F1	ae digraph: æ
B2	Superscript 2: [2]	D2	Registered: ®	F2	d-stroke: đ
B3	Superscript 3: [3]	D3	Copyright: ©	F3	Icelandic eth: ð
B4	Multiplication: ×	D4	Trademark: ™	F4	h-stroke: ħ
B5	Micro (mu): μ	D5	Musical note: ♪	F5	i-dotless: ı
B6	Pilcrow: ¶	D6	*Reserved*[1]	F6	ij digraph: ij
B7	Middle dot: ·	D7	*Reserved*[1]	F7	l-middle dot: l̇
B8	Division: ÷	D8	*Reserved*[1]	F8	l-stroke: ł
B9	R. single quote: '	D9	*Reserved*[1]	F9	o-slash: ø
BA	R. double quote: "	DA	*Reserved*[1]	FA	oe digraph: œ
BB	R. angle quote: »	DB	*Reserved*[1]	FB	German ess: ß
BC	One fourth: 1/4	DC	One eighth: 1/8	FC	Icelandic thorn: þ
BD	One half: 1/2	DD	Three eighths: 3/8	FD	t-stroke: ŧ
BE	Three fourths: 3/4	DE	Five eighths: 5/8	FE	Lappish eng: ŋ
BF	Inverted question: ¿	DF	Seven eighths: 7/8	FF	*Not defined*

Note: 1. Reserved for future standardization.

TABLE 13.15 ISO Standard Alphabets 8859/1, 8859/2, and 8859/3: Descriptive Listing of Additional Characters Beyond ASCII

Hex.	8859/1 Latin Alphabet 1	8859/2 Latin Alphabet 2	8859/3 Latin Alphabet 3
A0	No-break space	No-break space	No-break space
A1	Inverted excl.: ¡	A-ogonek: Ą	H-stroke: Ħ
A2	Cent: ¢	Breve: ˘	Breve: ˘
A3	Sterling: £	L-stroke: Ł	Sterling: £
A4	Currency: ¤	Currency: ¤	Currency: ¤
A5	Yen: ¥	L-caron: Ľ	*Not defined*
A6	Broken bar: ¦	S-acute: Ś	H-circumflex: Ĥ
A7	Paragraph: §	Paragraph: §	Paragraph: §
A8	Umlaut: ¨	Umlaut: ¨	Umlaut: ¨
A9	Copyright: ©	S-caron: Š	I-dot: İ
AA	Ordinal, fem.: ª	S-cedilla: Ş	S-cedilla: Ş
AB	L. angle quote: «	T-caron: Ť	G-breve: Ğ
AC	Not sign: ¬	Z-acute: Ź	J-circumflex: Ĵ
AD	Soft hyphen	Soft hyphen	Soft hyphen
AE	Registered: ®	Z-caron: Ž	*Not defined*
AF	Macron: ¯	Z-dot: Ż	Z-dot: Ż
B0	Degree: °	Degree: °	Degree: °
B1	Plus/minus: ±	a-ogonek: ą	h-stroke: ħ
B2	Super 2: ²	Ogonek: ˛	Super 2: ²
B3	Super 3: ³	l-stroke: ł	Super 3: ³
B4	Acute: ´	Acute: ´	Acute: ´
B5	Greek mu: μ	l-caron: ľ	Greek mu: μ
B6	Pilcrow: ¶	s-acute: ś	h-circumflex: ĥ
B7	Middle dot: ·	Caron: ˇ	Middle dot: ·
B8	Cedilla: ¸	Cedilla: ¸	Cedilla: ¸
B9	super 1: ¹	s-caron: š	i-dotless: ı
BA	Ordinal, masc.: º	s-cedilla: ş	s-cedilla: ş
BB	R. angle quote: »	t-caron: ť	g-breve: ğ
BC	One fourth: 1/4	z-acute: ź	j-circumflex: ĵ
BD	One half: 1/2	Double acute: ˝	One half: 1/2
BE	Three fourths: 3/4	z-caron: ž	*Not defined*
BF	Inverted question: ¿	z-dot: ż	z-dot: ż

TABLE 13.15 ISO Standard Alphabets 8859/1, 8859/2, and 8859/3: Descriptive Listing of Additional Characters Beyond ASCII (continued)

Hex.	8859/1 Latin Alphabet 1	8859/2 Latin Alphabet 2	8859/3 Latin Alphabet 3
C0	A-grave: À	R-acute: Ŕ	A-grave: À
C1	A-acute: Á	A-acute: Á	A-acute: Á
C2	A-circumflex: Â	A-circumflex: Â	A-circumflex: Â
C3	A-tilde: Ã	A-breve: Ă	Not defined
C4	A-umlaut: Ä	A-umlaut: Ä	A-umlaut: Ä
C5	A-ring: Å	L-acute: Ĺ	C-dot: Ċ
C6	Æ digraph: Æ	C-acute: Ć	C-circumflex: Ĉ
C7	C-cedilla: Ç	C-cedilla: Ç	C-cedilla: Ç
C8	E-grave: È	C-caron: Č	E-grave: È
C9	E-acute: É	E-acute: É	E-acute: É
CA	E-circumflex: Ê	E-ogonek: Ę	E-circumflex: Ê
CB	E-umlaut: Ë	E-umlaut: Ë	E-umlaut: Ë
CC	I-grave: Ì	E-caron: Ě	I-grave: Ì
CD	I-acute: Í	I-acute: Í	I-acute: Í
CE	I-circumflex: Î	I-circumflex: Î	I-circumflex: Î
CF	I-umlaut: Ï	D-caron: Ď	I-umlaut: Ï
D0	Icelandic Eth: Ð	D-stroke: Đ	Not defined
D1	N-tilde: Ñ	N-acute: Ń	N-tilde: Ñ
D2	O-grave: Ò	N-caron: Ň	O-grave: Ò
D3	O-acute: Ó	O-acute: Ó	O-acute: Ó
D4	O-circumflex: Ô	O-circumflex: Ô	O-circumflex: Ô
D5	O-tilde: Õ	O-double acute: Ő	G-dot: Ġ
D6	O-umlaut: Ö	O-umlaut: Ö	O-umlaut: Ö
D7	Multiplication: ×	Multiplication: ×	Multiplication: ×
D8	O-slash: Ø	R-caron: Ř	G-circumflex: Ĝ
D9	U-grave: Ù	U-ring: Ů	U-grave: Ù
DA	U-acute: Ú	U-acute: Ú	U-acute: Ú
DB	U-circumflex: Û	U-double acute: Ű	U-circumflex: Û
DC	U-umlaut: Ü	U-umlaut: Ü	U-umlaut: Ü
DD	Y-acute: Ý	Y-acute: Ý	U-breve: Ŭ
DE	Icelandic Thorn: Þ	T-cedilla: Ţ	S-circumflex: Ŝ
DF	German ess: ß	German ess: ß	German ess: ß

TABLE 13.15 ISO Standard Alphabets 8859/1, 8859/2, and 8859/3: Descriptive Listing of Additional Characters Beyond ASCII (continued)

Hex.	8859/1 Latin Alphabet 1	8859/2 Latin Alphabet 2	8859/3 Latin Alphabet 3
E0	a-grave: à	r-acute: ŕ	a-grave: à
E1	a-acute: á	a-acute: á	a-acute: á
E2	a-circumflex: â	a-circumflex: â	a-circumflex: â
E3	a-tilde: ã	a-breve: ă	Not defined
E4	a-umlaut: ä	a-umlaut: ä	a-umlaut: ä
E5	a-ring: å	l-acute: ĺ	c-dot: ċ
E6	æ digraph: æ	c-acute: ć	c-circumflex: ĉ
E7	c-cedilla: ç	c-cedilla: ç	c-cedilla: ç
E8	e-grave: è	c-caron: č	e-grave: è
E9	e-acute: é	e-acute: é	e-acute: é
EA	e-circumflex: ê	e-ogonek: ę	e-circumflex: ê
EB	e-umlaut: ë	e-umlaut: ë	e-umlaut: ë
EC	i-grave: ì	e-caron: ě	i-grave: ì
ED	i-acute: í	i-acute: í	i-acute: í
EE	i-circumflex: î	i-circumflex: î	i-circumflex: î
EF	i-umlaut: ï	d-caron: ď	i-umlaut: ï
F0	Icelandic eth: ð	d-stroke: đ	Not defined
F1	n-tilde: ñ	n-acute: ń	n-tilde: ñ
F2	o-grave: ò	n-caron: ň	o-grave: ò
F3	o-acute: ó	o-acute: ó	o-acute: ó
F4	o-circumflex: ô	o-circumflex: ô	o-circumflex: ô
F5	o-tilde: õ	o-double acute: ő	g-dot: ġ
F6	o-umlaut: ö	o-umlaut: ö	o-umlaut: ö
F7	Division: ÷	Division: ÷	Division: ÷
F8	o-slash: ø	r-caron: ř	g-circumflex: ĝ
F9	u-grave: ù	u-ring: ů	u-grave: ù
FA	u-acute: ú	u-acute: ú	u-acute: ú
FB	u-circumflex: û	u-double acute: ű	u-circumflex: û
FC	u-umlaut: ü	u-umlaut: ü	u-umlaut: ü
FD	y-acute: ý	y-acute: ý	u-breve: ŭ
FE	Icelandic thorn: þ	t-cedilla: ţ	s-circumflex: ŝ
FF	y-umlaut: ÿ	Dot: ˙	Dot: ˙

TABLE 13.16 ISO Standard Alphabets 8859/4 and 8859/9: Descriptive Listing of Additional Characters Beyond ASCII

Hex.	8859/4 Latin Alphabet 4	8859/9 Latin Alphabet 5
A0	No-break space	No-break space
A1	A-ogonek: Ą	Inverted exclamation: ¡
A2	Greenlandic kra: ĸ	Cent: ¢
A3	R-cedilla: Ŗ	Sterling: £
A4	Currency: ¤	Currency: ¤
A5	I-tilde: Ĩ	Yen: ¥
A6	L-cedilla: Ļ	Broken bar: ¦
A7	Paragraph: §	Paragraph: §
A8	Umlaut: ¨	Umlaut: ¨
A9	S-caron: Š	Copyright: ©
AA	E-macron: Ē	Ordinal, fem.: ª
AB	G-cedilla: Ģ	L. angle quote:«
AC	T-stroke: Ŧ	Not sign: ¬
AD	Soft hyphen	Soft hyphen
AE	Z-caron: Ž	Registered: ®
AF	Macron: ¯	Macron: ¯
B0	Degree: °	Degree: °
B1	a-ogonek: ą	Plus/minus: ±
B2	ogonek: ˛	Super 2: ^{2}
B3	r-cedilla: ŗ	Super 3: ^{3}
B4	Acute: ´	Acute: ´
B5	i-tilde: ĩ	Greek mu: μ
B6	l-cedilla: ļ	Pilcrow: ¶
B7	Caron: ˇ	Middle dot:·
B8	Cedilla: ¸	Cedilla: ¸
B9	s-caron: š	Super 1: ^{1}
BA	e-macron: ē	Ordinal, masc.: º
BB	g-cedilla: ģ	R. angle quote: »
BC	t-stroke: ŧ	One fourth: 1/4
BD	Lappish Eng: Ŋ	One half: 1/2
BE	z-caron: ž	Three fourths: 3/4
BF	Lappish eng: ŋ	Inverted question: ¿

TABLE 13.16 ISO Standard Alphabets 8859/4 and 8859/9: Descriptive Listing of Additional Characters Beyond ASCII (continued)

Hex.	8859/4 Latin Alphabet 4	8859/9 Latin Alphabet 5
C0	A-macron: Ā	A-grave: À
C1	A-acute: Á	A-acute: Á
C2	A-circumflex: Â	A-circumflex: Â
C3	A-tilde: Ã	A-tilde: Ã
C4	A-umlaut: Ä	A-umlaut: Ä
C5	A-ring: Å	A-ring: Å
C6	Æ digraph: Æ	Æ digraph: Æ
C7	I-ogonek: Į	C-cedilla: Ç
C8	C-caron: Č	E-grave: È
C9	E-acute: É	E-acute: É
CA	E-ogonek: Ę	E-circumflex: Ê
CB	E-umlaut: Ë	E-umlaut: Ë
CC	E-dot: Ė	I-grave: Ì
CD	I-acute: Í	I-acute: Í
CE	I-circumflex: Î	I-circumflex: Î
CF	I-macron: Ī	I-umlaut: Ï
D0	D-stroke: Đ	G-breve: Ğ
D1	N-cedilla: Ņ	N-tilde: Ñ
D2	O-macron: Ō	O-grave: Ò
D3	K-cedilla: Ķ	O-acute: Ó
D4	O-circumflex: Ô	O-circumflex: Ô
D5	O-tilde: Õ	O-tilde: Õ
D6	O-umlaut: Ö	O-umlaut: Ö
D7	Multiplication: ×	Multiplication: ×
D8	O-slash: Ø	O-slash: Ø
D9	U-ogonek: Ų	U-grave: Ù
DA	U-acute: Ú	U-acute: Ú
DB	U-circumflex: Û	U-circumflex: Û
DC	U-umlaut: Ü	U-umlaut: Ü
DD	U-tilde: Ũ	I-dot: İ
DE	U-macron: Ū	S-cedilla: Ş
DF	German ess: ß	German ess: ß

TABLE 13.16 ISO Standard Alphabets 8859/4 and 8859/9:
Descriptive Listing of Additional Characters Beyond ASCII
(continued)

Hex.	8859/4 Latin Alphabet 4	8859/9 Latin Alphabet 5
E0	a-macron: ā	a-grave: à
E1	a-acute: á	a-acute: á
E2	a-circumflex: â	a-circumflex: â
E3	a-tilde: ã	a-tilde: ã
E4	a-umlaut: ä	a-umlaut: ä
E5	a-ring: å	a-ring: å
E6	æ digraph: æ	æ digraph: æ
E7	i-ogonek: į	c-cedilla: ç
E8	c-caron: č	e-grave: è
E9	e-acute: é	e-acute: é
EA	e-ogonek: ę	e-circumflex: ê
EB	e-umlaut: ë	e-umlaut: ë
EC	e-dot: ė	i-grave: ì
ED	i-acute: í	i-acute: í
EE	i-circumflex: î	i-circumflex: î
EF	i-macron: ī	i-umlaut: ï
F0	d-stroke: đ	g-breve: ğ
F1	n-cedilla: ņ	n-tilde: ñ
F2	o-macron: ō	o-grave: ò
F3	k-cedilla: ķ	o-acute: ó
F4	o-circumflex: ô	o-circumflex: ô
F5	o-tilde: õ	o-tilde: õ
F6	o-umlaut: ö	o-umlaut: ö
F7	Division: ÷	Division ÷
F8	o-slash: ø	o-slash: ø
F9	u-ogonek: ų	u-grave: ù
FA	u-acute: ú	u-acute: ú
FB	u-circumflex: û	u-circumflex: û
FC	u-umlaut: ü	u-umlaut: ü
FD	u-tilde: ũ	i-dotless: ı
FE	u-macron: ū	s-cedilla: ş
FF	Dot: ˙	y-umlaut: ÿ

TABLE 13.17 ISO 8859/5, Latin/Cyrillic Alphabet: Descriptive Listing of Additional Characters Beyond ASCII

Hex.	Character	Hex.	Character	Hex.	Character
A0	No-break space	C0	Er: Р	E0	er: р
A1	Io: Ё	C1	Es: С	E1	es: с
A2	S.C. Dje: Ђ	C2	Te: Т	E2	te: т
A3	Mac. Gje: Ѓ	C3	U: У	E3	u: у
A4	Ukr. Ie: Є	C4	Ef: Ф	E4	ef: ф
A5	Mac. Dze: Ѕ	C5	Ha: Х	E5	ha: х
A6	Bye./Ukr. I: I	C6	Tse: Ц	E6	tse: ц
A7	Ukr. Yi: Ї	C7	Che: Ч	E7	che: ч
A8	Je: Ј	C8	Sha: Ш	E8	sha: ш
A9	Lje: Љ	C9	Shcha: Щ	E9	shcha: щ
AA	Nje: Њ	CA	Hard sign: Ъ	EA	hard sign: ъ
AB	S.C. Tshe: Ћ	CB	Yeru: Ы	EB	yeru: ы
AC	Mac. Kje: Ќ	CC	Soft sign: Ь	EC	soft sign: ь
AD	Soft hyphen	CD	E: Э	ED	e: э
AE	Bye. short U: Ў	CE	Yu: Ю	EE	yu: ю
AF	Dzhe: Џ	CF	Ya: Я	EF	ya: я
B0	A: А	D0	a: а	F0	Number: N°
B1	Be: Б	D1	be: б	F1	io: ё
B2	Ve: В	D2	ve: в	F2	S.C. dje: ђ
B3	Ghe: Г	D3	ghe: г	F3	Mac. gje: ѓ
B4	De: Д	D4	de: д	F4	Ukr. ie: є
B5	Ie: Е	D5	ie: е	F5	Mac. dze: ѕ
B6	Zhe: Ж	D6	zhe: ж	F6	Bye./Ukr. i: i
B7	Ze: З	D7	ze: з	F7	Ukr. yi: ї
B8	I: И	D8	i: и	F8	je: ј
B9	Short I: Й	D9	Short i: й	F9	lje: љ
BA	Ka: К	DA	ka: к	FA	nje: њ
BB	El: Л	DB	el: л	FB	S.C. tshe: ћ
BC	Em: М	DC	em: м	FC	Mac. kje: ќ
BD	En: Н	DD	en: н	FD	Paragraph: §
BE	O: О	DE	o: о	FE	Bye. short u: ў
BF	Pe: П	DF	pe: п	FF	dzhe: џ

Notes: S.C. = Serbo-Croatian, Mac. = Macedonian,
Bye. = Byelorussian, Ukr. = Ukrainian

TABLE 13.18 ISO 8859/6, Latin/Arabic Alphabet: Descriptive Listing of Additional Characters Beyond ASCII

Hex.	Character	Hex.	Character	Hex.	Character
A0	No-break space	C0	*Not defined*	E0	tatweel: ـ
A1	*Not defined*	C1	hamza: ء	E1	feh: ف
A2	*Not defined*	C2	madda on alef: آ	E2	qaf: ق
A3	*Not defined*	C3	hamza on alef: أ	E3	kaf: ك
A4	Currency: ¤	C4	hamza on waw: ؤ	E4	lam: ل
A5	*Not defined*	C5	hamza under alef: إ	E5	meem: م
A6	*Not defined*	C6	hamza on yeh: ئ	E6	noon: ن
A7	*Not defined*	C7	alef: ا	E7	ha: ه
A8	*Not defined*	C8	beh: ب	E8	waw: و
A9	*Not defined*	C9	teh marbuta: ة	E9	alef maksura: ى
AA	*Not defined*	CA	teh: ت	EA	yeh: ي
AB	*Not defined*	CB	theh: ث	EB	fathatan:
AC	Comma: ،	CC	jeem: ج	EC	dammatan:
AD	Soft hyphen	CD	hah: ح	ED	kasratan:
AE	*Not defined*	CE	khah: خ	EE	fatha:
AF	*Not defined*	CF	dal: د	EF	damma:
B0	*Not defined*	D0	thal: ذ	F0	kasra:
B1	*Not defined*	D1	ra: ر	F1	shadda:
B2	*Not defined*	D2	zain: ز	F2	sukun:
B3	*Not defined*	D3	seen: س	F3	*Not defined*
B4	*Not defined*	D4	sheen: ش	F4	*Not defined*
B5	*Not defined*	D5	sad: ص	F5	*Not defined*
B6	*Not defined*	D6	dad: ض	F6	*Not defined*
B7	*Not defined*	D7	tah: ط	F7	*Not defined*
B8	*Not defined*	D8	zah: ظ	F8	*Not defined*
B9	*Not defined*	D9	ain: ع	F9	*Not defined*
BA	*Not defined*	DA	ghain: غ	FA	*Not defined*
BB	Semicolon: ؛	DB	*Not defined*	FB	*Not defined*
BC	*Not defined*	DC	*Not defined*	FC	*Not defined*
BD	*Not defined*	DD	*Not defined*	FD	*Not defined*
BE	*Not defined*	DE	*Not defined*	FE	*Not defined*
BF	Question: ؟	DF	*Not defined*	FF	*Not defined*

TABLE 13.19 ISO 8859/7, Latin/Greek Alphabet: Descriptive Listing of Additional Characters Beyond ASCII

Hex.	Character	Hex.	Character	Hex.	Character
A0	No-break space	C0	iota-d-t: ΐ	E0	upsilon-d-t: ΰ
A1	L. single quote: '	C1	Alpha: A	E1	alpha: α
A2	R. single quote: '	C2	Beta: B	E2	beta: β
A3	Sterling: £	C3	Gamma: Γ	E3	gamma: γ
A4	*Not defined*	C4	Delta: Δ	E4	delta: δ
A5	*Not defined*	C5	Epsilon: E	E5	epsilon: ε
A6	Broken bar: ¦	C6	Zeta: Z	E6	zeta: ζ
A7	Paragraph: §	C7	Eta: H	E7	eta: η
A8	Dialytika: ¨	C8	Theta: Θ	E8	theta: θ
A9	Copyright: ©	C9	Iota: I	E9	iota: ι
AA	*Not defined*	CA	Kappa: K	EA	kappa: κ
AB	L. angle quote: «	CB	Lambda: Λ	EB	lambda: λ
AC	Not sign: ¬	CC	Mu: M	EC	mu: μ
AD	Soft hyphen	CD	Nu: N	ED	nu: ν
AE	*Not defined*	CE	Xi: Ξ	EE	xi: ξ
AF	Horizontal bar:—	CF	Omicron: O	EF	omicron: o
B0	Degree: ¤	D0	Pi: Π	F0	pi: π
B1	Plus/minus: ±	D1	Rho: P	F1	rho: ρ
B2	Super 2: 2	D2	*Not defined*	F2	Terminal sigma: ς
B3	Super 3: 3	D3	Sigma: Σ	F3	sigma: σ
B4	Tonos (accent): '	D4	Tau: T	F4	tau: τ
B5	Dialytika and Tonos: ¨'	D5	Upsilon: Y	F5	upsilon: υ
B6	Alpha-t: Ά	D6	Phi: Φ	F6	phi: φ
B7	Middle dot: ·	D7	Chi: X	F7	chi: χ
B8	Epsilon-t: Έ	D8	Psi: Ψ	F8	psi: ψ
B9	Eta-t: Ή	D9	Omega: Ω	F9	omega: ω
BA	Iota-t: Ί	DA	Iota-d: Ϊ	FA	iota-d: ϊ
BB	R. angle quote: »	DB	Upsilon-d: Ϋ	FB	upsilon-d: ϋ
BC	Omicron-t: Ό	DC	alpha-t: ά	FC	omicron-t: ό
BD	One half: 1/2	DD	epsilon-t: έ	FD	upsilon-t: ύ
BE	Upsilon-t: Ύ	DE	eta-t: ή	FE	omega-t: ώ
BF	Omega-t: Ώ	DF	iota-t: ί	FF	*Not defined*

Notes: -d = letter with dialytika.   -t = letter with tonos.
-d-t = letter with dialytika and tonos.
Dialytika is similar to umlaut.   Tonos is an accent.

TABLE 13.20 ISO 8859/8, Latin/Hebrew Alphabet: Descriptive Listing of Additional Characters Beyond ASCII

Hex.	Character	Hex.	Character	Hex.	Character
A0	No-break space	C0	*Not defined*	E0	aleph: א
A1	*Not defined*	C1	*Not defined*	E1	bet: ב
A2	Cent: ¢	C2	*Not defined*	E2	gimel: ג
A3	Sterling: £	C3	*Not defined*	E3	dalet: ד
A4	Currency: ¤	C4	*Not defined*	E4	he: ה
A5	Yen: ¥	C5	*Not defined*	E5	waw: ו
A6	Broken bar: ¦	C6	*Not defined*	E6	zain: ז
A7	Paragraph: §	C7	*Not defined*	E7	chet: ח
A8	Umlaut: ¨	C8	*Not defined*	E8	tet: ט
A9	Copyright: ©	C9	*Not defined*	E9	yod: י
AA	Multiplication: ×	CA	*Not defined*	EA	Terminal kaph: ך
AB	L. angle quote: «	CB	*Not defined*	EB	kaph: כ
AC	Not sign: ¬	CC	*Not defined*	EC	lamed: ל
AD	Soft hyphen	CD	*Not defined*	ED	Terminal mem: ם
AE	Registered: ®_	CE	*Not defined*	EE	mem: מ
AF	Line above: ‾	CF	*Not defined*	EF	Terminal nun: ן
B0	Degree: °	D0	*Not defined*	F0	nun: נ
B1	Plus/minus: ±	D1	*Not defined*	F1	samech: ס
B2	Super 2: ^{2}	D2	*Not defined*	F2	ayin: ע
B3	Super 3: ^{3}	D3	*Not defined*	F3	Terminal pe: ף
B4	Acute: ´	D4	*Not defined*	F4	pe: פ
B5	Greek mu: μ	D5	*Not defined*	F5	Terminal zade: ץ
B6	Pilcrow: ¶	D6	*Not defined*	F6	zade: צ
B7	Middle dot: ·	D7	*Not defined*	F7	qoph: ק
B8	Cedilla: ¸	D8	*Not defined*	F8	resh: ר
B9	Super 1: ^{1}	D9	*Not defined*	F9	shin: ש
BA	Division: ÷	DA	*Not defined*	FA	taw: ת
BB	R. angle quote: »	DB	*Not defined*	FB	*Not defined*
BC	One fourth: 1/4	DC	*Not defined*	FC	*Not defined*
BD	One half: 1/2	DD	*Not defined*	FD	*Not defined*
BE	Three fourths: 3/4	DE	*Not defined*	FE	*Not defined*
BF	*Not defined*	DF	Double low line:_	FF	*Not defined*

TABLE 13.21   Manufacturers' Extended Character Sets (Alphabetic and Some Punctuation Only)

Character	ISO 8859/1 Latin Alphabet 1	Apple Macintosh	DEC Multinational
a-acute: á	E1	87	E1
A-acute: Á	C1	E7	C1
a-circumflex: â	E2	89	E2
A-circumflex: Â	C2	E5	C2
æ	E6	BE	E6
Æ	C6	AE	C6
a-grave: à	E0	88	E0
A-grave: À	C0	CB	C0
a-ring: å	E5	8C	E5
A-ring: Å	C5	81	C5
a-tilde: ã	E3	8B	E3
A-tilde: Ã	C3	CC	C3
a-umlaut: ä	E4	8A	E4
A-umlaut: Ä	C4	80	C4
c-cedilla: ç	E7	8D	E7
C-cedilla: Ç	C7	82	C7
e-acute: é	E9	8E	E9
E-acute: É	C9	83	C9
e-circumflex: ê	EA	90	EA
E-circumflex: Ê	CA	E6	CA
e-grave: è	E8	8F	E8
E-grave: È	C8	E9	C8
e-umlaut: ë	EB	91	EB
E-umlaut: Ë	CB	E8	CB
i-acute: í	ED	92	ED
I-acute: Í	CD	EA	CD
i-circumflex: î	EE	94	EE
I-circumflex: Î	CE	EB	CE
i-dotless: ı	*Not defined*	F5	*Not defined*
i-grave: ì	EC	93	EC
I-grave: Ì	CC	ED	CC
i-umlaut: ï	EF	95	EF
I-umlaut: Ï	CF	EC	CF
n-tilde: ñ	F1	96	F1
N-tilde: Ñ	D1	84	D1

TABLE 13.21   Manufacturers' Extended Character Sets (Alphabetic and Some Punctuation Only) (continued)

Character	ISO 8859/1 Latin Alphabet 1	Apple Macintosh	DEC Multinational
o-acute: ó	F3	97	F3
O-acute: Ó	D3	EE	D3
o-circumflex: ô	F4	99	F4
O-circumflex: Ô	D4	EF	D4
o-grave: ò	F2	98	F2
O-grave: Ò	D2	F1	D2
o-slash: ø	F8	BF	F8
O-slash: Ø	D8	AF	D8
o-tilde: õ	F5	9B	F5
O-tilde: Õ	D5	CD	D5
o-umlaut: ö	F6	9A	F6
O-umlaut: Ö	D6	85	D6
u-acute: ú	FA	9C	FA
U-acute: Ú	DA	F2	DA
u-circumflex: û	FB	9E	FB
U-circumflex: Û	DB	F3	DB
u-grave: ù	F9	9D	F9
U-grave: Ù	D9	F4	D9
u-umlaut: ü	FC	9F	FC
U-umlaut: Ü	DC	86	DC
y-acute: ý	FD	*Not defined*	*Not defined*
Y-acute: Ý	DD	*Not defined*	*Not defined*
y-umlaut: ÿ	FF	D8	FD
Y-umlaut: Ÿ	*Not defined*	D9	DD
German ess: ß	DF	A7	DF

TABLE 13.21   Manufacturers' Extended Character Sets (Alphabetic and Some Punctuation Only) (continued)

Character	ISO 8859/1 Latin Alphabet 1	Apple Macintosh	DEC Multinational
α	Not defined	Not defined	Not defined
β	Not defined	Not defined	Not defined
δ	Not defined	Not defined	Not defined
ε	Not defined	Not defined	Not defined
φ	Not defined	Not defined	Not defined
Φ	Not defined	Not defined	Not defined
Γ	Not defined	Not defined	Not defined
μ	B5	B5	B5
π	Not defined	B9	Not defined
σ	Not defined	Not defined	Not defined
Σ	Not defined	B7	Not defined
τ	Not defined	Not defined	Not defined
Θ	Not defined	Not defined	Not defined
Ω	Not defined	BD	Not defined
Icelandic eth: ð	F0	Not defined	Not defined
Icelandic Eth: Ð	D0	Not defined	Not defined
Icelandic thorn: þ	FE	Not defined	Not defined
Icelandic Thorn: Þ	DE	Not defined	Not defined
£	A3	A3	A3
¥	A5	B4	A5
º	BA	BC	BA
ª	AA	BB	AA
¡	A1	C1	A1
¿	BF	C0	BF

TABLE 13.22 IBM PC and PS/2 Extended Character Sets (Alphabetic and Some Punctuation Only)

Character	CP437	CP850	CP860	CP863	CP865
a-acute: á	A0	A0	A0	Not defined	A0
A-acute: Á	Not defined	B5	86	Not defined	Not defined
a-circumflex: â	83	83	83	83	83
A-circumflex: Â	Not defined	B6	8F	84	Not defined
æ	91	91	Not defined	Not defined	91
Æ	92	92	Not defined	Not defined	92
a-grave: à	85	85	85	85	85
A-grave: À	Not defined	B7	91	8E	Not defined
a-ring: å	86	86	Not defined	Not defined	86
A-ring: Å	8F	8F	Not defined	Not defined	8F
a-tilde: ã	Not defined	C6	84	Not defined	Not defined
A-tilde: Ã	Not defined	C7	8E	Not defined	Not defined
a-umlaut: ä	84	84	Not defined	Not defined	84
A-umlaut: Ä	8E	8E	Not defined	Not defined	8E
c-cedilla: ç	87	87	87	87	87
C-cedilla: Ç	80	80	80	80	80
e-acute: é	82	82	82	82	82
E-acute: É	90	90	90	90	90
e-circumflex: ê	88	88	88	88	88
E-circumflex: Ê	Not defined	D2	89	92	Not defined
e-grave: è	8A	8A	8A	8A	8A
E-grave: È	Not defined	D4	92	91	Not defined
e-umlaut: ë	89	89	Not defined	89	89
E-umlaut: Ë	Not defined	D3	Not defined	94	Not defined
i-acute: í	A1	A1	A1	Not defined	A1
I-acute: Í	Not defined	D6	8B	Not defined	Not defined
i-circumflex: î	8C	8C	Not defined	8C	8C
I-circumflex: Î	Not defined	D7	Not defined	A8	Not defined
i-dotless: ı	Not defined	D5	Not defined	Not defined	Not defined
i-grave: ì	8D	8D	8D	Not defined	8D
I-grave: Ì	Not defined	DE	98	Not defined	Not defined
i-umlaut: ï	8B	8B	Not defined	8B	8B
I-umlaut: Ï	Not defined	D8	Not defined	95	Not defined
n-tilde: ñ	A4	A4	A4	Not defined	A4
N-tilde: Ñ	A5	A5	A5	Not defined	A5

TABLE 13.22 IBM PC and PS/2 Extended Character Sets (Alphabetic and Some Punctuation Only) (continued)

Character	CP437	CP850	CP860	CP863	CP865
o-acute: ó	A2	A2	A2	A2	A2
O-acute: Ó	*Not defined*	E0	9F	*Not defined*	*Not defined*
o-circumflex: ô	93	93	93	93	93
O-circumflex: Ô	*Not defined*	E2	8C	99	*Not defined*
o-grave: ò	95	95	95	*Not defined*	95
O-grave: Ò	*Not defined*	E3	A9	*Not defined*	*Not defined*
o-slash: ø	*Not defined*	9B	*Not defined*	*Not defined*	9B
O-slash: Ø	*Not defined*	9D	*Not defined*	*Not defined*	9D
o-tilde: õ	*Not defined*	E4	94	*Not defined*	*Not defined*
O-tilde: Õ	*Not defined*	E5	99	*Not defined*	*Not defined*
o-umlaut: ö	94	94	*Not defined*	*Not defined*	94
O-umlaut: Ö	99	99	*Not defined*	*Not defined*	99
u-acute: ú	A3	A3	A3	A3	A3
U-acute: Ú	*Not defined*	E9	96	*Not defined*	*Not defined*
u-circumflex: û	96	96	*Not defined*	96	96
U-circumflex: Û	*Not defined*	EA	*Not defined*	9E	*Not defined*
u-grave: ù	97	97	97	97	97
U-grave: Ù	*Not defined*	EB	9D	9D	*Not defined*
u-umlaut: ü	81	81	81	81	81
U-umlaut: Ü	9A	9A	9A	9A	9A
y-acute: ý	*Not defined*	EC	*Not defined*	*Not defined*	*Not defined*
Y-acute: Ý	*Not defined*	ED	*Not defined*	*Not defined*	*Not defined*
y-umlaut: ÿ	98	98	*Not defined*	*Not defined*	98
Y-umlaut:	*Not defined*	*Not defined*	*Not defined*	*Not defined*	*Not defined*
German ess: ß	*Not defined*	E1	*Not defined*	*Not defined*	*Not defined*

TABLE 13.22 IBM PC and PS/2 Extended Character Sets (Alphabetic and Some Punctuation Only) (continued)

Character	CP437	CP850	CP860	CP863	CP865
α	E0	*Not defined*	E0	E0	E0
β	E1	*Not defined*	E1	E1	E1
δ	EB	*Not defined*	EB	EB	EB
ε	EE	*Not defined*	EE	EE	EE
φ	ED	*Not defined*	ED	ED	ED
Φ	E8	*Not defined*	E8	E8	E8
Γ	E2	*Not defined*	E2	E2	E2
μ	E6	E6	E6	E6	E6
π	E3	*Not defined*	E3	E3	E3
σ	E5	*Not defined*	E5	E5	E5
Σ	E4	*Not defined*	E4	E4	E4
τ	E7	*Not defined*	E7	E7	E7
Θ	E9	*Not defined*	E9	E9	E9
Ω	EA	*Not defined*	EA	EA	EA
Icelandic eth: ð	*Not defined*	D0	*Not defined*	*Not defined*	*Not defined*
Icelandic Eth: Ð	*Not defined*	D1	*Not defined*	*Not defined*	*Not defined*
Icelandic thorn: þ	*Not defined*	E7	*Not defined*	*Not defined*	*Not defined*
Icelandic Thorn: Þ	*Not defined*	E8	*Not defined*	*Not defined*	*Not defined*
£	9C	9C	9C	9C	9C
¥	9D	BE	*Not defined*	*Not defined*	*Not defined*
º	A6	A6	A6	*Not defined*	A6
ª	A7	A7	A7	*Not defined*	A7
¡	AD	AD	AD	*Not defined*	AD
¿	A8	A8	A8	*Not defined*	A8

TABLE 13.23 Baudot Code

Lowercase	Uppercase	Baudot code
A	-	00011
B	?	11001
C	:	01110
D	$	01001
E	3	00001
F	!	01101
G	&	11010
H	#	10100
I	8	00110
J	'	01011
K	(	01111
L	)	10010
M	.	11100
N	,	01100
O	9	11000
P	0	10110
Q	1	10111
R	4	01010
S	BELL	00101
T	5	10000
U	7	00111
V	;	11110
W	2	10011
X	/	11101
Y	6	10101
Z	"	10001
Shift to lowercase		11111
Shift to uppercase		11011
Space		00100
Carriage-return		01000
Line-feed		00010
Blank		00000

TABLE 13.24 Binary Codes for Decimal Digits

Decimal digit	BCD 8421	2421	Excess-3	Gray code	Gray code excess 3
0	0000	0000	0011	0000	0010
1	0001	0001	0100	0001	0110
2	0010	0010	0101	0011	0111
3	0011	0011	0110	0010	0101
4	0100	0100	0111	0110	0100
5	0101	1011	1000	0111	1100
6	0110	1100	1001	0101	1101
7	0111	1101	1010	0100	1111
8	1000	1110	1011	1100	1110
9	1001	1111	1100	1101	1010

BCD = binary coded decimal. Note that in the 2421 and excess 3 codes, the 9's complement of a number is obtained by changing 1's to 0's and 0's to 1's.

13.9 Letter Frequency

Those who are concerned with character coding and text transmission may be interested in the statistics of letter frequencies in English and other languages. This information is particularly useful in the fields of cryptography and data compression (e.g., Huffman coding).

Many investigators have compiled tables of letter distributions in English, and different compilations tend to differ from each other. However, some broad features are agreed upon by nearly everyone. In English, "E" is always the most frequent letter, followed by "T." The third most common letter is usually "A" or "O." The same nine letters almost always top the frequency list.

Tables 13.25 and 13.26 below were compiled by Gaines (1939), and quoted by Salomaa (1990).

TABLE 13.25 Letter Frequency Distributions in English

Highest-frequency Letter	%	Medium-frequency Letter	%	Low-frequency Letter	%
E	12.31	L	4.03	B	1.62
T	9.59	D	3.65	G	1.61
A	8.05	C	3.20	V	0.93
O	7.94	U	3.10	K	0.52
N	7.19	P	2.29	Q	0.20
I	7.18	F	2.28	X	0.20
S	6.59	M	2.25	J	0.10
R	6.03	W	2.03	Z	0.09
H	5.14	Y	1.88		

TABLE 13.26 Highest-Frequency Letters in Various Languages

German Letter	%	French Letter	%	Spanish Letter	%
E	18.46	E	15.87	E	13.15
N	11.42	A	9.42	A	12.69
I	8.02	I	8.41	O	9.49
R	7.14	S	7.90	S	7.60
S	7.04	T	7.26	N	6.95
A	5.38	N	7.15	R	6.25
T	5.22	R	6.46	I	6.25
U	5.01	U	6.24	L	5.94
D	4.94	L	5.34	D	5.58

TABLE 13.26 Highest-Frequency Letters in Various Languages (continued)

Italian Letter	%	Finnish Letter	%
E	11.79	A	12.06
A	11.74	I	10.59
I	11.28	T	9.76
O	9.83	N	8.64
N	6.88	E	8.11
L	6.51	S	7.83
R	6.37	L	5.86
T	5.62	O	5.54
S	4.98	K	5.20

13.10   Digital Typography

Digital typography is not related directly to character coding, but because both it and character coding are so important for documents, and because the advent of desktop publishing has increased the need for information on digital typography, we include this discussion. Years ago, a computer user had no need to know anything of points, picas, fonts, or any of the other obscure concepts of typography. Typography was an arcane art, known only to copy editors, compositors, and proofreaders. However, these days almost every computer user has become something of a digital typographer.

There is still confusion in the minds of many people over the exact meanings of terms in typography. Typography is an art and science with centuries of tradition, and many of the terms have nothing to do with today's technology: they have an explicit origin in the days when letterforms were actually cast on to small lead blocks that would be inked and come into direct contact with the paper.

13.10.1   Units

Typographer's units are really nothing more than obscurely termed measures of *length*. The basic unit of measurement in typography in English-speaking countries is the *point*, with one inch equalling 72.27 points. The term *pica* is also used, and one pica equals 12 points. In Continental Europe, most measurements are now expressed simply in *millimeters*. However, an older unit called the *Didot point* may still be used, with one Didot point being slightly larger than an English-American point (1 Didot point = 1.07 points). The Continental analog of the pica is the *cicero*, with one cicero equalling 12 Didot points. The Japanese unit for typesetting is the "Q," equal to 0.25 mm. The conversion table below, Table 13.27, summarizes the relationships. Note that "A = B times some number" means: "to get the value of some quantity in unit A, multiply its value in unit B by some number." Thus, if a measurement is given in inches and we wish it in points, we must multiply by 72.27.

TABLE 13.27   Conversion Between Typographical Units

A = B times:	A	B	B = A times:
0.0393701	Inch	Millimeter	25.4
72.27	Point	Inch	0.013837
2.659136	Didot Point	Millimeter	0.37606
1.07	Point	Didot Point	0.934579
12	Point	Pica	0.083333
12	Didot Point	Cicero	0.083333
4	Japanese Q	Millimeter	0.25

Notes: Multiply quantity in unit B by the leftmost number in the table to obtain value expressed in unit A. For example, multiply quantity expressed in inches by 72.27 to obtain that quantity expressed in points. Likewise, multiply quantities expressed in unit A by the rightmost number in the table to obtain quantity expressed in unit B.

13.10.2   Other Typographic Terminology

Figure 13.2 illustrates the definition of several other terms used in typography.

Fig. 13.2 Illustration of typographical terminology.

A common misconception is that, say, a "12-point font" has a cap height equal to 12 points. In fact, the cap-height in a 12-point font is likely to be closer to 8 points. The concept of a *point size* comes to us from the lead-block days: the point size was the size of the actual pieces of lead used to hold the letters! Thus, the point size is something close to the maximum descent plus the maximum ascent plus any leftover lead. The "maximum ascent" may be the cap height, or it may be greater than the cap height, since in some fonts a few letters might be taller than capitals. The "b" in the figure above could conceivably be taller than the "F" in some typefaces, although we did not draw it that way.

Another concept that bears clarification is that of *leading*. This refers to the amount of extra interline spacing, beyond what would be obtained by letting successive lines of lead blocks touch each other. In this book, for example, the main font (which you are now reading) is 10-point New Century Schoolbook. Adjacent baselines are not 10 points apart, however, but 12 points apart. We say that there are 2 points of leading. The font is often denoted as 10/12 New Century Schoolbook.

13.10.3   Resolution

The quality of a typeface's appearance is intimately related to the resolution of the output device with which it is displayed. There are many different types of resolution. *Addressing resolution* tells us how many dot positions a given device can specify—e.g., 512 x 512 pixels. Addressing resolution does not specify the size of the pixels. *Spatial resolution* (sometimes called *addressability*) specifies the number of pixels per unit length, and is expressed typically as *dots per inch (dpi)*, or *dots per millimeter*. *Spot size* specifies the size of the smallest dot or spot that can be drawn by the output device. Conceivably, an output device might have excellent spatial resolution and a relatively large spot size, in which case adjacent spots may overlap. This may be a problem, or it may be used in some cases to advantage. Perceived resolution in dpi is thus determined by the spot size.

It is difficult to give rules of thumb, but we might safely state that type displayed at resolutions of 1200 dpi or greater (i.e., the resolution of a digital typesetter) will be of excellent quality, and type displayed at 600 dpi or so will be very good. At 300 dpi (the resolution of a medium-quality laser-printer such as the Apple Laserwriter), type should also look reasonably good. Type displayed at resolutions from 50 to 200 dpi is likely to be of fair quality. At resolutions lower than 50 dpi, type may still be legible, but will be of poor quality.

13.10.4 Representation of Fonts

Fonts may be represented in a number of ways, including bit maps, outline codes, and others. In a bit-mapped representation, each character is represented by a grid of 1's and 0's, with 1's (say) representing black, and 0's representing white. This simple representation is attractive because of its generality—any graphic object from line drawings to half-tones can be represented in this way, resulting in a complete equivalence between type and graphics. However, bit-mapped fonts are expensive to scale up and down, and require large amounts of storage (order n^2, where n is the size of the character). Outline-coded fonts using (for example) splines to represent the actual shape (outline) of each character are easy to scale up or down; the amount of storage does not depend on the size of the character involved. Postscript fonts are outline-coded and fully scalable.

13.11 List of Standards Relating to Character Codes

ANSI X3.4 (1986)	7-Bit American National Standard Code for Information Interchange (ASCII).
ISO 646 (1983)	ISO 7-Bit Coded Character Set for Information Interchange. (Same as ANSI x3.4-1986, with provisions for national variations in character sets.)
ANSI X3.41 (1974)	Code extension techniques for use with the 7-Bit American National Standard

	Code for Information Interchange (ASCII).
ANSI X3.64 (1979)	Additional controls for use with the American National Standard Code for Information Interchange (ASCII).
ANSI X3.32 (1973)	Graphic Representation of the Control Characters of the American national Standard Code for Information Interchange (ASCII). [*Note:* ISO 2047 (1975) is essentially identical.]
ANSI X3.42 (1975)	Representation of Numeric Values in Character Strings for Information Interchange (ASCII).
ISO 6937/1 (1983)	Coded Character Sets for Text Communication. Part 1: General Introduction.
ISO 6937/2 (1983)	Coded Character Sets for Text Communication. Part 2: Latin Alphabetic and Non-Alphabetic Graphic Characters.
ISO 8859/1 (1987)	8-Bit Single-Byte Coded Graphic Character Sets. Part 1: Latin Alphabet No. 1.
ISO 8859/2 (1987)	8-Bit Single-Byte Coded Graphic Character Sets. Part 2: Latin Alphabet No. 2.
ISO 8859/3 (1988)	8-Bit Single-Byte Coded Graphic Character Sets. Part 3: Latin Alphabet No. 3.
ISO 8859/4 (1988)	8-Bit Single-Byte Coded Graphic Character Sets. Part 4: Latin Alphabet No. 4.

ISO 8859/5 (1988)	8-Bit Single-Byte Coded Graphic Character Sets. Part 5: Latin/Cyrillic Alphabet.
ISO 8859/6 (1987)	8-Bit Single-Byte Coded Graphic Character Sets. Part 6: Latin/Arabic Alphabet.
ISO 8859/7 (1987)	8-Bit Single-Byte Coded Graphic Character Sets. Part 7: Latin/Greek Alphabet.
ISO 8859/8 (1988)	8-Bit Single-Byte Coded Graphic Character Sets. Part 8: Latin/Hebrew Alphabet.
ISO 8859/9 (1989)	8-Bit Single-Byte Coded Graphic Character Sets. Part 9: Latin Alphabet No. 5.
ISO 2022 (1986)	ISO 7-Bit and 8-Bit Coded Character Sets—Code Extension Techniques, 3rd Edition.
ISO/IEC DP10646	Draft Proposal for a Multiple Octet Coded Character Set (Reference Number ISO/IEC JTC1/SC2N, 1989-01-17, ISO).

13.12 Bibliography

There are few books treating the topic of character coding; one is the short work by Maslin et al. (1984). Important information can be found in the research papers by d'Cruz et al. (1988), Jerman-Blazic (1988), and Lua (1990).

An excellent reference for digital typography is Rubinstein (1989). Donald Knuth's massive "Computers and Typesetting" series, particularly Knuth (1986a,b), is indispensible for the serious student of typography. Van Vliet (1988) and André and Hersch (1989) are good compilations of recent research. Adobe (1990) describes the format of Adobe postscript fonts.

Adobe Systems Inc. (1990), *Adobe Type I Font Format, Version 1.1*, Addison-Wesley, Menlo Park, California.

André, J., and R. D. Hersch, *Raster Imaging and Digital Typography*, Cambridge University Press, New York, New York.

d'Cruz, M., E. Kulinek, and E. Lee (1988), "Character Sets of Today and Tomorrow," *Computer Standards and Interfaces* 8, 199–208.

Gaines, H. F. (1939), *Cryptoanalysis*, Dover, New York, New York.

Gianone, C. (1990), *Using MS-DOS Kermit*, Digital Press, Bedford, Massachusetts.

Jerman-Blazic, B. (1988), "Will the Multi-Octet Standard Character Set Code Solve the World Coding Problems for Information Interchange?" *Computer Standards and Interfaces* 8, 127–136.

Knuth, D. D. (1986a), *The METAFONT Book*, Computers and Typesetting Volume B, Addison-Wesley, Menlo Park, California.

Knuth, D. D. (1986b), *Computer Modern Typefaces*, Computers and Typesetting Volume E, Addison-Wesley, Menlo Park, California.

Lua, K. T. (1990), "A Proposal for Multilingual Computing Code Standardization," *Computer Standards and Interfaces* 10, 117–124.

Maslin, J. M., C. A. Cameron, M. Thomson, and M. Y. Gates (1984), *A Study of Character Sets and Coding* (prepared for the Commission of the European Communities), Learned Information Inc., Medford, New Jersey.

Rubinstein, R. D. (1989), *Digital Typography*, Addison-Wesley, Menlo Park, California.

Salomaa, A. (1990), *Public-Key Cryptography*, Springer Verlag, Berlin.

Van Vliet, J. C. (1988), *Document Manipulation and Typography*, Cambridge University Press, New York, New York.

14

Floating-Point Format

Floating-point numbers are generally represented in a computer as
$$N = M r^E$$
where N is the number, M is the mantissa, r is the radix, and E is the exponent. A floating-point format specifies a radix (usually 2 these days), and also how many bits are allocated to the exponent and to the mantissa. Typically, the mantissa is represented as an unsigned value, with a special bit (the sign bit) allocated to determine the sign of the number to be represented.

There are many different floating-point formats. Until recently, there was no accepted standard to follow. In 1985, however, a standard for binary floating-point arithmetic was published by the IEEE [ANSI/IEEE 754 (1985)], and now many manufacturers are striving for compatibility with this standard. We can thus expect some convergence in the representation of floating-point numbers in the future, although differences are likely to persist, particularly since some of the specifications of ANSI/IEEE 754 are minima that may be exceeded.

14.1   Precision and Range

Since the IEEE standard is a radix-2 (binary) standard, we will assume a radix of 2 in what follows. A basic property of a floating-point representation that may be of interest to computer users is the *precision* of the representation. This is the minimum difference between two mantissa representations, and is equal to the value of the least significant bit of the mantissa. The precision can be represented as

Precision $= 2^{-p}$

where p is the number of bits allocated to represent the mantissa. Another property of interest is the *range* of numbers that can be represented by the format. The largest and smallest numbers that can be represented are given by:

Maximum $= 2^{E_{max}} (1 - 2^{-p})$

Minimum $= 2^{(E_{min} - 1)}$

where E_{max} and E_{min} are, respectively, the largest and smallest exponents. Note that the numbers above are really the largest and smallest *positive* numbers that can be represented. Typically, their negative analogs can also be represented.

14.2   Bias

In evaluating the information below, it is necessary to understand the meaning of exponent *bias*. Both positive and negative exponents must be represented, but floating-point formats do not generally provide a sign bit for the exponent the way they do for the mantissa. Rather, a biased exponent is used, such that

Biased exponent $=$ Exponent + Bias

In this way, both positive and negative exponents are represented by a positive range of exponent values. Provisions are also made for certain values of the biased exponent to represent $\pm\infty$ and ±0. In this chapter, we use the lowercase symbol e to represent biased exponents, and the uppercase symbol E to represent regular exponents.

14.3   ANSI/IEEE Single-Precision Formats

The ANSI/IEEE standard 754 provides for a basic single-precision format and an extended single-precision format. The basic format is just called the "single" format, and it is quite rigidly specified. The "single extended" format, on the other hand, only provides guidelines and minimum specifications, and implementations of the standard may vary.

The basic "single" format is 32 bits wide, with the following three fields:

One-bit sign s

8-bit biased exponent e with bias $= 127$ ($e = E + $ Bias)

23-bit mantissa M.

The single format also has the following properties:

E_{max} = +127

E_{min} = −126

Exponent bias = +127

Largest representable number = 1.7×10^{38}

Smallest representable number = 5.877×10^{-39}

Precision = 1.19×10^{-7}

The number N represented is evaluated according to the following rules (e is the biased exponent):

If e = 255 and $M \neq 0$, then N is NaN (not a number).

If e = 255 and $M = 0$, then $N = (-1)^s \infty$.

If $0 < e < 255$, then $N = (-1)^s 2^{(e-127)} (1.M)$.

If $e = 0$ and $M \neq 0$, then $N = (-1)^s 2^{-126} (0.M)$.

If $e = 0$ and $M = 0$, then $N = (-1)^s 0$ (i.e., ±0).

The single-extended format is at least 43 bits wide, subject to the following constraints:

Number of bits in mantissa ≥ 32 (including sign bit)

Number of bits in exponent ≥ 11

$E_{max} \geq +1023$

$E_{min} \leq -1022$

Exponent bias: Unspecified

14.4   ANSI/IEEE Double-Precision Formats

The ANSI/IEEE standard provides for a basic double-precision format and an extended double-precision format. As in the case of single-precision, the basic "double" format is rigidly specified, while the "double extended" format allows leeway in implementation.

The basic "double" format is 64 bits wide, with the following three fields:

One-bit sign s

11-bit biased exponent e with bias = 1023 ($e = E + $Bias)

52-bit mantissa M

The double format also has the following properties:

E_{max} = +1023

E_{min} = −1022

Exponent bias = +1023

Largest representable number = 0.9×10^{308}

Smallest representable number = 0.1×10^{-307}

Precision = 2.2×10^{-16}

The number N represented is evaluated according to the following rules (e is the biased exponent):

If e = 2047 and $M \neq 0$, then N is NaN (not a number).

If e = 2047 and M = 0, then N = $(-1)^s \infty$.

If $0 < e < 2047$, then N = $(-1)^s 2^{(e - 1023)} (1.M)$.

If e = 0 and $M \neq 0$, then N = $(-1)^s 2^{-1022} (0.M)$.

If e = 0 and M = 0, then N = $(-1)^s 0$ (i.e., ±0).

The double-extended format is at least 79 bits wide, subject to the following constraints:

Number of bits in mantissa ≥ 64 (including sign bit)

Number of bits in exponent ≥ 15

E_{max} ≥ +16383

E_{min} ≤ −16382

Exponent bias: Unspecified

14.5   List of Floating-Point Standards

ANSI/IEEE 754 (1985)   Binary Floating-Point Arithmetic.

ANSI/IEEE 854 (1988)   A Radix-Independent Standard for Floating-Point Arithmetic.

14.6   Bibliography

A good discussion of the principles of floating-point computation and floating-point formats can be found in Waser and Flynn (1982). Waser and Flynn provide some discussion of the IEEE standard, although at the time their book was published, the standard had not yet been finalized. Wallis (1990), a work devoted mostly to recent research in floating-point programming, provides a more up-to-date treatment of the standard.

Wallis, P. J. L. (1990), *Improving Floating-Point Programming*, John Wiley & Sons, New York, New York.

Waser, S., and Flynn, M. J. (1982), *Introduction to Arithmetic for Digital Systems Designers*, Holt, Rinehart, and Winston, San Francisco, California.

15

Network Standards

15.1 Open Systems Interconnection (OSI) Model

The Open Systems Interconnection (OSI) model conceptually divides the communication process into seven discrete functional layers. The structure is hierarchical. Higher layers embody increasing levels of abstraction. Each layer provides services to the layer above, and uses the services of the layer below to provide communications to its counterpart layer in some other communicating node. The interfaces between the layers are well-defined, so that changes in technology will hopefully not cause a complete reorganization of the entire model. For example, if a cable network is replaced by a fiber-optic network, only the specifications of the lowest (physical) layer will have to be changed, and the upper layers can function as before. The layers are as follows, from lowest to highest level:

1. Physical layer   The physical layer is concerned with the extremely-low-level details of the communications process. A specification of the physical layer will involve actual electrical characteristics, modulation mechanisms, physical interface details, etc. The EIA's famous RS-232 serial interface is an example of the type of specification that might belong in the physical layer.

2. Data link layer	The data link layer adds such services as error detection, maintenance of flow control, maintenance of data sequencing, etc. It may also organize data into blocks, packets, messages, or some other format.
3. Network layer	The network layer provides sufficient addressing features to enable a message to be directed to any other part of the network (or networks).
4. Transport layer	The transport layer guarantees end-to-end message delivery across the network(s).
5. Session layer	The session layer establishes a communication session. In order to do this, it may accomplish such goals as determining the type of interaction (for example, two-way simultaneous interaction vs two-way alternate interaction).
6. Presentation layer	The presentation layer determines the representation of data. For example, the presentation layer may determine whether data are encoded as ASCII or EBCDIC. If the applications on the communicating nodes do not use the same data representation, the presentation layer may provide the necessary translation.
7. Applications layer	The applications layer constitutes the interface between application programs and the network.

The first three layers (physical, data link, and network) operate on a point-by-point basis. A node acting as a relay between two networks operates only up to the network layer. The first four layers, up to and including the transport layer, actually constitute a complete communications service. The upper three layers are applications-oriented. It is worth noting that the highest level of application program, that employed directly by the user, is considered to be outside the scope of the OSI model—it is above the seventh layer. However, unlike the internal interlayer interfaces of the model, the top of the applications layer is not well delineated. For example, common services such as file transfer and terminal emulation generally are considered to reside in the applications layer, even though one could reasonably argue that such services are actually user applications.

Another point worth noting is that OSI by itself only provides an overall framework in which to place communication protocols. In each layer, however, there are several protocols from which one can choose. Thus, two networking products could conceivably conform fully to the OSI reference model and still not be able to talk to each other. SPAG, the Standards Promotion and Applications Group (a

European users' organization which works with CEN, CENELEC, and EWOS), has developed a number of *profiles*. Each profile embodies selections of appropriate protocols at each layer. Two products conforming to the same profile should be able to internetwork successfully.

15.2 TCP/IP and the OSI Model

Although the OSI model has received much enthusiasm on a conceptual level, wholesale compliance has not been achieved. Conversion can be difficult, and older technology that does not fit exactly into the framework is likely to remain in use for a considerable period of time. There are many protocols and internetworking schemes in existence. One of the most important is the TCP/IP series of protocols (Rose, 1991; Comer, 1991), used on the Internet. The Internet is a global collection of interconnected networks. It began in the United States with funding from the United States Department of Defense. It is popularly and erroneously still known as the ARPANET, although it is much more extensive than the original ARPANET (see Chap. 9).

The Internet model can also be viewed conceptually as a series of layers, although they are not exactly the same layers as those in the OSI model. The transmission control protocol (TCP) resides in the Internet's "transport layer," which is similar in scope to the transport layer of OSI. The Internet protocol (IP) resides in the Internet's "internet layer." This corresponds roughly to the upper part of the OSI network layer. Quarterman and Hoskins (1986) have published a table comparing the conceptual layers of the Internet to those of the OSI model. Figure 15.1 has been drawn with the aid of Quarterman and Hoskin's comparison.

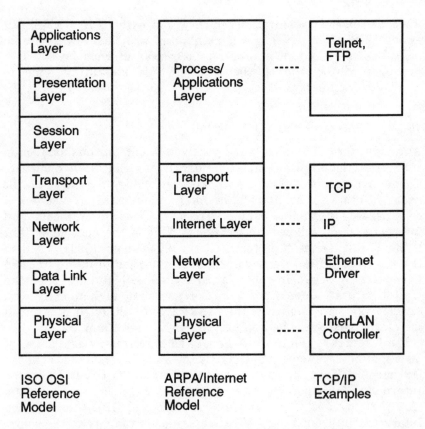

Fig. 15.1 ISO OSI and ARPA/Internet reference models.

15.3   IEEE Local Area Network Standards

An important step in network standardization was achieved by the IEEE in its 802 series. The IEEE 802 series of standards has largely been adopted by the ISO as the 8802 series. While the IEEE was concerned specifically with local area networks (LANs), such networks can be related conceptually to the lower layers of the overall OSI model. The IEEE strived for as much compatibility as possible with the OSI framework. However, the IEEE felt the need to subdivide the data-link layer into two sublayers, in order to allow for different link configurations.

The two sublayers are the medium access control (MAC) sublayer and the logical link control (LLC) sublayer. The LLC is the higher layer, and was standardized as IEEE 802.2. Thus the LLC was designed to be independent of specific access protocols; all the protocol specificity was placed in MAC. The various choices for access methods in the MAC include Carrier-Sense Multiple Access (IEEE 802.3), Token Bus (IEEE 802.4), Token Ring (IEEE 802.5), and Metropolitan Area (IEEE 802.6). The relationship of the IEEE 802 series of LAN standards to the lower layers of the OSI framework is illustrated in Fig. 15.12.

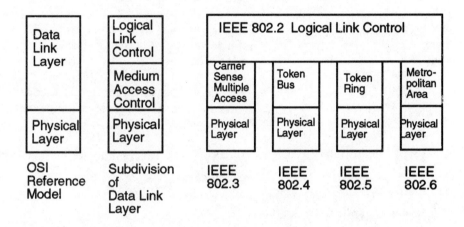

Fig. 15.12 Relationship between IEEE 802 standards and ISO OSI model.

15.4 List of Network Standards

Below we list many pertinent network standards, concentrating on international standards. The various standards are classified according to which layer of the OSI reference model they address. IEEE network standards, for example, are listed in the data-link layer. Many of the fundamental data-communication interface standards (e.g., RS-232) that belong in the physical layer are listed in Chap. 17.

The reader should note that there are also several CCITT X-Series recommendations relating to OSI; some of these are noted below. A full list of CCITT X- and V-Series recommendations can be found in Chap. 17.

15.4.1   General OSI Reference Model

ISO 7498 (1984)	Open Systems Interconnection. Basic Reference Model (corrected 1988).
ISO 7498-2 (1989)	Open Systems Interconnection. Basic Reference Model, Part 2: Security Architecture.
ISO 7498-3 (1989)	Open Systems Interconnection. Basic Reference Model, Part 3: Naming and Addressing.
ISO 7498-4 (1989)	Open Systems Interconnection. Basic Reference Model, Part 4: Management Framework.
ISO TR8509 (1987)	Open Systems Interconnection. Service Conventions.

15.4.2   Application Layer

ISO 8571-1 (1988)	Open Systems Interconnection. File Transfer, Access, and Management, Part 1: General Introduction.
ISO 8571-2 (1988)	Open Systems Interconnection. File Transfer, Access, and Management, Part 2: Virtual Filestore Definition.
ISO 8571-3 (1988)	Open Systems Interconnection. File Transfer, Access, and Management, Part 3: File Service Definition.
ISO 8571-4 (1988)	Open Systems Interconnection. File Transfer, Access, and Management, Part 4: File Protocol Specification.
ISO 8649 (1988)	Open Systems Interconnection. Service Definition for the Association Control Service Element.

ISO 8650 (1988)	Open Systems Interconnection. Protocol Specification for the Association Control Service Element.
ISO 8831 (1989)	Open Systems Interconnection. Job Transfer and Manipulation Concepts and Services.
ISO 8832 (1989)	Open Systems Interconnection. Specification of the Basic Class Protocol for Job Transfer and Manipulation.
ISO TR9007 (1987)	Concepts and Terminology for the Conceptual Schema and the Information Base.
ISO 9545 (1989)	Open Systems Interconnection. Application Layer Structure.

Also relevant: CCITT Recommendation X.400 provides another example of an application-level protocol. See Chap. 17 for a listing of CCITT recommendations.

15.4.3 Session Layer

ISO 8326 (1987)	Open Systems Interconnection. Basic Connection Oriented Session Service Definition.
ISO 8327 (1987)	Open Systems Interconnection. Basic Connection Oriented Session Protocol Specification.
ISO 8822 (1988)	Open Systems Interconnection. Connection Oriented Presentation Service Definition.
ISO 8823 (1988)	Open Systems Interconnection. Connection Oriented Presentation Protocol Specification.

ISO 8824 (1987)   Open   Systems   Interconnection.
                                Specification of Abstract Syntax
                                Notation One (ASN.1).

ISO 8825 (1987)   Open   Systems   Interconnection.
                                Specification of Basic Encoding Rules
                                for Abstract Syntax Notation One
                                (ASN.1).

Also relevant: CCITT Recommendations X.215 and X.225. See
Chap. 17.

15.4.4   Transport Layer

ISO 8072 (1986)   Open   Systems   Interconnection.
                                Transport Service Definition.

ISO 8073 (1988)   Open   Systems   Interconnection.
                                Connection Oriented Transport Protocol
                                Specification.

ISO 8073 Corrigendum 1 (1990)

ISO 8073 Addendum 2 (1989)
                                Class   Four   Operation   Over
                                Connectionless Network Service.

ISO 8602 (1987)   Open Systems Interconnection. Protocol
                                for Providing the Connectionless Mode
                                Transport Service.

Also relevant: CCITT Recommendations X.214 and X.224. See
Chap. 17 for listing of CCITT recommendations.

15.4.5   Network Layer

ISO 8208 (1987)   Data Communications.   X.25 Packet
                                Level Protocol for Data Terminal
                                Equipment.

ISO 9574 (1989)   Telecommunications and Information
                                Exchange Between Systems. Provision

of the OSI Connection-Mode Network Service by Packet Mode Terminal Equipment Connected to an Integrated Services Digital Network (ISDN).

15.4.6 Data-Link Layer

ISO 1745 (1975)	Basic Mode Control Procedures for Data Communications Systems.
ISO 3309 (1984)	Data Communication. High Level Data Link Control Procedures, Frame Structure.
ISO 7776 (1986)	Data Communication. High Level Data Link Control Procedures—Description of the X.25 LAPB-Compatible DTE Data Link Procedures.
ISO 8471 (1987)	Data Communication. High Level Data Link Control Balanced Classes of Procedures—Data Link Layer Address Resolution/Negotiation in Switched Environments.

15.4.7 Data-Link Layer: IEEE LAN Standards

ANSI/IEEE 802 (1990)	IEEE Standards for Local and Metropolitan Area Networks: Overview and Architecture.
IEEE 802.1D (1990)	IEEE Standards for Local and Metropolitan Area Networks: Media Access Control (MAC) Bridges.
IEEE 802.1 E (1990)	IEEE Standards for Local and Metropolitan Area Networks: System Load Protocol.

ANSI/IEEE 802.2 (1989)   Logical Link Control. Supersedes ANSI/IEEE 802.2 (1985). Adopted by ISO as ISO 8802-2 (1989).

ANSI/IEEE 802.3 (1985)   Carrier Sense Multiple Access with Collision Detection (CSMA/CD) Access Method and Physical Layer Specifications. Modified version adopted by ISO as ISO 8802-3 (1989, 1990). Superseded by ISO standards and the equivalent ANSI/IEEE 802.3 (1990).

ISO 8802-3 (1990) 2 (E)   Local Area Networks, Part 3: Carrier Sense Multiple Access with Collision Detection (CSMA/CD) Access Method and Physical Layer Specifications. This document includes the ISO-approved versions of IEEE 802.3c and IEEE 802.3d. This is also ANSI/IEEE 802.3 (1990), superseding ANSI/IEEE 802.3 (1985).

ANSI/IEEE 802.3b,c,d,e (1989)

IEEE Supplements to Carrier Sense Multiple Access with Collision Detection (CSMA/CD) Access Method and Physical Layer Specifications. Supplements ANSI/IEEE 802.2 (1985) and ISO 8802-3 (1989); ISO-approved versions of 802.3c and 802.3d included in ISO 8802-3 (1990) 2 (E).

IEEE 802.3h (1990)   IEEE supplement to Carrier Sense Multiple Access with Collision Detection (CSMA/CD) Access Method and Physical Layer Specifications: Layer Management.

IEEE 802.3i (1990)   IEEE supplement to Carrier Sense Multiple Access with Collision Detection (CSMA/CD) Access Method and Physical Layer Specifications: System Considerations for Multisegment 10

Mb/s Baseband Networks and Twisted-Pair Medium Attachment Unit (MAU) and Baseband Medium, Type 10BASE-T .

ANSI/IEEE 802.4 (1990)   Token Passing Bus Access Method and Physical Layer Specifications. Supersedes ANSI/IEEE 802.4 (1985); adopted by ISO as ISO 8802-4 (1990).

ANSI/IEEE 802.5 (1989)   Token Ring Access Method and Physical Layer Specifications.

IEEE 802.6 (1989)   Metropolitan Network Access Method and Physical Layer Specifications.

ANSI/IEEE 802.7 (1989)   IEEE Recommended Practices for Broadband Local Area Networks.

15.4.8   Physical Layer

(See also Chap. 17)

ISO 2110 (1989)   Data Communication.   25-Pole DTE/DCE Interface Connector and Contact Number Assignments.

ISO 2593 (1984)   Data Communication. 34 Pin DTE/DCE Interface and Pin Assignments.

ISO 4902 (1989)   Data Communication.   37-Pole DTE/DCE Interface Connector and Contact Number Assignments.

ISO TR7477 (1985)   Data Communication. Arrangements for DTE to DTE Physical Connection using V.24 and X.24 Interchange Circuits.

ISO 8480 (1987)   Data Communication.   DTE/DCE Interface Back-up Control Operation Using the 25-Pole Connector.

ISO 8481 (1986)	Data Communication. DTE to DTE Physical Connection Using X.24 Interchange Circuits with DTE Provided Timing.
ISO 8482 (1987)	Data Communication. Twisted Pair Multipoint Interconnections.
ISO 8877 (1987)	Systems. Interface Connector and Contact Assignments for ISDN Basic Access Interface Located at Reference Points S and T.

15.5   Bibliography

The book by Black (1991) offers a complete and up-to-date discussion of OSI. Comer (1991) and Rose (1991) do not focus on OSI but on the TCP/IP protocols, which represent an important deviation from OSI.

Black, U. (1991), *OSI: A Model for Computer Communications Standards*, Prentice-Hall, Englewood Cliffs, New Jersey.

Comer, D. E. (1991), *Internetworking with TCP/IP, Volume 1: Principles, Protocols and Architectures*, Second Edition, Prentice Hall, Englewood Cliffs, New Jersey.

Quarterman, J. S., and J. C. Hoskins (1986), "Notable Computer Networks," *Communications of the ACM* 29, 932–971. [Reprinted in Denning (1990), 20–96. See Chap. 9 Bibliography.]

Rose, M. T. (1991), *The Simple Book: An Introduction to Management of TCP/IP-Based Internets*, Prentice-Hall Series in Innovative Technology, Prentice-Hall, Englewood Cliffs, New Jersey.

16

Programming Language Standards

Programming language standards are often of direct concern to many computer users, and much confusion exists on the topic given the plethora of language versions that are commercially available. For these reasons, we preface our lists of standards with comments on the history and standardization of some important languages.

16.1 Ada

Ada, developed under the sponsorship of the United States Department of Defense, has a simpler standardization history than other languages such as FORTRAN and Pascal. The preliminary design of Ada was completed by 1979, and revised in 1980 after extensive public comment. The revised version was proposed to ANSI as a standard. The standardization process took over two years, producing minor changes that were often nonetheless subtly significant, particularly for compiler design. The standard ANSI/MIL 1815A was adopted finally in 1983. The ANSI standard was submitted for international approval, and was accepted as ISO 8652 in 1987. Unlike other languages, Ada was designed methodically, with a view to standardization, from the beginning.

The Ada standard is now under revision. Recently, the U.S. Federal Advisory Board to the Ada Joint Program Office published a statement (quoted in Long, 1991) stating that "some omissions, limitations, and minor errors have been discovered... since the ANSI standard was approved. Although a major revision does not appear to be necessary to correct these problems, some revision is warranted." The new version of the language is being referred to as "Ada 9X," and a draft Requirements Document has been prepared (it is reproduced in Long, 1991). Among the guidelines to be adopted for the revision is that of compatibility with the 1983 standard in the sense that "legal" Ada 83 programs should also be "legal" Ada 9X programs. Interestingly, Ada 9X is intended to increase support for international users, by adopting the 8-bit ISO 8859 standard as its character set in place of the 7-bit ASCII/ISO 646 set (see Chap. 13). It also appears that Ada 9X will allow different subsets to be operative. According to Long (1991), the Ada 9X committee has given consideration to the conflicting concerns of members of the Ada community, and established the policy that "...it should be possible for an Ada 9X implementation to address just the needs of a selected group of users, e.g., hard real-time applications developers, information systems developers, educators, etc." The way has thus been opened, for better or worse, to allowing variations in Ada implementations.

The Ada 9X project is coordinating closely with a parallel ISO Working Group, in order to ensure that ISO standardization occurs soon after ANSI approval.

16.2   BASIC

BASIC is a language designed to be implemented by an interpreter, but whose most effective versions are now compiled; it is a FORTRAN IV-inspired language whose best versions now seem closer to Pascal. Its history has been quite complex.

BASIC (Beginners All-purpose Symbolic Instruction Code) was first developed in 1964 by two Dartmouth College professors, John G. Kemeny and Thomas E. Kurtz. It was intended as an educational tool, to help Dartmouth students learn programming without delving into the mysteries of FORTRAN compilers and IBM job-control language. It was developed as an interactive language—in fact, it was the first such language.

The original Dartmouth language in its first and second editions consisted of the following core statements: LET, DATA, READ, PRINT, IF-THEN, FOR, NEXT, GOSUB, RETURN, DIM, STOP, END, REMARK, and single line DEFs. The third edition of the language, whose manual appeared in 1966, added INPUT and MAT, among other things.   Enhancements continued, until in 1979 the seventh edition added multicharacter identifiers, graphics statements, IF-THEN-ELSE, a DO-LOOP with WHILE and UNTIL options, and SELECT CASE among other features.

As the microcomputer explosion of the late 1970s and early 1980s gathered force, BASIC became entrenched as the language of choice for a large part of the programming public.   Numerous dialects and versions were born, many of them containing several enhancements to the original language.   With the introduction of the IBM personal computer in 1981, IBM-PC BASIC became a *de facto* standard.

Early versions of IBM-PC BASIC came in a number of different forms: Cassette BASIC (for computers with no floppy disk drives), Disk BASIC (for computers with floppy disk drives but limited memory) and BASICA ("Advanced" BASIC, a superset of disk BASIC).   Cassette BASIC and Disk BASIC are no longer being released.   GW-BASIC is a product of Microsoft and essentially equivalent to BASICA (also a product of Microsoft, but released through IBM).   BASICA already has some significant enhancements to original BASIC, such as WHILE..WEND statements.

Versions of the language with even more enhancements now exist.   Microsoft's QuickBASIC and Borland's Turbo BASIC are structured versions that rival Pascal and C in many ways.

The American National Standards Institute (ANSI) formed a committee (X3J2) in 1974 to propose a standard for BASIC.   Early ANSI standardization activity centered around developing a standard for "Minimal BASIC." Minimal BASIC, proposed finally in 1978, was intended to represent the minimal set of commands and features that every dialect had to have if it were to claim to be BASIC.   It was to include the familiar "core" statements: LET, PRINT, READ, DATA, RESTORE, INPUT, IF, GOTO, GOSUB, RETURN, FOR, NEXT, ON, RANDOMIZE, DEF, DIM, and REM.   A Minimal BASIC standard is not currently listed in the ANSI catalog, but Minimal BASIC standards are still distributed by the ISO and several national bodies (Table 16.1).

More recently, ANSI standardization activity has concentrated on developing a truly enhanced standard that would embody some of the good features in the various dialects, and incorporate the philosophy of structured programming.   A draft standard was proposed in 1984, with a final standard (ANSI X3.113) approved in 1987.   The new ANSI standard is most closely implemented by "True BASIC," announced in 1984 by Kemeny and Kurtz, the original developers of BASIC at Dartmouth.   The ANSI standard includes such constructs as IF-THEN-ELSE, CASE, nested IF's, DO-UNTIL, and DO-WHILE; it also supports subroutines.

16.3   C Language

The C programming language developed in close association with the UNIX operating system; C was the language developed to write UNIX. C grew from an earlier language named (of course) B, developed by Kenneth Thompson at AT&T Bell Laboratories. B itself was based on BCPL, an earlier systems programming language. The first recognizable version of C was produced in 1972, and evolution continued for several years in the 1970s. The language was "standardized" *de facto* in the book by Kernighan and Ritchie (1978). The version of the language described in that document is referred to as "K&R C." In 1983, ANSI committee X3J11 began working to produce an American National Standard for C, and that standard was finally published in 1989 as ANSI X3.159 (1989). The standard is now in the Draft International Standard stage at the ISO. To the user, the ANSI standard is very similar to K&R C. The standard, however, is a more precise definition of the language. Quoting from the standard itself, "The de facto C programming language standard, *The C Programming Language* by Brian W. Kernighan and Dennis M. Ritchie, is an excellent book; however, it is not precise nor complete enough to specify the C language fully." Kernighan and Ritchie have published a revised edition (1989) of their famous work, incorporating the modifications introduced by the new standard.

16.4   COBOL

COBOL (*Co*mmon *B*usiness *O*riented *L*anguage) arose out of a perceived need in the late 1950s for a higher-level language for data processing applications. The CODASYL (Conference on Data Systems and Languages) Committee for COBOL was formed in 1959, with representatives from industry and government, and this committee produced a draft language called COBOL-60 within a year. Several versions offering extensions and enhancements followed. The 1965 version, known as "COBOL, Edition 65, " was approved by ANSI as a standard in 1968. COBOL development continued, with new versions and enhancements being published every year or two in the *Cobol Journal of Development*. ANSI approved a standard in 1974 incorporating the new developments up to that time. A further draft revision to the standard was published in 1981, and a new standard was adopted by ANSI in 1985 [ANSI X3.23 (1985)]. The ANSI standard was endorsed by the ISO as ISO 1989 (1985).

16.5 FORTRAN

FORTRAN is one of the oldest high-level languages, and still one of the most widely used. It reigns supreme in the world of scientific and engineering computation, despite some recent challenge from C. The continuing success of FORTRAN is at least partly explainable by the size of the existing investment in FORTRAN software, but also by the fact that implementations of the language tend to be efficient, producing fast executable code.

The first version of FORTRAN was implemented on the IBM 704 computer in 1956. FORTRAN II appeared in 1958 and embodied several enhancements, among them support for subroutines. During the next five years, FORTRAN was implemented on many computers. FORTRAN III contained many machine-dependent features. FORTRAN IV was developed in 1962 for the IBM 7090 and 7094.

FORTRAN was the first language to be standardized in the United States. The first ASA (soon to become ANSI) subcommittee on the language was formed in May, 1962. The subcommittee was designated ASA/X3.4.3, and proposed two draft standards in 1964; they were accepted in 1966. One standard [ANSI X3.9 (1966)] was for a full language, the other [ANSI X3.10 (1966)] for a subset. The former is widely known as FORTRAN 66, and is very similar to FORTRAN IV.

The ink was barely dry on the 1966 standard before the need for a new one became apparent. Many implementations of FORTRAN had useful and advanced features not embodied in the standard. This was true even before 1966, and the discrepancies only increased with time. Moreover, the movement towards structured programming and rational top-down design was making people realize the inadequacies of FORTRAN 66, which did not provide much support for this programming methodology. FORTRAN 66 did not have such constructs as IF-THEN-ELSE that are conducive to good programming; instead, FORTRAN 66 programmers had to rely excessively on GOTO statements. ALGOL, in many ways, was a much better language than FORTRAN, and there was a movement to make FORTRAN more ALGOL-like. Thus the late 1960s and early 1970s saw the development of a new standard, known widely as FORTRAN 77. FORTRAN 77 is an American standard, but has been adopted without alteration as the ISO FORTRAN standard as well.

The new committee, ANSI/X3J3, was guided by the principle of downward compatibility. They intended that the new standard be a superset of FORTRAN 66. The committee came close to achieving this goal, but FORTRAN 66 is not completely contained in FORTRAN 77. The Hollerith type, for example, has been removed. FORTRAN 77 added improved string-handling capabilities by introducing a CHARACTER type, and also added an IF-THEN-ELSE construct. However, FORTRAN still lags behind the ALGOL family of languages, including Pascal, Ada, C, and Modula-2, in useful and rational programming features. The discontent is growing, and yet another standard is under development.

A working version known as FORTRAN 90 (formerly FORTRAN 8x) exists and is being considered. This proposed ANSI standard is a superset of FORTRAN 77, although many old features are designated as "obsolescent." This means that they are considered undesirable and are recommended for deletion in the *next* revision (FORTRAN 2000?). The obsolescent features include the arithmetic IF; real and double-precision DO variables; shared DO termination; DO termination on a statement other than a CONTINUE or an END DO; assigned GOTO; and PAUSE. FORTRAN 90 has added many new features, for example: a CASE construct; a WHERE statement for arrays allowing operations to be performed only on a certain subset of elements; and derived data types, similar to Pascal records.

16.6 Pascal

Pascal has had a complex standardization history. The language was first designed by Professor Niklaus Wirth, and defined in Jensen and Wirth (1974). Pascal began as a teaching language, but it soon gained a significant following, and extended versions began to be used for commercial purposes and serious software development. Standardization efforts began in the late 1970s. In the United States, the IEEE and ANSI authorized a joint committee in early 1979 to develop a standard. The joint ANSI/IEEE standard 770X3.97 was finalized in 1983. Meanwhile, an International (ISO) standard was under development in Europe, under an initiative launched by the United Kingdom in 1977. The British Standards Institution produced the standard BS 6132 in 1982. The ISO adopted the British standard formally in 1983 as ISO 7185.

There were a number of differences between the BSI/ISO standard and the ANSI/IEEE standard. For example, the BSI/ISO standard included conformant arrays, whereas the ANSI/IEEE standard did not. There were also some ambiguities of definition in the BSI/ISO standard that were corrected by the ANSI/IEEE standard. Both BS 6192 and ISO 7185 were revised and corrected in 1988-1989, as was the American standard.

Even before the initial British, American, and International standards were approved, work was under way in both Europe and the United States to produce an additional standard for "Extended Pascal" that would correct some of Pascal's shortcomings. Both ANSI/IEEE and BSI have had input in the development of the international standard, still not published in final form. However, ANSI/IEEE have published their own standard in the United States: ANSI/IEEE 770X3.160 (1989). This Extended Pascal standard was explicitly intended to be compatible with the earlier standard ANSI/IEEE 770X3.97 (1983). Among the features added by the extended language standard are the following:

- Modularity and separate compilation. The user's lack of ability to compile subroutines separately into libraries was a *major* weakness in Pascal, one that had already been remedied in many available (nonstandard) compilers.

- Increased power and flexibility in the handling of strings.

- Direct-access file handling.

- Enhancements in the `case` statement and in variant records. Each `case-constant-list` may now include ranges of values. An `otherwise` clause represents values not listed in the `case-constant-list`.

- Support for complex arithmetic.

- Exponentiation. Previously, standard Pascal had no operator equivalent to the FORTRAN ** !

- Conformant arrays. ANSI/IEEE 770X3.97 (1983) did not have them, although ISO 7185 did. ANSI/IEEE 770X3.160 (1989) provides a conformant array specification that is compatible with the international standard.

16.7　List of Programming Language Standards (ANSI, ISO)

ANSI/MIL 1815A (1983)　　Reference Manual for the Ada Programming Language. Standardized by the ISO as ISO 8652 (1987).

ISO 1538 (1984)　　Programming Language ALGOL-60.

ISO 8485 (1989)　　Programming Language APL.

ANSI X3.37 (1987)　　Programming Language Apt.

ANSI/IEEE 416 (1984)　　Programming Language Atlas.

ANSI X3.113 (1987)　　FULL BASIC standard. [Minimal BASIC standard is no longer listed in current ANSI catalog; may still be available from ISO as ISO 6373 (1984).]

ANSI X3.159 (1989)　　Programming Language C. (The ISO has also prepared a Draft International Standard, DIS 9899, released June, 1990)

ANSI X3.23 (1985)　　Programming Language COBOL. First approved in 1968; currently under revision. ANSI X3.23 (1985) has been endorsed by the ISO as ISO 1989 (1985).

ANSI X3.165 (1988)　　Programming Language Dibol.

ANSI X3.9 (1978)　　Programming Language FORTRAN. First Approved 1966. Currently under revision. ANSI X3.9 (1978) has been endorsed by the ISO as ISO 1539 (1980).

ANSI/IEEE 770X3.97 (1989)

　　Programming Language Pascal. Revision of ANSI/IEEE 770 X3.97 (1983).

ISO 7185 (1983)　　Programming Language Pascal. An endorsement of the British Standard BS 6132 (1982).

ANSI/IEEE 770X3.160 (1989)

Programming Language Extended Pascal. New proposed standard, 1990. (The ISO has also prepared a Draft International Standard for Extended Pascal, DIS 10206, released June, 1990).

ANSI X3.53 (1976)

Programming Language PL/I. Reaffirmed 1987. Endorsed by the ISO as ISO 6160 (1979).

ANSI X3.74 (1987)

Programming Language PL/I. General Purpose Subset. Also ISO 6522 (1985).

Table 16.1 shows the language standards listed above, along with standards from various other national and industry organizations. The European standards (AFNOR, DIN, BS) are often very similar or identical to the corresponding ISO standard (which in turn is often heavily influenced by the corresponding ANSI standard).

TABLE 16.1   Programming Language Standards

Language	Standards	
Ada	ANSI/MIL 1815 (1983) DIN 66268 (1988)	ISO 8652 (1988) FIPS 119
Algol-60	ISO 1538 (1984) ECMA 2 (1965)	AFNOR NF-Z-65-010 (1967)
APL	ISO 8485 (1989) BS 7301 (1990)	AFNOR NF-Z-65-800 (1990)
Apt	ANSI X3.37 (1987)	
ATLAS	ANSI/IEEE 416 (1984)	ARINC 626-1 (1989)
Minimal BASIC	ISO 6373 (1984) ECMA 55 (1978) JIS C 6207 (1982) FIPS 68-1	DIN 66284 (1988) SAA AS 2797 (1985) JIS X 3003 (1982)
BASIC	ANSI X3.113 (1987)	ECMA 116 (1986)
C	ANSI X3.159 (1989)	ISO DIS 9899 (1990)

TABLE 16.1   Programming Language Standards (continued)

Language	Standards	
COBOL	ANSI X3.23 (1985)	ISO 1989 (1985)
	AFNOR NF-Z-65-210 (1976)	DIN 66028 (1986)
	AFNOR NF-Z-65-220 (1984)	JIS C 6205 (1980)
	JIS X 3002 (1980)	FIPS 21-2
	SAA AS 1209 (1978)	
Coral 66	BS 5905 (1980)	
FORTRAN	ANSI X3.9 (1978)	ISO 1539 (1980)
	AFNOR NF-Z-65-110 (1983)	DIN 66027 (1980)
	CSA Z243.18 (1980)	SAA AS 1486 (1983)
	JIS C 6201 (1982)	JIS X 3001 (1982)
	FIPS 69-1	
Pascal	ANSI/IEEE 770 X3.97 (1983)	ISO 7185 (1983)
	ANSI/IEEE 770 X3.160 (1989)	FIPS 109
	AFNOR NF-Z-65-300 (1984)	DIN 66256 (1985)
	BS 6192 (1982)	SAA AS 2580 (1983)
Pearl	DIN 66253 T2 (1982)	DIN 66253 T3 (1989)
PL/I	ANSI X3.53 (1976)	ISO 6160 (1979)
	ANSI X3.74 (1987)	ISO 6522 (1985)
	ECMA 50 (1976)	DIN 66255 (1980)
	DIN 66255 T2 (1984)	

Notes: AFNOR = Association Française de Normalization (France).
ARINC = Aeronautical Radio, Inc.
BS = British Standard.
CSA = Canadian Standards Association.
DIN = Deutsches Institut für Normung (Germany).
ECMA = European Computer Manufacturers' Association.
JIS = Japanese Industrial Standard.
SAA = Standards Association of Australia; AS = Australian Standard.
FIPS = (U.S.) Federal Information Processing Standard.

16.8   Programming Language Standards under Development

Some important programming languages have not yet been standardized. LISP is an example. Various standards are still under development, for a variety of languages. The list below is of programming language standards at the ANSI Project Proposal (PP) stage, an early phase in the process. Drafts may not be currently available to the public. We are not aware of any parallel efforts outside the United States.

ANSI X3-PP-743	Project Proposal for a C++ programming language standard.
ANSI X3-PP-610	Project Proposal for a FORTH programming language standard.
ANSI X3-PP-574	Project Proposal for a Common LISP programming language standard.
ANSI X3-PP-748	Project Proposal for a Prolog programming language standard.
ANSI X3-PP-823	Project Proposal for a REXX programming language standard.

16.9 Bibliography

Many important references on standardization are listed in the bibliography to Chap. 12. The references below are mostly to texts on computer languages that provide a good treatment of the *standard* versions of their respective languages. In addition, there are references to texts that provide some treatment of the standardization of languages per se: Long (1991) for Ada, Kemeny and Kurtz (1985) for BASIC, and Hill and Meek (1980) for several languages. Hill and Meek is somewhat out-of-date, as we noted in Chap. 12, but is nevertheless a good source. Wilson and Clark (1988) is a superb general survey text of programming languages that also provides some historical perspective on their development. Tucker (1986) is another useful general text.

Barnes, J. G. P. (1989), *Programming in Ada,* Third Edition, Addison-Wesley, Menlo Park, California.

Brainerd, W. S., C. H. Goldberg, and J. C. Adams (1990), *Programmer's Guide to FORTRAN 90*, McGraw-Hill, San Francisco, California.

Clark, R. G. (1985), *Programming in Ada: A First Course*, Cambridge University Press, New York, New York.

Davis, W. S. (1986), *True BASIC Primer*, Addison-Wesley, Menlo Park, California.

Gottfried, B. S. (1985), *Programming with Pascal*, Schaum's Outline Series, McGraw-Hill, San Francisco, California.

Hill, I. D., and B. L. Meek (1980), *Programming Language Standardisation*, Ellis Horwood, Chichester, U.K. (in U.S.: John Wiley, New York, New York).

Kemeny, J. G., and T. E. Kurtz (1985), *Back to BASIC*, Addison-Wesley, Menlo Park, California.

Jensen, K., and N. Wirth (1974), *Pascal User Manual and Report*, Springer Verlag, New York, New York.

Kernighan, B. W., and D. M. Ritchie (1978), *The C Programming Language*, Prentice-Hall, Englewood Cliffs, New Jersey. (This is the original version of "K&R" C, before modifications by ANSI.)

Kernighan, B. W., and D. M. Ritchie (1989), *The C Programming Language*, Revised Edition, Prentice-Hall, Englewood Cliffs, New Jersey. (This edition includes the revisions to the original version of the language made by the ANSI standardization committee.)

Long, F. (1991) (ed.) *ADA Yearbook 1991*, Chapman and Hall, New York , New York.

Metcalf, M. (1988), *Effective FORTRAN 77*, Oxford University Press, New York, New York.

Metcalf, M., and J. Reid (1991), *FORTRAN 90 Explained*, Oxford University Press, New York, New York. [Previous editions (1987,1989) published by Oxford under the title *FORTRAN 8X Explained*.]

Tucker, A. B. (1986), *Programming Languages*, Second Edition, McGraw-Hill, San Francisco, California.

Wilson, L. B., and R. G. Clark (1988), *Comparative Programming Languages*, Addison-Wesley, Menlo Park, California.

Chapter

17

Other Hardware and Software Standards

In this chapter, we list many other useful standards for information technology, in areas other than those covered by Chaps. 13 to 16. We list standards from international organizations, as well as ANSI and IEEE standards.

17.1 Operating Systems

Although operating system interfaces constitute an area in dire need of standardization, activity has been limited. The IEEE recently released the POSIX standard (based on the UNIX system), an important step. The IEEE standard was accepted by ANSI and was modified by the ISO as an international standard. It remains to be seen whether POSIX will gain widespread acceptance.

ISO/IEC 9945-1 (1990)   Portable Operating System Interface (POSIX) Part 1: System Application Program Interface (API) [C Language] [Note: Based on the UNIX operating System. Adapted from IEEE 1003.1 (1988); equivalent to IEEE 1003.1 (1990); known informally as POSIX.1.]

17.2   Microprocessors

ANSI/IEEE 694 (1985)   Microprocessor Assembly Language.

ANSI/IEEE 855 (1990)   Standard for Microprocessor Operating
                              Systems Interface (MOSI).

17.3   Software Engineering

ANSI/IEEE 1042 (1987)   Guide to Software Configuration
                              Management.

ANSI/IEEE 828 (1990)   Software Configuration Management
                              Plans.

ANSI/IEEE 1016 (1987)   Software Design Descriptions.

ANSI/IEEE 1058.1 (1987)   Software Project Management Plans.

ANSI/IEEE 730 (1989)   Software Quality Assurance Plans.

ANSI/IEEE 983 (1986)   Software Quality Assurance Planning.

ANSI/IEEE 729 (1983)   Software Engineering Terminology.

ANSI/IEEE 829 (1983)   Software Test Documentation.

ANSI/IEEE 1008 (1987)   Software Unit Testing.

ANSI/IEEE 1063 (1987)   Software User Documentation.

ANSI/IEEE 1012 (1987)   Software Verification and Validation
                              Plans.

ANSI X3.88 (1981)   Computer Program Abstracts.
                              Reaffirmed 1987.

ANSI/ANS 10.3 (1986)   Guidelines for the Documentation of
                              Digital Computer Programs.

ANSI/ANS 10.5 (1986)   Guidelines for Considering User Needs
                              in Computer Program Development.

17.4 Computer Graphics

ANSI X3.124 (1985)   Graphical Kernel System (GKS) Functional Description.

BSI DPS 13/WG5/25 (Dec. 1978)
Graphical Kernel System (GKS) Functional Description.

ISO DIS 7942   Graphical Kernel System (GKS) Functional Description: GKS Version 7.2, ISO/TC97/SC5/WG2 N163 (1982).

ISO 8805 (1988)   Graphical Kernel System for Three Dimensions.

ANSI X3.124.1 (1985)   Graphical Kernel System (GKS) FORTRAN Binding.

ANSI X3.124.2 (1989)   Graphical Kernel System (GKS) Pascal Binding.

ISO 8651-1 (1988)   Graphical Kernel System Language Bindings Part 1: FORTRAN.

ISO 8651-2 (1988)   Graphical Kernel System Language Bindings Part 2: Pascal.

ISO 8651-3 (1988)   Graphical Kernel System Language Bindings Part 3: Ada.

ISO/IEC JTC1/SC24 N180   Graphical Kernel System Language Bindings Part 4: C.

ISO DIS 8806-1   Graphical Kernel System for Three Dimensions (GKS) 3-D Language Bindings Part 1: FORTRAN.

ISO/IEC JTC1/SC24 N190   Graphical Kernel System for Three Dimensions (GKS) 3-D Language Bindings Part 2: Pascal.

ISO/IEC JTC1/SC24 N189   Graphical Kernel System for Three Dimensions (GKS) 3-D Language Bindings Part 3: Ada.

ISO/IEC JTC1/SC24 N181   Graphical Kernel System for Three Dimensions (GKS) 3-D Language Bindings Part 4: C.

ANSI X3.122 (1986)   Computer Graphics Metafile for the Storage of and Transfer of Picture Description Information.

ISO 8632 1-4 (1987)   Computer Graphics Metafile for the Storage of and Transfer of Picture Description Information.

17.5 Text and Document Processing

ANSI X3.98 (1983)   Text Information Interchange in Page Image Format (PIF).

ISO 8613-1 (1989)   Office Document Architecture (ODA) and Interchange Format, Part 1: Introduction and General Principles.

ISO 8613-2 (1989)   Office Document Architecture (ODA) and Interchange Format, Part 2: Document Structures.

ISO 8613-4 (1989)   Office Document Architecture (ODA) and Interchange Format, Part 4: Document Profile.

ISO 8613-5 (1989)   Office Document Architecture (ODA) and Interchange Format, Part 5: Office Document Interchange Format (ODIF).

ISO 8613-6 (1989)   Office Document Architecture (ODA) and Interchange Format, Part 6: Character Content Architectures.

ISO 8613-7 (1989)   Office Document Architecture (ODA) and Interchange Format, Part 7: Raster Graphics Content Architectures.

ISO 8613-8 (1989)   Office Document Architecture (ODA) and Interchange Format, Part 8: Geometric Graphics Content Architectures.

ISO 8879 (1986)   Standard Generalized Markup Language (SGML).

17.6   Data Communications

Chapter 15 covers standards relating to Open Systems Interconnection (OSI) and local area networks. In this section we list other standards relevant for data communications. We list standards produced by the EIA, by the ISO and national bodies, and the CCITT (the last are referred to as "recommendations").

17.6.1   EIA Standards

The Electronic Industries Association (U.S.) has published many "Recommended Standards" (RSs) for data communications interfaces. These are among the best known standards in the world. Chapter 8 describes some of these standards, particularly RS-232 and RS-422, in more detail. An EIA recommended standard is properly referred to as EIA-(standard number), but is popularly referred to simply as RS-(standard number). Thus, EIA-232-D is almost universally referred to as RS-232.

These interface standards can be fit into the OSI framework: they would reside in the lowest (physical) layer (see Chap. 15).

EIA 232-D (1987)   Interface Between Data Terminal Equipment and Data Circuit-Terminating Equipment Employing Serial Binary Data Interchange. Related standards: CCITT V.24, V.28; ISO 2110.

EIA 422-A (1978)   Electrical Characteristics of Balanced Voltage Digital Interface Circuits. Related standards: CCITT V.11, X.27.

EIA 423-A (1978) Electrical Characteristics of Unbalanced Voltage Digital Interface Circuits. Related standards: CCITT V.10, X.26.

EIA 449 (1977) General Purpose 37-Position and 9-Position Interface for Data Terminal Equipment and Data Circuit-Terminating Equipment Employing Serial Binary Data Interchange. Related Standards: CCITT V.24, V.54, X.21*bis*.

EIA 530 (1987) High Speed 25-Position Interface for Data Terminal Equipment and Data Circuit-Terminating Equipment.

17.6.2   ISO and National Bodies

ANSI X3.15 (1976) Bit Sequencing of the American National Standard Code for Information Interchange (ASCII) in Serial-by-Bit Data Transmission. Reaffirmed 1983.

ANSI X3.16 (1976) Character Structure and Character Parity Sense for Serial-by-Bit Data Communication in the American National Standard Code for Information Interchange (ASCII). Reaffirmed 1983.

ANSI X3.25 (1976) Character Structure and Character Parity Sense for Parallel-by-Bit Data Communication in the American National Standard Code for Information Interchange (ASCII). Reaffirmed 1983.

ANSI X3.28 (1976) Procedures for the Use of the Communications Control Characters of the American National Standard Code for Information Interchange (ASCII) in Specified Data-Communication Links. Reaffirmed 1986.

ANSI X3.57 (1977)　　　　　Structure for Formatting Message headings for Information Interchange Using the American National Standard for Information Interchange for Data Communication System Control. Reaffirmed 1986.

ANSI X3.1 (1987)　　　　　Synchronous Signaling Rates in Data Transmission.

ANSI X3.131 (1986)　　　　Small Computer Systems Interface (SCSI) (Endorsed by the ISO, as ISO 9316-89).

ANSI/IEEE 488.1 (1988)　　IEEE Standard Digital Interface for Programmable Instrumentation.

ANSI/IEEE 488.2 (1988)　　IEEE Standard Codes, Formats, Protocols, and Common Commands for Use with IEEE Std. 488.1.

ANSI/IEEE 696 (1983)　　　Interface Devices.

17.6.3　CCITT Recommendations

V Series:　Data Communication Over the Telephone Network

V.1　　　　　　　　　　Equivalence between binary notation symbols and the significant conditions of a two-condition code.

V.2　　　　　　　　　　Power levels for data transmission over telephone lines.

V.3　　　　　　　　　　International alphabet no. 5.

V.4　　　　　　　　　　General structure of signals of international alphabet no. 5 code for data transmission over public telephone networks.

V.5　　　　　　　　　　Standards of modulation rates and data signaling rates for synchronous data transmission in the general switched network.

V.6

Standards of modulation rates and data signaling rates for synchronous data transmission on leased telephone type circuits.

V.7

Definitions of terms concerning data transmission over the telephone network.

V.10

Electrical characteristics for unbalanced double-current interchange circuits for general use with integrated circuit equipment in the field of data communications (equivalent to EIA RS-423).

V.11

Electrical characteristics for balanced double-current interchange circuits for general use with integrated circuit equipment in the field of data communications (equivalent to EIA RS-422).

V.13

Answerback unit simulator.

V.15

Use of acoustic coupling for data transmission.

V.16

Recommendations for modems for the transmission of medical dialog data.

V.19

Modems for parallel data transmission using signaling frequencies.

V.20

Parallel data transmission modems standardized for universal use in the general switched network.

V.21

1200-bps modem standardized for use in the switched telephone network.

V.22	1200-bps full-duplex 2-wire modem standardized for use in the general switched telephone network and on leased lines.
V.22*bis*	2400-bps full-duplex 2-wire modem using frequency division techniques standardized for use in the general switched telephone network.
V.23	600/1200-bps modem standardized for use in the general switched telephone network.
V.24	List of definitions for interchange circuits between data terminal equipment and data circuit-terminating equipment (equivalent to EIA RS-232C.)
V.25	Automatic calling and/or answering equipment on the general switched telephone network including disabling echo suppressors on manually established calls.
V.25*bis*	Automatic calling and/or answering equipment on the general switched telephone network using the 100 series interchange circuits.
V.26	2400-bps modem for use on 4-wire point-to-point leased telephone circuits.
V.26*bis*	2400/1200-bps modem standardized for use in the general switched telephone network.
V.26*ter*	2400-bps duplex modem using echo cancellation standardized for use in the general switched telephone network and on point-to-point 2-wire leased telephone circuits.

V.27	4800-bps modem with manual equalizer standardized for use on leased telephone circuits.
V.27*bis*	4800/2400-bps modem with automatic equalizer standardized for use on leased circuits.
V.27*ter*	4800/2400-bps modem with automatic equalizer standardized for use in the general switched telephone network.
V.28	Electrical characteristics for unbalanced double-current interchange circuits.
V.29	9600-bps modem standardized for use on leased circuits.
V.31	Electrical characteristics for single-current interchange circuits controlled by contact closure.
V.32	Duplex modems operating at data rates of up to 9600-bps standardized for use in the general switched telephone network and in 2-wire leased telephone circuits.
V.33	Full duplex synchronous or asynchronous transmission at 14.4 kbps for use in the public telephone network.
V.35	Interface between DTE and DCE using electrical signals defined in V.11 (equivalent to EIA RS-449)
V.36	Modems for synchronous data transmission using 60–108 kHz group band circuits.

V.37	Synchronous data transmission at data rates in excess of 72 kbps using 60–108 kHz group band circuits.
V.40	Error indication with electromagnetic equipment.
V.41	Code-independent error control system.
V.50	Standard limits for transmission quality of data transmission.
V 51	Organization of the maintenance of international telephone-type circuits used for data transmission.
V.52	Characteristics of distortion and error rate measuring apparatus for data transmission.
V.53	Limits for the maintenance of telephone-type circuits used for data transmission.
V.54	Loop test devices for modems.
V.55	Specification for an impulsive noise measuring instrument for telephone-type circuits.
V.56	Comparative tests for modems for use over telephone-type circuits.
V.57	Comprehensive data test set for high signaling rates.
V.110	Support of DTEs with V-series type interfaces by an ISDN (I.463)

X-Series: Public Data Networks

X.1	International user classes of service in public data networks and ISDN.

X.2	International user facilities in public data networks.
X.3	Packet assembly/disassembly facility in a public data network.
X.4	General structure of signals of international alphabet no. 5 code for data transmission over public data networks.
X. 15	Definitions of terms concerning public data networks.
X.20	Interface between data terminal equipment and data circuit-terminating equipment for start-stop transmission services on public data networks.
X.20*bis*	V.21-compatible interface between data terminal equipment and data circuit-terminating equipment or start-stop transmission services on public data networks.
X.21	General-purpose interface between data terminal equipment and data circuit-terminating equipment for synchronous operation on public data networks.
X.21*bis*	Use on public data networks of data terminal equipments which are designed for interfacing to synchronous V-series modems.
X.22	Multiplex data terminal equipment/data circuit-terminating equipment for user classes 3–6.
X.24	List of definitions of interchange circuits between data terminal equipment and data circuit-terminating equipment on public data networks.

X.25	Interface between data terminal equipment and data circuit-terminating equipment for terminals operating in the packet mode on public data networks.
X.26	Electrical characteristics for unbalanced double-current interchange circuits for general use with integrated circuit equipment in the field of data communications (identical to V.10).
X.27	Electrical characteristics for balanced double-current interchange circuits for general use with integrated circuit equipment in the field of data communications (identical to V.11).
X.28	Data terminal equipment/data circuit-terminating equipment interface for a start/stop mode data terminal equipment accessing the packet assembly/ disassembly facility on a public data network situated in the same country.
X.29	Procedures for exchange of control information and user data between a packet mode data circuit-terminating equipment and a packet assembly/ disassembly facility.
X.30	Support of X.21 and X.21*bis* based data terminal equipment by an ISDN (I.461).
X.31	Support of packet mode terminal equipment by an ISDN (I.462).
X.32	Interface between data terminal equipment and data circuit-terminating equipment for terminals operating in packet mode and accessing a packet switched public data network through a public switched network.

X.50

Fundamental parameters of a multiplexing scheme for the international interface between synchronous data networks.

X.50*bis*

Fundamental parameters of a 48-kbps user data signaling rate transmission scheme for the international interface between synchronous data networks.

X.51

Fundamental parameters of a multiplexing scheme for the international interface between synchronous data networks using 10-bit envelope structure.

X.51*bis*

Fundamental parameters of a 48-kbps user data signaling rate transmission scheme for the international interface between synchronous data networks using 10-bit envelope structure.

X.52

Method of encoding asynchronous signals into a synchronous user bearer.

X.53

Number of channels on international multiplex links at 64 kbps.

X.54

Allocations of channels on international multiplex links at 64-kbps applications.

X.60

Common channel signaling for circuit-switched data applications.

X.61

Signaling system no. 7 (data user part).

X.70

Terminal and transit control signaling system on international circuits between asynchronous data networks.

X.71	Decentralized terminal and transit control signaling system on international circuits between synchronous data networks.
X.75	Terminal and transit call control procedures and data transfer systems on international circuits between packet switched data networks.
X.80	Interworking of interexchange signaling systems for circuit switched data services.
X.87	Principles and procedures for realization of international test facilities and network utilities in public data networks.
X.92	Hypothetical reference connections for public synchronous data networks.
X.95	Network parameters in public data networks.
X.96	Call progress signals in public data networks.
X.110	Routing principles for international public data services through switched public data networks of the same type.
X.121	International numbering plan for public data networks.
X.130	Provisional objectives for call set-up and clear-down times in public synchronous data networks (circuit switching).
X.132	Provisional objectives for grade of service in international data

communications over circuit-switched public data networks.

X.150   Data terminal equipment and data circuit-terminating equipment test loops for public data networks.

X.180   Administration arrangements for international closed user groups.

The following CCITT X-series recommendations relate to OSI (see Chap. 15):

X.200   Reference model of OSI for CCITT applications.

X.210   OSI layer service definition conventions.

X.213   Network service definition for OSI for CCITT applications.

X.214   Transport service definition for OSI for CCITT applications.

X.215   Session service definition for OSI for CCITT applications.

X.224   Transport protocol specification for OSI for CCITT applications.

X.225   Session protocol specification for OSI for CCITT applications.

X.244   Procedure for the exchange of protocol identical during virtual call establishment on packet switched public data networks.

X.250   Formal description techniques for data communications protocols and services.

| X.400 | Message handling service for all test communications and electronic mail. |

Note: *bis* refers to the second part of a CCITT recommendation. *ter* refers to the third part. *bis* and *ter* are generally addenda providing enhancements to the original recommendation.

17.6.4   European Communications Standards (NETs)

European communication standards (NETs) are developed by ETSI in cooperation with CEPT. They tend to focus on amplifying CCITT recommendations.

NET1	X.21 Access.
NET2	X.25 Access.
NET3	ISDN Basic Access.
NET4	PSTN Basic Access.
NET5	ISDN Primary Rate Access.
NET6	Switched Access to PSPDN (X.32).
NET7	ISDN Terminal Adaptor.
NET10	European 900 MHz Digital Cellular Mobile Telecommunications Network Access.
NET20	General Requirements for Voiceband Modems.
NET21	Specific Requirements for Modem V.21.
NET22	Specific Requirements for Modem V.22.
NET23	Specific Requirements for Modem V.22*bis*.
NET24	Specific Requirements for Modem V.23.
NET25	Requirements for Modem V.32.

17.7   Standard Paper Sizes

A fairly large part of computer development and computer use today lies in the area of document preparation. Those with an interest in document preparation, particularly those with European connections, will find it useful to have tables of international paper sizes [ISO 216 (1975)]; see Tables 17.1 to 17.3. It will come as a surprise to many Americans that their familiar letter size (8.5" × 11") and legal size (8.5" × 14") sheets of paper are not international standard sizes. There are three families of paper sizes, indicated by the letters A, B, and C. The basic sheet in the A family (indicated by A0) is 1189 mm by 841 mm; the basic sheet (B0) in the B family is 1414 mm by 1000 mm; and the basic sheet (C0) in the C family is 1297 mm by 917 mm. The reader will notice that each of the three basic sheets has a length-to-breadth ratio of $\sqrt{2}$ (i.e., about 1.414...).

Each of the three basic sheets can be folded to create another standard size. If the A0 sheet is folded so as to halve its longer dimension, a sheet 841 mm by 594 mm is created; this is the A1 sheet. Folding the A1 sheet so as to halve its longer dimension creates the A2 sheet; and so on. The A4 sheet, which is 297 × 210 mm (8.27" × 11.69") is a particularly common size; U.S. readers may recognize it as the size of many "long and skinny" British magazines they see on newsstands next to more familiar American ones.

TABLE 17.1 International Paper Sizes: "A" Series

Code	Breadth (mm)	Length (mm)
A0	841	1189
A1	594	841
A2	420	594
A3	297	420
A4	210	297
A5	148	210
A6	105	148

TABLE 17.2 International Paper Sizes: "B" Series

Code	Breadth (mm)	Length (mm)
B0	1000	1414
B1	707	1000
B2	500	707
B3	353	500
B4	250	353
B5	176	250
B6	125	176

TABLE 17.3 International Paper Sizes: "C" Series

Code	Breadth (mm)	Length (mm)
C0	917	1297
C1	648	917
C2	458	648
C3	324	458
C4	229	324
C5	162	229
C6	114	162

Glossary of Acronyms

AFNOR	Association Française de Normalisation. National standards body of France.
ANSI	American National Standards Institute.
ARPANET	Advanced Research Projects Agency Network.
AS	Australian Standard.
ASCII	American Standard Code for Information Interchange.
BARRNet	Bay Area Regional Research Network.
BITNET	"Because It's Time" Network.
bps	Bits per second.
BS	British Standard.
BSD	Berkeley Software Distribution.
BSI	British Standards Institution.
BSR	Bureau of Standards Research (ANSI).
CCIR	Comité Consultatif International de Radio (International Radio Consultative Committee) of ITU.
CCITT	Comité Consultatif International Télégraphique et Téléphonique (International Telegraph and Telephone Consultative Committee) of ITU.
CDC	Control Data Corporation.
CEN	Comité Européen de Normalisation (European Committee for Standardization).
CENELEC	Comité Européen de Normalisation Électrotechnique (European Committee for Electrical Standardization).
CEPT	Conférence Européenne des Administrations des Postes et Télécommunications (European Conference of Postal and Telecommunications Administrations).

CLIST	Command List (MVS-TSO).
CMS	Conversational Monitor System.
CP/M	Control Program for Microprocessors.
CREN	Corporation for Research and Educational Networking.
CSNET	Computer and Science Research Network.
CTSS	Compatible Time-Sharing System.
DARPA	Defense Advanced Research Projects Agency.
DCE	Data Communications Equipment, or Data Circuit-terminating Equipment.
DCL	Digital Command Language.
DDN	Defense Data Network.
DECnet	Digital Equipment Corporation Network.
DIN	Deutsches Institut für Normung. National standards body of Germany.
DIS	Draft International Standard (ISO/IEC).
DOS	Disk Operating System.
DP	Draft Proposal (ISO).
DPANS	Draft Proposal American National Standard.
DTE	Data Terminal Equipment.
EARN	European Academic and Research Network.
EBCDIC	Extended Binary Coded Decimal Interchange Code.
ECMA	European Computer Manufacturers' Association.
EIA	Electronic Industries Association.
EPS	Encapsulated PostScript.
ETSI	European Telecommunications Standards Institute.
EUnet	European UNIX Network.
EWOS	European Workshop on Open Systems.
FIPS	(U.S.) Federal Information Processing Standard.
FSK	Frequency Shift Keying.
FTP	File Transfer Protocol.
HEPnet	High Energy Physics Network.
IEC	International Electrotechnical Commission.
IEEE	Institute of Electrical and Electronics Engineers.

ISDN	Integrated Services Digital Network.
ISO	International Organization for Standardization.
ISO/IEC JTC1	Joint Technical Committee of ISO and IEC concerned with information technology issues.
ISPF	Interactive System Productivity Facility.
ITU	International Telecommunications Union.
JANET	Joint Academic Network.
JCL	Job Control Language.
JIS	Japanese Industrial Standard.
JISC	Japanese Industrial Standards Committee.
JTC1	Joint Technical Committee of ISO and IEC concerned with information technology issues.
JUNET	Japan UNIX Network.
MIDnet	Midwestern States Network.
MILNET	Military Network (Same as DDN).
MS-DOS	Microsoft Disk Operating System.
MVS	Multiple Virtual Storages.
MVS/XA	Multiple Virtual Storages/Extended Architecture.
NET	European Telecommunications Standard.
NIC	Network Information Center.
NIST	(U.S.) National Institute of Standards and Technology.
NJE/NJI	Network Job Entry/Network Job Interface.
NNI	Nederlands Normalisatie Instituut. National standards body of the Netherlands.
NSFNET	National Science Foundation Network.
NSN	NASA (National Aeronautics and Space Administration) Science Network.
NWI	New Work Item (ISO).
ODA	Office Document Architecture.
OSI	Open Systems Interconnection.
PDN	Public Data Network.
PP	Project Proposal (ANSI).
PSK	Phase Shift Keying.
PSPDN	Packet-Switched Public Data Network.

PSTN	Public-Switched Telephone Network.
QAM	Quadrature Amplitude Modulation.
RS	Recommended Standard, issued by EIA.
SAA	Standards Association of Australia.
SC	Subcommittee of ISO/IEC JTC1.
SCC	Standards Council of Canada.
SCSI	Small Computer Systems Interface.
SG	CCITT Study Group.
SGML	Standard Generalized Markup Language.
SPAG	Standards Promotion and Applications Group.
SPAN	Space Physics Analysis Network.
SURANet	Southeastern Universities Research Association Network.
TAG	Technical Advisory Group (ANSI).
TCM	Trellis Code Modulation.
TCP/IP	Transmission Control Protocol/Internet Protocol.
THEnet	Texas Higher Education Network.
TIFF	Tagged Image File Format.
TRAC	Technical Recommendations Application Committee of CEPT.
TSO	Time Sharing Option (MVS).
USAN	University Satellite Network.
UUCP	UNIX-to-UNIX Copy Program.
V-Series	Recommendations issued by CCITT Study Group SGXVII, on data transmission over the telephone network.
VAX	Virtual Address eXtension.
VM	Virtual Machine.
VMS	Virtual Memory System.
WD	Working Draft (ISO).
X-Series	Recommendations issued by CCITT Study Group SGVII, on data communications networks.
X3	ANSI TAG responsible for information technology (roughly a U.S. national equivalent of ISO/IEC JTC1).

Index

2421 Code, 188
Accented letters:
  illustration of, 165–166
  ISO representation, 153–155,
    165–166
Accents:
  acute, 165, 166
  breve, 166
  caron, 165
  cedilla, 165
  circumflex, 165
  dot, 166
  double acute, 166
  grave, 165
  Macintosh, 64
  macron, 166
  ogonek, 166
  ring, 166
  slash, 166
  stroke, 165, 166
  tilde, 165
  umlaut, 165
Acute accent, 165, 166
Ada, 215–216, 222, 223
  Ada 83, 216
  Ada 9X, 216
Adobe Illustrator, 69
Adobe Photoshop, 70
Adobe Type 1 font, 67
Adobe Type Manager, 67
AFNOR, 143, 145
  address, 145
Algol, 222, 223
Alphabets see Character sets

Amphenol connector, 96
  pin numbering, 96
ANSI, 141–142, 145
  address, 145
  standardization process, 142
  X3 subcommittees, 141–142
  X3 technical advisory group,
    141
ANSI BASIC, 217
ANSI C language, 218
ANSI COBOL, 218
APL, 222, 223
Apple Laserwriter, 66
Apple Macintosh see Macintosh
Apt, 222, 223
Arabic character set, ISO, 153, 178
  table, 178
ARPANET, 113, 205
Atlas, 222, 223
ASCII, 77, 78, 79, 149–151, 156–159,
    162, 164, 167–169, 181–186
  British version, 167
  Danish version, 169
  French version, 167
  German version, 167
  international variations, 150–151,
    167–169
  Italian version, 168
  manufacturers' extended versions,
    153, 164, 181–186
    tables, 164, 181-186
  Norwegian version, 169
  replacement characters, 151,
    167–169

ASCII (*Continued*):
  Spanish version, 168
  Swedish version, 168
  tables, 156–159, 162, 164,
    167–169, 181–186
AT&T Bell Laboratories, 3

B language, 218
B-splines, 67
Background processes
  see Batch jobs
Balanced interface, RS-422, 89
BARRNet, 114
BASIC, 216–218, 222, 223
  ANSI BASIC, 217
  Dartmouth BASIC, 216
  GW BASIC, 217
  IBM-PC BASIC, 217
  Minimal BASIC, 217, 223
  QuickBASIC, 56, 217
  True BASIC, 217
  Turbo BASIC, 217
BASICA, 217
Batch files, MS-DOS, 57
Batch jobs:
  MVS-TSO, 35
  UNIX, 12
  VMS, 23
Baud vs. bits per second, 107
Baudot code, 187
BCPL, 218
Bell 113B/208A, 83, 85
Berkeley UNIX, 4, 6, 8, 11, 12
Bezier splines, 67
Biased exponent, 198
Binary coded decimal, 188
Binary codes for decimal digits,
    188
  2421 code, 188
  binary coded decimal, 188
  Excess-3, 188
  Gray code, 188
  Gray code excess-3, 188
BITNET, 115
Bits per second, 107
Bourne shell, UNIX, 11
bps *see* Bits per second

Breve accent, 166
British ASCII, 167
BSD UNIX, 4
BSI, 143, 145
  address, 145
Bus, IEEE 488, 97–98

C language, 218, 222, 223
  ANSI C, 218
  Kernighan-Ritchie C (K&R C),
    218
C shell, UNIX, 11
C++ language, 225
Canvas, 70
Caron accent, 165
Case sensitivity, 4
CCITT, 83, 139–140
  address *see* ITU, address
  recommendations, 140
  study groups, 140
CCITT V.24, 83, 85
CCITT V-series, 104, 107, 140,
    233–237
CCITT X.25, 115, 116
CCITT X-series, 140, 237–243
CDC Cyber Systems, 79
  byte size, 79
  end-of-file marker, 79
  end-of-line marker, 79
  word size, 79
Cedilla accent, 165
CEN, 140–141, 145, 205
  address, 145
CENELEC, 140–141, 205
CEPT, 140
Centronics interface, 96–97
Character code tables, 156–159,
    162–164, 167–188
Character codes *see* Character sets
Character sets, 149–188
  ASCII, 149–151, 156–159, 162,
    164, 167–169, 181–186
    tables, 156–159, 162, 164,
      167–169, 181–186
  ASCII, extended, 153, 164,
    181–186
    tables, 164, 181–186

Character sets (*Continued*):
  Baudot, 187
  DEC multinational, 153, 181–183
  EBCDIC, 150, 156–159, 162, 163
    tables, 156–159, 162, 163
  IBM-PC, PS/2, 153, 164, 184–186
  ISO 646, 150–151, 167–169
  ISO 6937/2, 151, 170
    table, 170
  ISO 8859, 152–153, 171–180
    languages covered, 152–153
    tables, 171–180
  ISO Arabic, 153, 178
    table, 178
  ISO Cyrillic, 152, 177
    table, 177
  ISO Greek, 153, 179
    table, 179
  ISO Hebrew, 153, 180
    table, 180
  ISO Latin, 152–153, 171–180
    tables, 171–180
  Macintosh, 181–183
    tables, 181–183
Cicero, typography, 191
Circumflex accent, 165
CLISTs, MVS-TSO, 32, 34
  See also Command procedures
CMS, 37-43, 78
  byte size, 78
  command procedures, invoking, 43
  compiling and linking, 42–43
  copying a file, 40
  deleting a file, 41
  editing files, 42
  end-of-file marker, 78
  end-of-line marker, 78
  file system, 37–39
  file type, 37–38
  file mode, 37–38
  filenames, 37–38
  help, online, 37
  listing contents of a file, 41
  listing directory contents, 39–40
  minidisks, 38
  printing a file, 42

CMS (*Continued*):
  renaming a file, 41
  running programs, 42–43
  wild cards, 39–40
  word size, 78
CMS commands:
  COPYFILE, 40
  ERASE, 41
  EXEC, 43
  LISTFILE, 39–40
  LOAD, 43
  PRINT, 42
  RENAME, 41
  TYPE, 41
  XEDIT, 42
COBOL, 218, 222, 224
  ANSI COBOL, 218
Code pages, IBM-PC, 153, 184–186
Command procedures:
  CMS, 43
  MS-DOS, 57
  MVS-TSO, 34
  UNIX, 11–12
  VMS, 22–23
Common LISP, 225
Compiling and linking:
  CMS, 42–43
  MS-DOS, 55–57
  MVS-TSO, 32–34
  UNIX, 10
  VMS, 22
Connections:
  computer to computer, 86–87, 92–96
  computer to modem, 85–86, 95
  IBM-PC to Macintosh, 92-94
  Macintosh to Macintosh, 95–96
  Macintosh to modem, 95
  RS-232, 85–89
  RS-422, 91
Connectors:
  DB-25, 83, 84, 90
  DB-37, 90
  DB-9, 87, 88, 90
  Mini-DIN, 90
  SCSI, 98–99

Control characters, 162–164
  ASCII, 162, 164
    standard graphical
      representation, 164
  EBCDIC, 162, 163
  IBM-PC, 164
Conversational Monitor System
  see CMS
Copying a file:
  CMS, 40
  MS-DOS, 50–51
  MVS-TSO, 29
  UNIX, 6
  VMS, 18
Coral 66, 224
CP/M, 79
  byte size, 79
  end-of-file marker, 79
  end-of-line marker, 79
  word size, 79
CREN, 115
CSNET, 114
CTSS, 3
Cyber see CDC Cyber Systems
Cyrillic character set, ISO, 152, 177
  table, 177

Danish ASCII, 169
Dartmouth BASIC, 216
Data circuit-terminating equipment
  see DCE
Data communications, 83–133,
    203–214, 231–243
  connections, 86–89, 92–96
  file transfers, 121–130, 131–133
    FTP, 131–133
    Kermit, 121–130
  interfaces, 83–92, 96–102
  modems, 102–109
  networks, 113–119, 203–214
  standards, 203–214, 231–243
  system characteristics, 109–110
Data communications equipment
  see DCE
Data sets, MVS-TSO, 26–28
Data terminal equipment see DTE

DB-25 connector, 83, 84, 90
  pin numbering, 84
DB-37 connector, 90
DB-9 connector, 87, 88, 90
  pin numbering, 88
DCE, 85, 86
DDN, 114
DEC, 15
DEC multinational character set,
    153, 181–183
DECnet , 115
DECSYSTEM-10, 78
  byte size, 78
  end-of-file marker, 78
  end-of-line marker, 78
  word size, 78
DECSYSTEM-20, 78
  byte size, 78
  end-of-file marker, 78
  end-of-line marker, 78
  word size, 78
Deleting a file:
  CMS, 41
  Macintosh, TRASH, 64
  MS-DOS, 52
  MVS-TSO, 29–30
  UNIX, 7
  VMS, 18–19
Deneba Canvas, 70
Dibol, 222
Didot point, typography, 191
Digital Equipment Corporation
  see DEC
DIN, 143, 145
  address, 145
DIN connector see
    Mini-DIN connector
Directories see Subdirectories
Directory structure:
  MS-DOS, 47–48
  UNIX, 5
  VMS, 16
Disks:
  dominant, Macintosh, 65
  duplicating, MS-DOS, 58
  formatting, MS-DOS, 57–58

Disks (*Continued*):
  verifying, MS-DOS, 59
Document processing, standards,
    230–231
DOS *see* MS-DOS
Dot accent, 166
Double acute accent, 166
DTE, 85, 86

E-mail, addresses, 117–118
EARN, 115
EBCDIC, 78, 150, 156–159, 162,
    163
  tables, 156–159, 162, 163
ECMA, 144, 146
  address, 146
Editing files:
  CMS, 42
  MS-DOS, 54–55
  MVS-TSO, 31–32
  UNIX, 8–10
  VMS, 20–22
EIA, 83, 144, 146, 231–232
  address, 146
  standards, 231–232
EIA 232-D *see* RS-232
Electronic mail *see* E-mail, addresses
Encapsulated PostScript, 68, 69
Ethernet, 115, 116
ETSI, 141
EUnet, 116
European communications
    standards, 243
EWOS, 141, 205
Excess-3 code, 188
Exponent, 197–198
  bias, 198
Extended Pascal, 221, 223, 224

File system:
  CMS, 37-39
  MS-DOS, 46–49
  MVS-TSO, 26–28
  UNIX, 4–5
  VMS, 15–17
File transfer protocol *see* FTP

File transfers, 121–130, 131–133
  FTP, 131–133
  Kermit, 121–130
  overhead, 129
Filenames:
  CMS, 37–38
  MS-DOS, 46–47
  MVS-TSO, 26–27
  UNIX, 4
  VMS, 15–16
FIPS, 143
Floating point, 197–201
  exponent, 197–198
    bias, 198
  IEEE formats, 197, 198–200, 201
  mantissa, 197, 198
  precision, 197–198
  range, 198
Flow control, 109–110, 125, 126
  ENQ/ACK, 110
  XON, 109
  XON/XOFF, 110, 125, 126
Fonts:
  Adobe Type 1, 67
  Adobe Type Manager, 67
  bit-mapped, 66, 193
  Macintosh, 66–68
    identification, 67
    printer, 66
    screen, 66
  outline-coded, 66–67, 193
  representation, 193
  Truetype, 67
Formatting disks, MS-DOS, 57–58
FORTH, 225
FORTRAN, 219–220, 222, 224
  FORTRAN 66, 219
  FORTRAN 77, 219
  FORTRAN 8X, 220
  FORTRAN 90, 220
French ASCII, 167
Frequencies:
  modem signalling, 105
  touch-tone, 105
Frequency shift keying, 103, 104,
    107

FTP, 131–133
  sample session, 131–133
FTP commands:
  CD, 133
  DIR, 133
  GET, 133
  HELP, 133
  LOGIN, 133
  PUT, 133
  SET, 133
    SET LOCAL_DEFAULT, 133
    SET TYPE, 133
Full duplex, 109, 125, 126

German ASCII, 167
Graphics, standards, 229–230
Grave accent, 165
Gray code, 188
Gray code excess-3, 188
Greek character set, ISO, 153, 179
  table, 179
GW-BASIC, 217

Half duplex, 109, 125, 126
Handshake, 125, 126
Hayes modems, 95, 106–107
  commands, 106
  connections, 95
  result codes, 107
Help, online:
  CMS, 37
  MVS-TSO, 25
  UNIX, 4
  VMS, 15
Hebrew character set, ISO, 153, 180
  table, 180
HEPnet, 115
Hewlett-Packard, 110
  communication characteristics,
    110
Hexadecimal/decimal conversion,
  160–161
Honeywell, 110
  communication characteristics,
    110

IBM mainframes, 25, 37, 124,
    126–127
  Kermit, 124, 126–127
IBM-PC, 45, 110, 153, 164,
    184–186
  ASCII control characters, 164
  code pages, 153, 184–186
  communication characteristics,
    110
IBM-PC/AT, 87
IBM-PC BASIC, 217
IBM system/370, 25, 37
IEC, 138–139, 144
  address, 144
IEEE, 144, 146
  address, 146
IEEE 488 interface, 97–98, 233
IEEE 802 series, 206–207
  logical link control, 206
  medium access control, 206
  relationship to OSI, 207
IEEE Computer Society, 144
IEEE floating-point format,
    197, 198–200, 201
  double extended, 200
  double precision, 199–200
  single extended, 199
  single precision, 198–199
Input/output redirection:
  MS-DOS, 59
  UNIX, 13
Interfaces, 83–102, 231–233
  Centronics, 96–97
  IEEE 488, 97–98, 233
  parallel, 96–102
  RS-232, 83–89, 231
  RS-422, 89–92, 231
  RS-423, 232
  RS-449, 90, 232
  RS-530, 90, 232
  SCSI, 98–102, 233
  serial, 83–92
Internet, 113–115, 131, 205
  information *see also*
    NIC.DDN.MIL

Internet model, 205–206
  layers, 205–206
  relationship to OSI, 205–206
ISDN, 102
ISO, 138-139, 144
  address, 144
ISO 2110, 83
ISO 646 character set ,150–151,
  167–169
ISO 6937/2 character set, 151, 170
  table, 170
ISO 8859 character sets, 152–153,
  171–180
  languages covered, 152–153
  tables, 171–180
ISO/IEC JTC1, 138–139
  standardization process, 139
  subcommittees, 138–139
ISO Latin character sets, 152–153,
  171–180
  languages covered, 152–153
  tables, 171–180
ISPF, 25
Italian ASCII, 168
ITU, 139–140, 144
  address, 144

JANET, 116
JCL, 25, 35
JISC, 143, 145
  address, 145
Job control language *see* JCL
JTC1 *see* ISO/IEC JTC1
JUNET, 116

Kermit, 121–130, 131
  File transfer protocol, 128–130
  IBM mainframe parameters, 124,
    126–127
  overhead, 129
  packet format, 128–130
  parity, 127
  sample session, 121–122
Kermit commands:
  connect, 124
  get, 128
  receive, 127–128

Kermit commands (*Continued*):
  send, 127
  set, 125–127
    set baud, 125
    set delay, 125
    set duplex, 125
    set escape, 125
    set file byte, 126
    set file type, 126
    set flow, 126
    set handshake, 126
    set IBM, 126
    set parity, 127
Kernighan-Ritchie C language
  (K&R C), 218
Korn shell, UNIX, 11

Languages, programming,
  215–226
  Ada, 215–216, 222, 223
    Ada 83, 216
    Ada 9X, 216
  Algol, 222, 223
  APL, 222, 223
  Apt, 222, 223
  Atlas, 222, 223
  B language, 218
  BASIC, 216–218, 222, 223
    ANSI BASIC, 217
    Dartmouth BASIC, 216
    GW BASIC, 217
    IBM-PC BASIC, 217
    Minimal BASIC, 217, 223
    QuickBASIC, 56, 217
    True BASIC, 217
    Turbo BASIC, 217
  BASICA, 217
  BCPL, 218
  C language, 218, 222, 223
    ANSI C, 218
    Kernighan-Ritchie C (K&R C),
      218
  C++ language, 225
  COBOL, 218, 222, 224
    ANSI COBOL, 218
  Common LISP, 225
  Coral 66, 224

Languages, programming
  (*Continued*):
  Dibol, 222
  FORTH, 225
  FORTRAN, 219–220, 222, 224
    FORTRAN 66, 219
    FORTRAN 77, 219
    FORTRAN 8X, 220
    FORTRAN 90, 220
  LISP *see* Common LISP *above*
  Pascal, 220–221, 222, 223, 224
    Extended Pascal, 221, 223, 224
  Pearl, 224
  PL/I, 223, 224
  Prolog, 225
  REXX, 225
Leading, typography, 192
Letter frequency, 188–190
  English, 189
  Finnish, 190
  French, 189
  German, 189
  Italian, 190
  Spanish, 189
LISP *see* Common LISP
Listing contents of a file:
  CMS, 41
  MS-DOS, 52–53
  MVS-TSO, 30
  UNIX, 7
  VMS, 19
Listing directory contents:
  CMS, 39–40
  MS-DOS, 49–50
  MVS-TSO, 28
  UNIX, 6
  VMS, 17–18
Local area networks, 206–207
Los Nettos, 114

Macintosh, 61-76, 78, 90–91, 92–96,
  98–102, 110, 181–183
  abort operation, 62
  accents, 64
  adapter cable, DB-9 to Mini-DIN,
    91
  Adobe Illustrator, 69

Macintosh (*Continued*):
  Adobe Photoshop, 70
  Adobe Type Manager, 67
  byte size, 78
  Canvas, 70
  character set, 181–183
    tables, 181–183
  clean up, 64
  communication characteristics,
    110
  connections, 92–96
  connectors, 90–91, 99
  Deneba Canvas, 70
  disk,dominant, 65
  end-of-file marker, 78
  end-of-line marker, 78
  Finder, 61–62
  FOND resource, 67–68
  FONT resource, 67–68
  fonts, 66–68
    Adobe Type 1, 67
    bit-mapped, 66
    formats, 67
    identification, 67
    outline-coded, 66–67
    printer, 66
    screen, 66
    Truetype, 67
  graphics:
    format conversions, 70–75
    formats, 68-75
  MacDraw format, 68, 70
  MacPaint format, 68
  Multifinder, 65
  NFNT resource, 67
  Pixelpaint, 70
  Pixelpaint Professional, 70
  punctuation marks, 64
  QuickDraw, 68
  resources, 67
  SCSI interface, 98–102
  serial port pin assignments, 91
  shortcuts, 62–63
  Supermac Pixelpaint, 70
  Supermac Pixelpaint Professional,
    70
  System, 61–62

Macintosh (*Continued*):
  System 7, 62, 66, 67
  TRASH, 64
  Truetype, 67
  windows, 63, 64
  word size, 78
MacDraw format, 68, 70
MacPaint format, 68
Macron accent, 166
Mail, electronic
  see E-mail, addresses
Mantissa, 197, 198
MERIT, 114
Microprocessors, standards, 228
Microsoft corporation, 217
Microsoft Windows, 46
MIDnet, 114
MILNET, 114, 115
Mini-DIN connector, 90
  pin numbering, 90
Minidisks, CMS, 38
Minimal BASIC, 217, 223
Modems, 95, 102-109
  AT&T Bell series, 103, 107
  CCITT V-series, 104, 107
  Hayes, 95, 106–107
    commands, 106
    connections, 95
    result codes, 107
  modulation methods, 107
  signal frequencies, 105
  smart, 106
  standards, 103
  transmission speed, 107–108
MS-DOS, 45-60, 78
  abort operation, 57
  batch files, invoking, 57
  byte size, 78
  command procedures, invoking, 57
  compiling and linking, 55–57
  copying a file, 50–51
  deleting a file, 52
  directories *see*
    subdirectories *below*
  directory, current, 48
  directory structure, 47–48

MS-DOS (*Continued*):
  disk drives, moving between, 57
  disks:
    duplicating, 58
    formatting, 57–58
    verifying, 59
  drivenames, 47
  editing files, 54–55
  end-of-file marker, 78
  end-of-line marker, 78
  file system, 46-49
  filenames, 46–47
  history and development, 45–46
  input/output redirection, 59
  listing contents of a file, 52–53
  listing directory contents, 49–50
  pathnames, 47–48
  pipes, 53, 59
  printing a file, 53
  rebooting system, 57
  renaming a file, 51
  running programs, 55–57
  subdirectories:
    creating, 53
    moving between, 53–54
    removing, 53
  version variations, 45–46, 47, 48, 52, 58
  wild cards, 48–49
  word size, 78
MS-DOS commands:
  CD, 53–54
  CHKDSK, 59
  COPY, 50–51
  DEL *see* ERASE *below*
  DISKCOPY, 58
  DIR, 49–50
  EDLIN, 54–55
  ERASE, 52
  FORMAT, 57–58
  LINK, 56-57
  MD, 53
  MKDIR *see* MD *above*
  MORE, 53, 59
  PRINT, 53
  RENAME, 51
  RD *see* RMDIR *below*

MS-DOS commands (*Continued*):
  RMDIR, 53
  SORT, 59
  TYPE, 52–53
Multics, 3
Multifinder, Macintosh, 65
Multiple virtual storages
  see MVS-TSO
MVS *see* MVS-TSO
MVS-TSO, 25-35, 78
  batch jobs, 35
  byte size, 78
  CLISTs, 32, 34
  command procedures, invoking,
    34
  compiling and linking, 32–34
  copying a file, 29
  data sets, 26–28
  deleting a file, 29–30
  editing files, 31–32
  end-of-file marker, 78
  end-of-line marker, 78
  file system, 26–28
  filenames, 26–27
  help, online, 25
  listing contents of a file, 30
  listing directory contents, 28
  partitioned data sets, 27
  printing a file, 30
  renaming a file, 29
  running programs, 32
  wild cards, 27–28
  word size, 78
MVS-TSO commands:
  COPY, 29
  DELETE, 29–30
  DSPRINT, 30
  EDIT, 31–32
  EXEC, 34
  LIST, 30
  LISTCAT, 28
  LISTDS, 28
  RENAME, 29
MVS/XA, 25

NetNorth, 115
NETs, 141, 243

Networks, 113–119, 203–214
  ARPANET, 113
  BARRNet, 114
  BITNET, 115
  cooperative, 115
  CREN, 115
  CSNET, 114
  DDN, 114
  DECnet , 115
  E-mail, addresses, 117–118
  EARN, 115
  electronic mail *see*
    E-mail, addresses *above*
  Ethernet, 115, 116
  EUnet, 116
  gateways, 116–117
  HEPnet, 115
  hubs, 116–117
  Internet, 113–115
    information *see also*
      NIC.DDN.MIL
  JANET, 116
  JUNET, 116
  Los Nettos, 114
  MERIT, 114
  MIDnet, 114
  MILNET, 114, 115
  NetNorth, 115
  NorthWestNet, 114
  NSFNET, 114, 115
  NSN, 114
  regional, 113–119
  Sesquinet, 114
  SPAN, 115
  standards, 203–214
  SURANet, 114
  THEnet, 115
  USAN, 114
  USENET, 116
  UUCP, 116
    protocol, 116
  Westnet, 114
  worldwide, 113–119
NIC.DDN.MIL, 118—119
  whois command, 119
NIST, 142–143
NJE/NJI protocols, 115

NNI, 143, 145
  address, 145
NorthWestNet, 114
Norwegian ASCII, 169
NSFNET, 114, 115
NSN, 114
Nyquist rate, 108

Office Document Architecture
    (ODA), 230
Ogonek accent, 166
Open systems interconnection
    see OSI
Operating systems:
  CDC Cyber Systems, 79
  CMS (VM-CMS), 37–43, 78
  CP/M, 79
  DECSYSTEM-10, 78
  DECSYSTEM-20, 78
  Macintosh, 61-76, 78
  MS-DOS, 45–60, 78
  MVS-TSO, 25-35, 78
  POSIX, 3, 227
  PRIMOS, 79
  RT-11, 78
  standards, 3, 227
  UCSD p System, 79
  UNIX, 3–14, 77
  VMS (VAX-VMS), 15-24, 77
OS/2, 46
OSI, 203–205, 206, 207, 208
  applications layer, 204, 208–209
  data link layer, 204, 211–213
  layers, 203–205
  network layer, 204, 210–211
  physical layer, 203, 213–214
  presentation layer, 204
  relationship to IEEE 802, 207
  relationship to TCP/IP, 205–206
  session layer, 204, 209–210
  transport layer, 204, 210

p System see UCSD p System
Paper sizes, standard, 244–245
Parallel interface, 96–102

Parity, 109, 127
  even, 109
  mark, 109
  odd, 109
  space, 109
Partitioned data sets, MVS-TSO,
    27
Pascal, 220–221, 222, 223, 224
  Extended Pascal, 221, 223, 224
PC-DOS see MS-DOS
PDP-11, 110
  communication characteristics,
    110
Pearl, 224
Pica, typography, 190
PICT format, 68
PICT2 format, 69
Pipes:
  MS-DOS, 53, 59
  UNIX, 13
Pixelpaint, 70
Pixelpaint Professional, 70
PL/I, 223, 224
Point , typography, 190
Point size, typography, 192
POSIX, 3, 227
PostScript, 66, 68, 69
PRIME, 110
  communication characteristics,
    110
  operating system see PRIMOS
PRIMOS, 79
  byte size, 79
  end-of-file marker, 79
  end-of-line marker, 79
  word size, 79
Printing a file:
  CMS, 42
  MS-DOS, 53
  MVS-TSO, 30
  UNIX, 8
  VMS, 19
Prolog, 225
Punctuation marks, Macintosh,
    64

Q, typography, 191
Quadrature amplitude modulation,
    103, 104, 107
QuickBASIC, 56, 217
QuickDraw, 68

Rebooting system, MS-DOS, 57
Renaming a file:
    CMS, 41
    MS-DOS, 51
    MVS-TSO, 29
    UNIX, 7
    VMS, 18
Research UNIX, 3
REXX, 225
Ring accent, 166
Ritchie, Dennis, 3
RS-232, 83–89, 231
    9-pin connector, 87, 88
        adapter cable, DB-9 to DB-25,
        88
    connections, 85–89
    null modem:
        DB-9 to DB-25, 89
        DB-9 to DB-9, 89
        DB-25 to DB-25, 87
    pin assignments, 85
    subsets, 84
    voltage levels, 84
RS-422, 89–92, 231
    connections, 91
    pin assignment, 91
    voltage levels, 90
RS-423, 232
RS-449, 90, 232
RS-530, 90, 232
RSX system, 15
RT-11, 78
    byte size, 78
    end-of-file marker, 78
    end-of-line marker, 78
    word size, 78
Running programs:
    CMS, 42–43
    MS-DOS, 55–57
    MVS-TSO, 32
    UNIX, 10

Running programs (Continued):
    VMS, 22

SAA, 145
    address, 145
SCC, 145
    address, 145
SCSI interface, 98–102, 233
Serial interfaces, 83–92
Sesquinet, 114
Shannon's law, 108
Shells, UNIX, 11
Slash accent, 166
Software engineering, standards,
    228
SPAG, 204
SPAN, 115
Spanish ASCII, 168
Sperry, 110
    communication characteristics,
    110
Standard Generalized Markup
    Language (SGML), 231
Standards:
    Ada, 215–216, 222, 223
    Algol, 222, 223
    alphabets see character sets below
    APL, 222, 223
    Apt, 222, 223
    ASCII character sets, 149–151,
        156–159, 162, 164, 167–169,
        181–186
    Atlas, 222, 223
    BASIC, 216–218, 222, 223
    C language, 218, 222, 223
    C++ language, 225
    character sets, 149–188,
        193–195
    CCITT, 233–243
    COBOL, 218, 222, 224
    Common LISP, 225
    Coral 66, 224
    data communications, 83–105,
        203–214, 231–243
    Dibol, 222
    document processing, 230–231
    EIA, 231–232

Standards (*Continued*):
European communications, 243
FORTH, 225
FORTRAN, 219–220, 222, 224
graphics, computer, 229–230
IEEE 488 interface, 97–98, 233
IEEE 802 series, 206–207
interfaces, 83–102, 231–233
ISO character sets, 150–153,
   153–155, 165–180
LISP *see* Common LISP *above*
local area networks, 206–207
microprocessors, 228
modems, 103
NETs, 243
networks, 203–214
Office Document Architecture
   (ODA), 230
operating systems, 3, 227
organizations *see*
   Standards organizations
OSI, 203–205, 206, 207, 208
paper sizes, 244
Pascal, 220–221, 222, 223, 224
Pearl, 224
PL/I, 223, 224
POSIX, 227
programming languages,
   215–226
Prolog, 225
REXX, 225
RS-232, 83–89, 231
RS-422, 89–92, 231
RS-423, 232
RS-449, 90, 232
RS-530, 90, 232
software engineering, 228
Standard Generalized Markup
   Language (SGML), 231
text processing, 230–231
Standards organizations, 137–147
addresses, 144–146
AFNOR, 143, 145
ANSI, 141–142, 145
   standardization process, 142
   X3 subcommittees, 141–142

Standards organizations
   (*Continued*):
ANSI (*Continued*):
   X3 technical advisory group,
   141
British, 143
BSI, 143, 145
CCITT, 139–140
   address *see* ITU, address
   recommendations, 140
   study groups, 140
CEN, 140–141, 145
CENELEC, 140–141
CEPT, 140
DIN, 143, 145
Dutch, 143
ECMA, 144, 146
EIA, 144, 146
ETSI, 141
European, 140
EWOS, 141
French, 143
German, 143
IEC, 138–139, 144
IEEE, 144, 146
international, 138–140
ISO, 138-139, 144
ISO/IEC JTC1, 138–139
   standardization process, 139
   subcommittees, 138–139
ITU, 139–140, 144
Japanese, 143
JISC, 143, 145
national, 141–143
NIST, 142–143
NNI, 143, 145
SAA, 145
SCC, 145
professional and industry,
   143–144
U.S., 141–142
Stroke accent, 165, 166
Subdirectories, creating:
   MS-DOS, 53
   UNIX, 8
   VMS, 20

Subdirectories, moving between:
  MS-DOS, 53–54
  UNIX, 8
  VMS, 20
Subdirectories, removing:
  MS-DOS, 53
  UNIX, 8
  VMS, 20
Supermac Pixelpaint, 70
Supermac Pixelpaint Professional,
  70
SURANet, 114
Swedish ASCII, 168
System 7, Macintosh, 62, 66, 67
System V, UNIX, 4, 6, 8, 11, 12

TCP/IP, 113, 118, 131, 205–206
  relationship to OSI, 205–206
Telephone:
  channel bandwidth, 108
  touch-tone frequencies, 105
Telnet, 118
Terminals, IBM 3270, 35
Text processing, standards,
      230–231
THEnet, 115
Thompson,Ken, 3
TIFF format, 68, 69
Tilde accent, 165
TOPS-20, 110
  communication characteristics,
      110
TRAC, 141
Transmission speeds:
  BITNET, 115
  Internet, 115
  JANET, 116
  MILNET, 115
  modem, 107–108
  NSFNET, 115
  USENET, 116
  UUCP, 116
TRASH, Macintosh, 64
True BASIC, 217
Truetype, 67
TSO see MVS-TSO
Turbo BASIC, 217

Typography, 190–193
  cicero, 191
  Didot point, 191
  leading, 192
  pica, 190
  point, 190
  point size, 192
  Q, 191
  resolution, 192–193
  units, 190–191

UCSD p System, 79
  byte size, 79
  end-of-file marker, 79
  end-of-line marker, 79
  word size, 79
Umlaut accent, 165
UNIX, 3–14, 77
  abort operation, 13
  batch jobs, 12
  Berkeley UNIX, 4, 6, 8, 11, 12
  Bourne shell, 11
  byte size, 77
  C shell, 11
  case sensitivity, 4
  command procedures, invoking,
      12
  compiling and linking, 10
  copying a file, 6
  deleting a file, 7
  directory structure, 5
  directories see
      subdirectories below
  editing files, 8–10
  editors, 9
  end-of-file marker, 77
  end-of-line marker, 77
  file system, 4–5, 12
  filenames, 4, 12
  help, online, 4
  input/output redirection, 13
  Korn shell, 11
  listing contents of a file, 7
  listing directory contents, 6
  pathnames, 5
  PID (process identification), 12
  pipes, 13

UNIX (*Continued*):
  printing a file, 8
  renaming a file, 7
  Research UNIX, 3
  running programs, 10
  shells, 11
  stopping batch jobs, 12
  subdirectories:
    creating, 8
    moving between, 8
    removing, 8
  System V, 4, 6, 8, 11, 12
  versions, 3–4
  wild cards, 5
  word size, 77
UNIX commands:
  cat, 7, 13
  cc, 10–11
  cd, 8
  cp, 6
  csh, 12
  ed, 8–10
  ex, 9
  f77, 11
  grep, 13
  kill, 12
  ksh, 12
  lp, 8
  lpr, 8
  ls, 6, 13
  make, 11
  man, 4
  mkdir, 8
  more, 7, 13
  mv, 7
  pg, 7
  ps, 12
  pwd, 8
  rm, 7
  rmdir, 8
  sh, 12
UNIX support group, 3
USAN, 114
USENET, 116
UUCP, 116
  protocol, 116

VAX computers, 15
VAX-VMS *see* VMS
VM *see* CMS
VM-CMS *see* CMS
VMS, 15-24, 77, 110
  abort operation, 23
  batch jobs, 23
  byte size, 77
  command procedures, invoking,
    22–23
  communication characteristics,
    110
  compiling and linking, 22
  copying a file, 18
  DCL, 22
  deleting a file, 18–19
  directories *see*
      subdirectories *below*
  directory structure, 16
  editing files, 20–22
  end-of-file marker, 77
  end-of-line marker, 77
  file system, 15–17
  filenames, 15–16
  help, online, 15
  listing contents of a file, 19
  listing directory contents, 17–18
  pathnames, 16
  printing a file, 19
  renaming a file, 18
  running programs, 22
  stopping batch jobs, 23
  subdirectories:
    creating, 20
    moving between, 20
    removing, 20
  versions of files, 16
  wild cards, 17
  word size, 77
VMS commands:
  cc, 22
  COPY, 18
  CREATE/DIRECTORY, 20
  DELETE, 18–19, 20
  DIR, 17–18
  EDT, 20–22

VMS commands (*Continued*):
 FOR, 22
 HELP, 15
 PRINT, 19
 PURGE, 19
 RENAME, 18
 SET DEFAULT, 20
 SET PROTECTION, 20
 SHOW QUEUE, 23
 STOP, 23
 SUBMIT, 23
 TYPE, 19

Westnet, 114
Wild cards:
 CMS, 39–40
 MS-DOS, 48–49
 MVS-TSO, 27–28
 UNIX, 5
 VMS, 17
Windows, Macintosh, 63, 64
Windows, Microsoft, 46

X.PC, 129
XMODEM, 129

ABOUT THE AUTHORS

Marius S. Vassiliou is a research scientist at the Rockwell International Science Center in Thousand Oaks, California. He holds a Ph.D. in geophysics and electrical engineering from the California Institute of Technology, and an M.S. in computer science from the University of Southern California. He also holds degrees from Harvard and UCLA. He has taught engineering and science at the University of Texas at Dallas and Moorpark College, and has published widely in a number of scientific fields. Dr. Vassiliou's experience as a practicing computational scientist who has used and programmed many different computers inspired this book. He is a member of ACM and a senior member of IEEE.

Jack A. Orenstein is a computer scientist at Object Design, Inc., in Burlington, Massachusetts. He has worked extensively with state-of-the-art programs and applications. He was formerly professor of computer and information science at the University of Massachusetts at Amherst. He has also taught computer science courses at McGill University, where he earned his B.S., M.S., and Ph.D. in computer science. Dr. Orenstein is a member of ACM and the IEEE Computer Society.